Finally
FIT!

Finally FIT!

LORRAINE BOSSÉ-SMITH

A STRANG COMPANY

Most STRANG COMMUNICATIONS/CHARISMA HOUSE/SILOAM products are available at special quantity discounts for bulk purchase for sales promotions, premiums, fund-raising, and educational needs. For details, write Strang Communications/Charisma House/Siloam, 600 Rinehart Road, Lake Mary, Florida 32746, or telephone (407) 333-0600.

FINALLY FIT! by Lorraine Bossé-Smith
Published by Siloam
A Strang Company
600 Rinehart Road
Lake Mary, Florida 32746
www.siloam.com

Unless otherwise noted, all Scripture quotations are from The Holy Bible, New International Version. Copyright © 1973, 1978, 1984, International Bible Society. Used by permission of Zondervan.

Cover design by Judith McKittrick

Library of Congress Cataloging-in-Publication Data

Bosse-Smith, Lorraine, 1966-
  Finally fit! / Lorraine Bosse-Smith.
  p. cm.
  Includes bibliographical references.
  ISBN 1-59185-416-4 (pbk.)
  1. Exercise. 2. Physical fitness. 3. Health. I. Title.
RA781.B676 2004
613.7--dc22
                        2004002476

As with any exercise program, readers are advised to check with their healthcare professional before starting this exercise regimen. Neither the author nor the publisher assumes any responsibility for incidents that may arise from following this program.

04 05 06 07 08 — 987654321
Printed in the United States of America

I dedicate this book to my beloved husband, Steven,
whom God gave to me as a special gift.

Besides unconditional love
like I've never known before,
you have given me the freedom to discover my true self
and actually see my real reflection
for the first time in my life.
You believed in me when I doubted,
and you gave me courage to come into myself.
Because of you, I can celebrate who I am
and accept who I am not.
Sweetheart, you changed my life and world.
I'll never be the same,
and my life is richer and better
with you in it.

Your dream girl,
Lorraine

ACKNOWLEDGMENTS

I WOULD LIKE to thank Bob Minotti, a dear friend and longtime peer, for connecting me to the team at Siloam. I appreciate your continued friendship and support. God brought our lives together for several reasons—this book being one of them. Your family will always be a part of my prayers, and Joey has a special place in my heart.

To the team at Siloam, thank you for catching the vision of this book and the possibilities it has to change people's lives. I appreciate all your hard work and effort to ensure this product is top quality and reaches the masses.

To Virginia Bowen, my friend and editor, thank you for coming alongside me in so many ways. Knowing I'm not the only one out there who thinks like I do is comforting! I appreciate our time together to vent, laugh…and eat! I value our friendship and look forward to redefining our lives as clarity comes.

To my agent and friend, Nancy Jernigan, many thanks for handling an array of details throughout the publishing process and being my "Border Buster." Here's to exciting days ahead!

To Pete and Susan Schownir, who are better than family to me. Thank you for being faithful, loyal, godly people. Pete, our conversation about what I should be doing with my life was instrumental for this health and fitness path. I appreciate you, bro!

To my fitness class participants and personal-training clients, you rock! You may think that I am the one inspiring you, but the truth is that *you* inspire me! Your dedication and commitment to health and fitness in the midst of very busy, full lives are incredible and honorable. I applaud each and every one of you for your hard work toward becoming *Finally FIT!* Thank you for letting me be a part of your lives. I am blessed.

To Jann Gentry, my photographer (www.janngentry.com), thank you for making me look good! You are a creative, talented, beautiful person, inside and out. I could not have done this project without you.

And most of all, a heart full of gratitude to my husband, Steve, for your faithful love and devotion to me. I'm blessed to be married to you! Here's to at least eighty-eight more wonderful years together. I love you.

CONTENTS

TABLE OF CHARTS

INTRODUCTION | HOUSTON, WE HAVE A PROBLEM!

LET'S FACE IT: for many people exercise is a dreaded, boring task they know they should do but find a million and one excuses to avoid.

Oh sure, some people decide they'd better do something before yet another size category appears in their closet, and they join a health club in January for their New Year's resolution. But by early March most of these people have given up and gone back to their old habits, which do not include exercise. Still others try every trendy diet that comes out. They purchase every weight-loss pill in hopes of finally winning the battle of the bulge, only to find themselves losing and gaining the same 30 pounds over and over again.

Can you relate? Do you have difficulty making exercise a priority? Do you struggle with living a healthy lifestyle? Are you just bored with exercise and in a rut?

This was the case for my mother, Millie Bossé. Between her full-time work schedule, raising kids, taking care of a house, and managing all other aspects of life, she just didn't seem to have time or energy for exercise. My mom retired and stopped smoking at around the same time, with the result being that she found herself about 50 pounds overweight. Discouraged and frustrated because she couldn't fit in her clothes anymore, she decided to embark on a health kick. Besides, she couldn't afford to buy more clothes.

So she began exercising and watching what she ate. She started walking three miles a day, seven days a week. My mom had long legs, which I thankfully inherited, so she was able to walk at a good clip. This helped get her heart going. Combined with better nutrition (lots of salads), she began to

1

feel stronger and more energetic. While her friends were taking afternoon naps, she had plenty of energy to play with the grandchildren and even help my brother unload a cord of wood…at an elevation of 10,000 feet! She felt young again.

However, though she was strict with her diet and exercise, it took time for the weight to melt away. Mom added some resistance training into her weekly routine. Sometimes she would use light hand weights, which she purchased at Wal-Mart, and other times she would simply use soup cans. The bottom line was that she began to rebuild her muscles.

Before long, Mom started shedding the pounds and shaving away the fatty tissue. In a year's time—and at the age of sixty-seven—she lost more than the 50 pounds she had gained over the course of her life. I had never seen her looking so healthy.

DO YOU HAVE DIFFICULTY MAKING EXERCISE A PRIORITY?

If you are discouraged and frustrated with your level of health today, you aren't alone—and I have very good news for you. Please read on to find out why. Or if you are the type of person who wants to know the bottom line right now, feel free to skip to chapter one, where you will learn about your particular personality style.

Over the years, I have discovered that we are all created uniquely by God. "Duh," you say. "Tell me something I didn't know." Well, follow me for a minute. Some people are very social, extroverted, and outgoing while others are quiet, introverted, and shy. Some people love to get stuff done while others like to stop and visit with people. Ever see someone who is incredibly fast paced while people around him move much slower? We're all different.

If we were created with different personalities and behavior patterns, then wouldn't it make sense that we would all approach fitness in different ways? Yet the fitness industry is full of one-size-fits-all approaches to good health. Although it may work for *some* people, it doesn't work for *all* people.

If all your life you have struggled with exercising, you might just be one of those people for whom the generic fitness thing doesn't work. If so, this book is for you! Instead of forcing a one-size-fits-all fitness approach on you, my book will help you customize a program that fits you perfectly.

Imagine a workout routine that you enjoy…one that you don't dread but actually look forward to!

I can't tell you how many times I have seen inexperienced personal trainers at gyms using the same workout format with a beginner that they would use with an accomplished athlete. The client is completely overwhelmed, sore, and discouraged. These personal trainers often wonder why their clients never return, and the clients depart with negative feelings about fitness.

Perhaps you have had a similar unfortunate experience that has prevented you from giving fitness another try. I can't blame you. This is such a tragedy! Fitness should be safe and fun, yet challenging. If classes and trainers are safe, then clients don't get hurt and can return. If workouts are fun yet challenging, clients will respond favorably and make a commitment to incorporate fitness into their lives.

■

INSTEAD OF FORCING A ONE-SIZE-FITS-ALL FITNESS APPROACH ON YOU, MY BOOK WILL HELP YOU CUSTOMIZE A PROGRAM THAT FITS YOU PERFECTLY.

■

Through the course of this book, consider me *your* experienced, knowledgeable, and caring personal trainer. I want you to experience success, not failure. And you can. If you've been frustrated with fitness in the past, perhaps you were not given the right formula or maybe you were trying programs that just didn't work for your unique personality style. *Finally FIT!* will provide your FIT formula, match you up with a program that will work for you, and help you find success where you may have failed in the past.

MEET YOUR PERSONAL TRAINER

I have been an active person my entire life. Even so, I wasn't always as healthy as I am today. Major stresses of life forced me to redefine my health habits even further. I embarked on a fitness-training journey that eventually led to me becoming a certified personal trainer. My goal and my desire are to help others improve the quality of their lives through nutrition and exercise, just as mine has been improved.

Today I combine my passion for fitness with my years of business experience in the corporate world and advanced certifications in human behavior consulting and professional coaching—all to address the "total person." I now coach, consult, and train people all across the country, helping them reach their personal and professional goals.

By reading this book you are entering into a personal training/coaching relationship with me. Thank you for your trust and the desire to improve. I am excited to be working with you!

THIS BOOK *IS* DIFFERENT

Finally FIT! is not like most fitness books. While other authors try to include all people and personality styles in their one-size-fits-all plan, I don't. I believe every person falls into one of four broad personality type categories and that no one fitness plan will work for all four types. *Finally FIT!* includes a personality type assessment test to help you identify your type. This is what I call your FIT, your *Fitness Individuality Trait*. Then I've written chapters for each of the four personality styles. Here's where you'll discover the kind of fitness program that will work best for *you*, your customized approach to fitness.

You'll want to be sure to read the chapters I've included for everyone: "Fitness Facts," "Seeing Is Believing," "Eat Right, Feel Right," and "Choose Wisely." I think you would also enjoy reading the chapters on the other personality styles—it might help you understand some of the people in your life—but these are optional.

This book is designed to help you understand how you are wired so you can make excellent choices about your lifestyle. In other words, it is designed to help you succeed. Because when you actually find something you like and it is a good "FIT" with your personality, aren't you more likely to stick to it? Yes!

You need to find some fitness plan you can stick with. Any fitness plan. Your health is at stake.

THE COSTS OF POOR HEALTH

I'm going to be honest here: our country is unhealthy. It's on the verge of a medical crisis.

A recent study by the *Archives of Internal Medicine* cited data showing that about two-thirds of U.S. adults—131 million people—are overweight.[1] The Aerobics and Fitness Association of America has found that 80 percent of Americans are not getting enough exercise on a weekly basis to have any health benefit.[2] One million people die of a heart attack each year. And now, for the first time in our history, women are dying at the same rate as men.[3]

What does all this mean for you? It means that chances are you aren't living a healthy lifestyle. And *that* means you are running an elevated risk for serious illness and premature death.

■

AN UNHEALTHY LIFE EQUALS
POOR QUALITY OF LIFE.

■

What is poor health costing *you*? Poor health can result in:

- Low energy
- Restless nights/lack of sleep
- Depression/anxiety
- Decreased productivity
- Unhappiness/mood swings
- Frequent sickness/illness
- Excessive hair loss
- Weight gain
- Diseases such as coronary heart disease, cancer, diabetes, emphysema, and osteoporosis
- Sexual dysfunction
- Premature death

Being overweight, in particular, causes you to be subject to a number of ailments that you'd likely never get if you were slimmer. Did you know that 70 percent of all illnesses and injuries in America are preventable?[4] Go online to www.WebMD.com or read health magazines and medical journals to see which sicknesses are caused by weighing too much. Carrying around those extra pounds contributes to heart attacks, diabetes, severe and constant back pain, and a myriad of other painful problems and diseases. You will discover that an unhealthy life leads you down the path of suffering. That is a fact. Decide today that once and for all you will take a different path.

I hate to be the one to tell you this, but no overnight remedy is going to work. Although you're being bombarded by media messages offering superpills that allow you to lose weight while eating whatever you want, the only real solutions for a life of good health are regular exercise and a healthy diet. It requires some work on your part, but I'm here to guide you to the right program that is more enjoyable and appropriate for you. Your health is worth the effort, and I want to help you.

Wellness involves not only our physical condition, but also our mental, emotional, and spiritual states. We need to take care of our entire being. Too often we work extremely hard on one aspect of our lives but fail to address the others. That was my story. I was working hard on my outward appearance but failed to address my internal stress. It negatively impacted me and caused illness nonetheless. I encourage you to consider your *total self* to ensure you are a complete, healthy package. The amazing thing about fitness is that as we pay more attention to our physical bodies and give them what they need, the other areas benefit as well.

An active lifestyle has many positive attributes:

- Exercise will reduce your stress.

- Being active will improve the quality of your sleep.

- Exercise can reduce your chances of becoming depressed and help you recover from depression more quickly.

- Staying fit will give you more energy, allowing you to be more productive at work and home.

- A healthy lifestyle reduces your chances of illness, improving the quality of your life.

- Being in shape maintains healthier muscles and joints, reducing injuries.

- Weight-bearing exercise will increase your bone density and decrease your blood pressure, reducing your risk for osteoporosis and coronary heart disease.

- Proper exercise will help prevent back pain, which 80 percent of adults suffer from at some point in their life.

- Above all, being in shape will help you *feel better* about yourself and help give you a more positive outlook on life.[5]

The list of benefits grows even longer when you add the results of eating right.

I know you desire these things. We all do. When we take care of ourselves and become healthy, everyone wins! You gain energy and the ability to perform every aspect of life at a higher level. You also get to support those who matter. What good are you to those you love if you are hospitalized from poor health? How can you meet your goals if you don't have the energy? How can you enjoy life if you are constantly run down? How can you carefully analyze anything if you are drained?

BALANCE IS THE KEY

To have a truly healthy, fulfilled life we must have balance in all four aspects of our being: emotional, mental, physical, and spiritual.

Ever been in a car on which one of the tires is out of balance with the rest? How about when one tire is completely flat? You get a very bumpy, rough ride, don't you? I recently got a flat tire on the way to our church, which is only one mile up the highway from where we live. Driving with the car out of balance made that one mile feel like ten. I prayed and prayed that I would make it. I felt desperate. When I finally arrived at my destination, I was emotionally and mentally exhausted. I didn't like the feeling of being out of balance, and I couldn't wait to get an inflated tire back on the vehicle.

Our bodies are the same way. When one aspect is out of balance, the entire body suffers.

I like to think of the emotional, mental, physical, and spiritual elements of our makeup as the four wheels of a car. We need to work on all four to ensure we have complete balance. Unfortunately, many people sacrifice their health to the point that one "tire" is completely flat. They may be emotionally, mentally, and spiritually on target, but if their physical health is not in good condition, they can't continue to expect their bodies to perform. When you ignore one aspect of your makeup, you're a blowout waiting to happen. People seemed shocked when their tire blows, but they should have known it was coming. Neglect your health, and it *will* catch up with you.

That was how it was with me. I was severely out of balance. I had the cardio health "tire" totally under control, but I wasn't as disciplined in other areas. I wasn't eating right, weight training, and so on. One day my body almost "blew out." After that, I learned how to get all aspects of my life in balance, and I arrived at a quality of health I'd never had before. With some work I was able to put balance back in my life

You can, too! The amazing thing about concentrating on your health is that as the other three areas (emotional, mental, and spiritual) automatically improve, the healthier you become.

A friend of mine is a perfect example of how changing one's habits can beat illness and create balance. Back in 1997, Marion was struggling with chronic fatigue syndrome and severe fibromyalgia. She was barely able to get out of bed due to pain, and when she did get up she didn't have any energy. Marion was forced to give up her active lifestyle. She became secluded and withdrawn. The doctors told Marion that this was her future: she would have to live with her symptoms for the rest of her life.

■

WHEN ONE ASPECT OF OUR LIVES IS OUT OF BALANCE, THE ENTIRE BODY SUFFERS.

■

But Marion, being the strong-willed and deeply spiritual person she is, decided to fight back. She began searching for ways to improve her health, not accepting poor health as an option and realizing that her mental state was contributing to her poor health.

In her search, Marion discovered she was allergic to several foods. When she ate these foods, her pain became more intense. So she began to watch her diet. She also began to slowly add exercise into her life again. She included prayer and meditation in her daily routine. She was addressing all four elements of her makeup.

Not only did all of this bring about a change in her attitude, but it also brought about a radical change in her condition. Her road to recovery was long and difficult, but today Marion is healthier at almost sixty than she was at forty. She is often complimented for her shapely physique and her inner energy that radiates from her entire being.

Marion is a wonderful example of good health. She got all aspects of her being into balance—and we can all do the same if we work at it. Marion works at her health every day. She eats right, exercises on a regular basis, and cares for her emotional and spiritual well-being.

What are *you* doing to move toward balanced health?

START WITH SMALL STEPS

Perhaps you really want to get in shape, but you can't seem to make it a priority. Or maybe you go full speed ahead for a short while but soon give up in frustration or boredom. Maybe your solution is to simply do absolutely nothing. That's OK, because we are about to change all of that and move you toward a healthier you, no matter what your personality style.

But first, you must commit to doing whatever it takes for a new you. I can show you the most enjoyable way for your personality type to exercise, but if you continue to do the same things you've always done, you will continue to end up at the same place. In order to achieve different results, you must be willing to do something different. Are you? Be honest with yourself. Your first steps toward health don't have to be huge. Baby steps are just right.

I recently spoke to a group of business professionals about health and wellness. During my presentation, I discussed the consequences of an inactive lifestyle and the benefits of an active one. I shared alarming statistics about stress-related illnesses and obesity. I encouraged them all to do something positive about their health that very day because each of them mattered to someone, and they are very special. I said that although caring for one's self can seem selfish, it is actually a very giving act. If you really love your family and friends, you will take care of yourself so that you will be around for a very long time.

The next month, I gave the same presentation to another group of business professionals in a nearby town. One of the women from my previous engagement was also at this function. Early in my speech she asked to speak to the group. She turned to them and said that I had changed her life. She had been overweight and inactive, but when she heard me speak she'd finally confronted the fact that she was in poor health, which could have severe consequences for her family that she loved. Immediately following my first talk she had started making better choices about her health: eliminating some fried foods, drinking more water, and purchasing (and using) a set of hand weights. She'd begun exercising at home and working in the yard more. After just one month of this she was already feeling healthier and more energetic. She was on her way to a healthier life.

The very good news is that you can also make huge improvements in a short time. It is not too late to start, and even small steps will make a difference.

THE SPIRITUAL SIDE OF HEALTH

I wouldn't be surprised if you're still feeling apprehensive about making that commitment. Maybe you've had a bad experience with fitness in the past or you're concerned about how much time and energy this will take. If that's you, consider the *spiritual* side of poor health. God created our bodies. He refers to them in Scripture as our *temples*. He commands us to take very good care of them because they are sacred:

> Don't you know that you yourselves are God's temple and that God's Spirit lives in you? If anyone destroys God's temple, God will destroy him. For God's temple is sacred, and you are that temple.
>
> —1 CORINTHIANS 3:16

Many people think that as long as they work on their spiritual relationship they are caring for God's temple. Wrong! That leaves out the other three tires on the car. Our physical bodies, our emotions, and our minds must be in good shape, too. We are to be a reflection of God. Personally, I think He wants us to have the best package possible so that we may draw people closer to His love. If we are not in shape, how can people *see* what God has done?

Besides owing it to ourselves to strive toward a healthier life, we owe it to God. He gave us a miraculous gift called life. Let us not waste it or take it for granted. We don't know how many days we will have in this life, but good health will ensure that whatever time we have *will* be more enjoyable and effective for Him.

I believe in you. I know you can do this. It will require some adjustments, but in the end you will be so very glad you did...and so will your family.

GETTING THE MOST FROM THIS BOOK

In order to move toward better health you must not only make a commitment; you must also take action. This is where a lot of people get stuck.

Recently, a client of mine decided to stop talking about running a half marathon and actually sign up for one. By paying the entrance fee and telling her friends she was going to race, she felt obligated to begin training for race day. Instead of thinking about it, she started taking steps toward completing it.

Have you tried numerous diets and workout plans but always gotten frustrated or bored and ended up quitting? Can you remember your reasons for stopping? You wanted to get healthier, but it didn't work out. Why? Again, be honest with yourself. Do you just dislike exercise as you have experienced it in the past? Do you feel you don't have the time? Are you afraid to try something new? Are you settling for poor health and accepting it as "good enough"?

I am simply the person delivering this message. Your attitude will determine the true value you receive from this book. So before you go any further, please read the following suggestions for getting the most out of this book. My corporate training and consulting experience have taught me that if we prepare ourselves for new information in advance, we are more likely to receive and apply it.

Try these out:

1. *Be receptive to new ideas and methods.* Keep your mind open to new information, concepts, and strategies. Even if you have heard some of the ideas in this book before, strive to apply them in a different manner.

2. *Delay final judgment until you have a chance to see if it works.* Give everything some time to sink in before you say yea or nay.

3. *Be flexible and adapt.* Take the information I provide and build upon it, making it personal and suitable for your particular situation. Although the book will address a variety of styles, every person is unique. Make it work for you.

4. *Desire to improve.* You will find what you seek. If you think fitness and health is a bunch of hogwash, you won't discover all the gems found within this book's pages. If, on the other hand, you come to it looking for ways to improve the quality of your life, you will find outstanding ways to do just that. It is in your power to determine what you get out of this book and whether or not you will succeed.

5. *Wear thicker skin as you read.* Do not get so caught up in how the message is delivered, but rather concentrate on what it can do for you. Remember that you want to learn how to live a healthier life.

LET'S GO!

As your personal trainer for the duration of this book, I look forward to providing you with information that will help you make better decisions regarding your health. I am eager to introduce you to yourself and help you understand how beautifully made you are and how you can make fitness FAST, FUN, FRIENDLY, or FACTUAL, depending upon your temperament.

You have made a commitment, are willing to take action, want to turn your health aspirations into realized goals, and are proceeding with an open mind—so let's get started! Get ready for a healthier you. Be prepared to achieve a more balanced life. As my mom did. As Marion did. As that woman who heard me speak did. And as I did.

You, dear friend, can finally be fit.

SET YOURSELF UP FOR SUCCESS

ONE | DISCOVER YOUR FIT!

WELCOME TO *FINALLY FIT!* I hope you read the introduction. If not, I encourage you to go back because it will help you find your motivation. Without it, you may be reducing your chances of success, and I want everyone to win!

Do you remember the television show *Simon & Simon*? It was a 1980s' series about two brothers operating a private eye business together in San Diego. Although they came from the same parents, they were complete opposites. AJ (the blonde) was warm, friendly, and personable, while Rick (the cowboy) was bold, aggressive, and task oriented. I won't make you tell me which one you liked best—and please don't embarrass me by saying you're too young to remember the show! Each brother had his strengths. On the show, however, they were constantly squabbling about how to approach a case or talk with people, and they never seemed to see eye to eye.

Can you relate? Do you have a family member you just don't understand?

I believe there are four basic personality traits that everyone possesses in some measure. God gives them to us at birth and arranges them differently in each of us. Typically they are called personality traits, styles, or human behavior temperaments. People have been noticing temperament differences at least as far back as 444 B.C.[1] They have been defined, labeled, and taught by an array of professionals through the course of history. But don't let any of that intimidate you: they are simply tools for helping us understand each other better and get along with less conflict.

You have probably encountered personality type or temperament systems in the past. If you read one person's book regarding personalities and human behavior, he or she may correlate temperaments with bodily fluids, as did Hippocrates long ago.[2] If you study another person's work, the traits may be given as colors that represent each style. Some network marketing companies use this method. Still other people have created labels, names, acronyms, and so forth in order to help define personality traits.

All of these schools of thought are attempting to accomplish the same thing: to help you understand yourself and people around you. They can give insight into how your personality traits are arranged and how you are different from other people.

You see, even though we all have the same four basic temperaments or traits, we each have them in varying degrees. The unique mix of these traits is what makes you *you* and not me or someone else. It explains why siblings from the same parents, who grew up in the same home—like AJ and Rick—can be complete opposites. Our unique profile determines how we approach everything: communication, conflict resolution, time management, social interaction, and yes, fitness.

And because you *are* different from everyone else, knowing how you are wired will help you determine what kind of fitness program you should implement. Why try to squeeze that square peg into a round hole when you can have a custom fit?

STRUCTURE OF THIS BOOK

Too often, we settle for programs that don't feel right or work for us because we don't think we have any other options. We grin and bear it, trying to make the most of a mismatched system. Our learning institutions are infamous for this. Those who don't fit the profile must simply persevere because the system will not change for them.

But when it comes to fitness, you do have a choice! You can make it fit your unique style. This book will take you on a journey of self-discovery that will help you understand how you view things and approach life. In just a moment you'll take an assessment that will determine your primary temperament type.

This book will also guide you through the process of finding your purpose or motivation. I'm a firm believer in the idea that if we don't know *why* we want to embark on a change, we won't be nearly as committed to making that change, which will likely reduce our chances of success.

With a better understanding of yourself and what motivates you, I will then give you some fitness basics. I hope to slowly bring you up to speed on a very practical and effective concept of a healthy lifestyle. I will even show you pictures and describe certain exercises. My hope is that this will all start to come together to prepare you for the chapter on your primary temperament type. That chapter (one of the four chapters in section three) gathers all this information and customizes it into a package just for you.

Then we will talk about good nutrition choices, because being healthy certainly includes eating right. Finally I've included a success contract for you to fill out and a number of success stories—including mine—to inspire you to become finally fit.

Your chances of succeeding at anything are greatly increased when you do it in a way that works for—not against—you. Fitness is no exception. In order to truly incorporate it into your life and obtain the results you are seeking, *it must fit your personality*.

THE FIT ASSESSMENT

The assessment I've provided will help you discover exactly what your personality profile looks like.

I wonder if you're thinking, *I've taken this kind of test before. I never get anything out of them.* Well, this isn't a *test*. No one can pass or fail my FIT questionnaire. What you will be taking is an assessment, which is basically going to take a snapshot of your personality profile as it reads *today*. Tomorrow you might answer somewhat differently. You're not stuck with this snapshot forever. We will simply use it for today for the purposes of this book.

Discovering your primary FIT (Fitness Individuality Trait) is easy! Just answer the questions. Remember, no one style is better or worse than any other; they are simply different. We are each a combination of several traits, and each combination is different.

Personality or behavior assessments are never intended to be a negative label to be used for judging others or placing them in a box. They do, however, provide incredible insight into how we are wired and how we approach life. Please also keep in mind that our backgrounds, upbringings, cultures, experiences, and faith influence who we become and how we behave.

Assessment instructions

As you go through the FIT Assessment:

- Circle the answer you feel *best* describes you *most* of the time.

- Circle your answers right on the book or on a separate sheet.

- Be honest and answer each question as you really are, not as you would like to be or wish you were. This assessment is only as accurate as your honesty. There are no right or wrong answers.

- Go with your first response or gut feeling, as it is likely the most accurate.

- Do not spend a lot of time analyzing an answer. This assessment should take no more than twenty to thirty minutes.

- If you would answer differently for yourself at work versus at home, use home as your reference.

FIT Assessment

1. I am reading this book because...
   a. I have specific fitness goals and this book can help me achieve them.
   b. I am interested in learning about a new approach to fitness.
   c. a friend or family member recommended the book to me.
   d. I want to obtain more details about a healthy lifestyle.

2. Regular exercise...
   a. can keep me healthy, benefiting all areas of my life.
   b. can help me perform better and achieve the results I seek.
   c. is a requirement for a healthy lifestyle.
   d. is good for me, is good for you, and can be fun to boot!

3. I presently approach fitness...
   a. by scheduling it in and honoring the commitment.
   b. by taking on the challenge and conquering it.
   c. by participating in group classes.
   d. by working out with my fitness partner/friend/spouse.

4. When I work out, I…
   a. like a high-energy club where I can interact with other people.
   b. prefer a steady, stable routine that includes many of the same exercises without a lot of change.
   c. prefer an exercise program that is goal oriented and gets me in and out quickly.
   d. prefer a structured, proven exercise program rather than trendy new classes.

5. I personally work out…
   a. to achieve my health and fitness goals.
   b. because it is an integral part of a healthy lifestyle.
   c. because I enjoy the atmosphere and interacting with others at the club.
   d. to see friends and catch up.

6. When selecting a facility to work out in, I prefer…
   a. a large gym that has a lot of equipment and no lines.
   b. a smaller, more intimate gym—maybe even a home gym.
   c. a large gym with a lot of options and variety of classes.
   d. any size facility that has proper equipment, regularly scheduled classes, and knowledgeable staff.

7. When it comes to exercise, I enjoy…
   a. small groups or one-on-one training without a lot of distractions.
   b. competitive sports such as basketball, tennis, racquet-ball, or baseball.
   c. participating in classes or exercise programs with lots of high-energy people!
   d. a steady routine, but not too "hard core."

8. I would describe myself as mostly…
   a. outgoing, but I like to get things done.
   b. outgoing, and I like interacting with people.
   c. reserved, but I enjoy one-on-one relationships.
   d. reserved, and I like systematically analyzing or planning things.

9. If you asked a close friend or family member about me, he or she would say that I am...
   a. a cautious, organized individual.
   b. a stable, supportive person.
   c. an inspirational, fun person.
   d. a driven and goal-oriented individual.

10. When I have a choice, I like...
    a. a fast, intense pace with purpose.
    b. a slow, methodical pace with no change.
    c. a fast, high-energy pace with little change.
    d. a structured, calculated pace with planned change.

11. In my opinion, rules...
    a. can help people get along by providing stability and certainty.
    b. are for other people.
    c. are necessary for a structured and orderly world.
    d. can be bent or broken (there are too many anyway).

12. Given a choice, I would prefer to wear...
    a. tried and true classic clothes that are practical.
    b. calming, subtle-colored clothes that are comfortable.
    c. sharp and classy suits or business attire.
    d. fun, bright-colored outfits that are hip and trendy.

13. Under stress, I may...
    a. retreat to solitude and withdraw emotionally.
    b. get impatient and bark.
    c. become quite talkative and disorganized.
    d. overanalyze and become critical.

14. My life motto is...
    a. go for it!
    b. all for one and one for all!
    c. we need each other.
    d. everything is done for a reason.

15. When making decisions, I…
    a. quickly decide and press on.
    b. gather information and research in order to make the right decision.
    c. tend to follow popular opinion.
    d. ask a close friend what he or she thinks.

16. At a party or large gathering, I am likely to…
    a. enjoy mingling and meeting new people.
    b. look for a friend or someone I know and usually hang out with just that person.
    c. make an appearance, shake some hands, and leave if there is no particular reason for me to be there.
    d. find an excuse not to attend. I don't like parties.

17. By making a lifestyle change, I want to…
    a. better plan and structure exercise into my life.
    b. lose a little weight and feel better about myself.
    c. reach specific health and/or fitness goals.
    d. meet other active people and have fun.

18. Given a choice, I would prefer to drive…
    a. a practical, economical car.
    b. a fun, new, and trendy vehicle.
    c. a fast sports car.
    d. a reliable, modest, mid-sized car.

19. My relationship to food is such that I believe eating…
    a. is a vital part of life, and I don't like to rush it.
    b. is social, and I enjoy sharing a good meal with a friend.
    c. can be a great social event, and I like trying all sorts of different dishes.
    d. is for fuel. I eat only when I'm hungry and get it over with quickly.

20. When communicating with others, I tend to…
    a. state my opinion directly.
    b. talk more than I listen.
    c. listen more than I talk.
    d. speak precisely and accurately.

Well, how did that go? For some people, this will be a quick and easy task. If this is you, you probably only needed a few minutes to complete the assessment. Another type of person would have actually labored over the questions for quite some time. Which are you?

Resist the temptation to go back and change your answers. Accept that it is good enough for today. You can always take the assessment again another time.

Let's score your assessment and discover your FIT profile.

SCORING YOUR FITNESS INDIVIDUALITY TRAITS (FIT)

Using the table below, circle the letter that corresponds to each question. If you circled letter *B* in Question #1, circle letter *B* in the table below. If you circled letter *C* in Question #2, circle the letter *C*, and so forth. Then count up the number of circles in each column and enter the total at the bottom. The column with the highest number is your FIT profile.

For example, Chart 1.1 on the next page shows how one person might fill out the test.

Note: If you have two columns that are the same number, review the brief descriptions below and select the FIT profile you relate with most. You may want to read both of those chapters in section three in order to truly customize your program for your style.

Chart 1.1 | FIT Assessment Sample Answer Sheet

Q#	Circle Answer			
1	A	Ⓑ	C	D
2	B	D	A	Ⓒ
3	B	C	Ⓓ	A
4	Ⓒ	A	B	D
5	A	C	D	Ⓑ
6	Ⓐ	C	B	D
7	B	Ⓒ	D	A
8	A	B	Ⓒ	D
9	Ⓓ	B	C	A
10	A	Ⓒ	B	D
11	Ⓑ	D	A	C
12	C	D	B	Ⓐ
13	B	Ⓒ	A	D
14	A	B	Ⓒ	D
15	A	C	Ⓓ	B
16	C	A	B	Ⓓ
17	Ⓒ	D	B	A
18	Ⓒ	B	D	A
19	D	Ⓒ	B	A
20	Ⓐ	B	C	D
Total	7	5	4	4
FIT Profile	FAST	FUN	FRIENDLY	FACTUAL

In the example above, the person scored highest in the FAST temperament, which is his or her primary style.

Now, find your FIT.

Chart 1.2 | FIT Assessment Answer Sheet

Q#	Circle Answer			
1	A	B	C	D
2	B	D	A	C
3	B	C	D	A
4	C	A	B	D
5	A	C	D	B
6	A	C	B	D
7	B	C	D	A
8	A	B	C	D
9	D	B	C	A
10	A	C	B	D
11	B	D	A	C
12	C	D	B	A
13	B	C	A	D
14	A	B	C	D
15	A	C	D	B
16	C	A	B	D
17	C	D	B	A
18	C	B	D	A
19	D	C	B	A
20	A	B	C	D
Total				
FIT Profile	FAST	FUN	FRIENDLY	FACTUAL

FIT profile descriptions

Read the brief descriptions that follow on page 24, and determine which one you relate with most often. Write it down.

FAST—Congratulations! You most likely tend to be a driven individual who enjoys competition, whether it be with yourself or others. You keep a fast pace and focus on results. I've dedicated chapter six to your FIT profile.

FUN—Congratulations! You most likely tend to be an interactive individual who enjoys people, whether in large or small groups. You are energetic and must have variety. I've dedicated chapter seven to your FIT profile.

FRIENDLY—Congratulations! You most likely tend to be a bit on the shy side and enjoy a supportive environment, whether it be from a class or a personal trainer. You prefer a slower pace and put relationships first. I've dedicated chapter eight to your FIT profile.

FACTUAL—Congratulations! You most likely tend to be a focused individual who enjoys structure, whether it be at the gym or outdoor activities. You analyze before you decide in order to ensure that you will be correct and accurate. I've dedicated chapter nine to your FIT profile.

Now you know which FIT you are, and you have some small idea of what that means. Chapter two will go into detail to help you understand your personality type and how temperaments relate to each other in groups. I think you'll be surprised at what you learn.

Two | Understanding Personality Types

WHAT ARE PERSONALITY types, anyway? Maybe you're familiar with these from one or more of the typing systems that are out there. Maybe you're not. Allow me to take a moment to explain.

I like to use the analogy of a stereo to explain how I view personality profiles because almost everyone is familiar with stereos. When you turn the volume knob to the right you increase the volume. In my model, turning the personality volume knob to the right indicates a more outgoing personality. Think of louder as more verbal. When turned back to the left, it reflects a quieter, more reserved personality. If you were to divide up everyone in the world, some of us would be more outgoing while others would be reserved. If we further divided this group, some would be oriented toward tasks, while the remaining people would enjoy being with people.

VOLUME   TUNER CONTROL

The tuner knob on a stereo changes the radio station. In my model, it points you to a "people" station or a "task" station. Some of us would like to just sit and visit with friends. The rest of us would prefer to get busy doing what needs to be done.

These two knobs together divide the world up into the four personality groups: those who are more verbal (outgoing), those who carefully select their words (reserved), those who tackle tasks, and those who like being around people. No group is better than any other. It is simply how the world is divided. God didn't want us to all be the same, so He created four temperaments. Each of us can relate more with one style than with any of the others. How boring the world would be if we were all alike and fell in the same quadrant.

Of course, it's not that simple. Just as a stereo is more complex than just the volume and tuner knobs, so is your personality. Each of us is *primarily* one temperament, but we also have some measure of the other types in us. The mix is one of the things that make us unique. In the assessment you may have related most with the FRIENDLY style, for example, but you can "visit" the other styles in the course of a normal day.

We can't always behave in the way that comes most naturally to us. If you're naturally brutally honest, it's OK to be that way with someone who is like you and wants you to shoot straight. But it could be disastrous to be brutally honest with some people or in some situations. The school of hard knocks has taught us that in some situations, it is in everyone's best interest if we curb our natural impulses and those words that come so easily to our tongue. We can even behave in ways that are completely different from who we are naturally—but only for short periods and with great effort.

There is much more to the temperaments and the way they are interrelated. If you are interested, I recommend *You've Got Style* by Robert A. Rohm, PhD, or other good books on the subject. I've given you just enough to help you understand the components of temperament styles that will make you successful in your journey toward becoming finally fit.

PUTTING YOUR FIT INTO FITNESS

In this book we will focus on your primary FIT trait and how it relates to fitness. FIT stands for Fitness Individuality Trait, after all. On the next page is a summary of the four primary temperaments. You'll find much greater detail in the chapters dedicated to the particular temperaments, but this will give you something about all of them. I believe it's important for us to understand not only ourselves, but also to understand a little of what makes other people tick.

If you found yourself in the FAST FIT category (like me), you prefer deciding for yourself. You assess things quickly without a lot of input from others. You are driven and goal oriented, as well. You can be demanding on yourself and others. Can you see how this information will impact what type of exercise programs you select? A FAST person, for instance, hates to wait in lines at the gym and may give up on fitness altogether rather than finding a faster way to work out. Understanding how you're wired will help you find success in fitness—and everything else, for that matter.

If your highest score was in the FUN FIT category, you like to interact with people. You blend or mingle well. You appreciate high-energy groups and a variety of options. You are an influencer, but you can also be easily influenced by others. You typically like large social or public gatherings. Can you imagine how you might approach fitness differently than the other styles? If you were to try to exercise alone all the time, you might get bored. It might not be very much fun, so you could end up quitting.

If your highest score was in the FRIENDLY FIT category, you prefer a slow pace. You would much rather be in a small group setting than a large social event. You do not like a lot of change, preferring a routine. Your steady pace can lead to stubbornness if not monitored. You need a unique fitness program that "fits" you. Don't try to go it alone. Work out with a friend.

If your highest score was in the FACTUAL FIT category, you like details and structure. You have a calculating and analytical mind that prefers working on tasks rather than engaging with people. Because of your attention to facts and figures, you may at times come across as cold. You approach fitness differently than others…more structured.

We're all different! A one-size-fits-all approach to fitness (or to anything, for that matter) will not work with any of these people. Probably all four types could *do* any fitness program, but to really succeed at it, it would have to be one that allowed them to operate as close as possible to their comfort zone.

It is the difference between buying a cheap suit off the rack or having one custom made from fine silk, tailored to your exact body shape. One gets the job done, but the other caresses your skin and makes you feel like a million bucks! It fits and is your favorite suit, so you wear it. You feel good in it, and you find you have more success when you're wearing it.

A customized approach to fitness will be that perfect FIT for you—one that you enjoy and that motivates you to stick with it. It's the program that will make *the* difference you have been hoping for.

How to FIT in With Others

The temperament information is fascinating, isn't it? Most people enjoy the self-discovery these personality-typing systems bring. But it's also great to learn a little about the people around you.

The more I study human behavior, the more fun I have interacting with people. Within seconds, I can usually determine a person's temperament style. This enables me to immediately adapt my natural temperament style to accommodate them as we converse. Everything goes smoothly because I'm speaking their language.

As you learn more about yourself and others, you can use this information to build relationships, not tear them down. The more we know about others and ourselves, the better we can communicate, if we use it properly. Soon you too will begin noticing other people's styles and adapting accordingly.

Discovering your style is not a license to say, "This is just the way I am." On the contrary, this information should enable you to be more understanding and compassionate with others. As you learn more about how each style is different, you should find yourself adapting more to others and attempting to communicate to *their* style.

[EFFECTIVE] COMMUNICATION DOES NOT BEGIN WITH BEING UNDERSTOOD BUT WITH FIRST UNDERSTANDING OTHERS.

—W. STEVEN BROWN

You now have a basic idea of how you are wired. This will be foundational in designing a fitness plan that is right for you. But good health will not simply come to you. You won't wake up one morning and be fit and trim just because you decided to. You must make a deliberate decision to pursue fitness, and you must actively engage in it each and every day, no matter what your style is.

The key to succeeding in fitness is not so much how you do, but why. When I coach or train people, motivation is *the* factor that will determine if they stick with their new program or not, no matter what their style is.

So, what is it that *you* want? *Who* is it that matters? *What* are you looking for? What *works* best for you? Let's find out together and ensure the greatest chances of success for your new life being *Finally FIT!*

THREE | UNDERSTANDING WHY YOU DO WHAT YOU DO

I HAVE TITLED section one "Set Yourself Up for Success" for two reasons. First, most people don't understand how they are wired. Without this knowledge, they are literally walking around blind. In many cases they are making things harder on themselves by trying to be someone they are not or trying to do things that don't work for them. We will change that for you with this book. My hope is that a huge weight will be lifted from your shoulders as a result of your reading *Finally FIT!*

THIS CHAPTER WILL HELP YOU UNCOVER YOUR WHY, YOUR MOTIVATION FOR MAKING A CHANGE AND ACHIEVING SUCCESS.

That's what happened to a woman in one of my seminars. She'd spent thirty years struggling to get along with her sister. After just one session of our communications training, she began to cry. She realized that it wasn't *her* that was the problem; it was simply that she had been created to be different from her sister. She wasn't less of a person; she was a different personality. She went straight home and called her sister, and her newly learned understanding of herself and her sister enabled her to communicate more effectively. They have a brand-new, loving relationship now.

Setting yourself up for success involves understanding yourself and others. That's what chapter one was about.

The other reason I named this section "Set Yourself Up for Success" is that most people don't know why they do some things and not others. Even people with goals may not have a clearly defined reason for their goal. Without a *why*, your chances of succeeding in anything are dramatically diminished. This chapter will help you not only define your goals but also help you uncover your motivation for making a change and achieving success.

DESIRES, DREAMS, AND GOALS

My husband has been a commercial fisherman, one of the most dangerous occupations in the world, for eighteen years. Out at sea he doesn't have road signs or landmarks to keep him on course. To manage—and stay alive—he must carefully map out his target location, calculate the path he should chart, anticipate obstacles, and then constantly monitor his course in order to arrive at his final destination. So far Steve has always arrived back safely, and *Deo valente* (Lord willing), he will continue to do so.

Our lives are no different. We have destinations we want to reach, but storms threaten to blow us off course. Have you ever felt like a tiny boat being tossed about by the fierce waves of the ocean? The pounding of each wave can wear you out and the undertow can pull you down—if you don't have a plan. This chapter will help you overcome disappointment that you may have faced in the past by helping you chart a clear course to reach your fitness goals.

Have you heard the saying, "No one plans to fail, but always will if they fail to plan"? Every aspect of our life, including fitness, requires planning. You must have clearly defined plans and smart goals if you hope to have a chance of hitting your target. Although our lives are not in immediate danger, like my husband's when he is out in the open waters, our long-term future health can be dramatically impaired if we get off course today. You must know where you are going *today* in order to reach the *tomorrow* you want to enjoy. Goal setting is the key.

■

GOALS ARE THE KEY TO SUCCESS—
BUT GOALS REQUIRE ACTION.

■

Goals are not the same thing as desires. Desires are things we talk about wanting but never really do anything about. I personally *desire* to win the lottery. I would love to have more money to spoil people I care about. But

I am not purchasing any tickets. Therefore, it is not a goal because I have not taken any *action* toward it. Goals require action. *Dreams* are not goals, either. We tend to feel more passionately about our dreams than we do about our desires, but still a dream does not become a goal until we take steps toward it.

Is a healthy lifestyle a goal for you? Or is it just a desire or a dream? In order for you to achieve it, it must be a true goal, which means it will require action on your part. You cannot hope to change; you must *decide and commit* that you will change.

I am constantly in awe of my fitness class participants. Though they all have very full and complex lives, they faithfully attend classes. When I talk with them, they never say their goal is just to be in shape. No, they have a deeper motivation, something that gets them to class on days when they just don't feel like it.

One man was told he was a walking heart attack waiting to happen. He joined my class six months ago, and now his cholesterol is so low the doctors thought he had been taking medication behind their backs. With a big smile on his face, he introduced me to his motivation: his wife. He wanted to be around to enjoy their golden years together. His wife was who kept him going, and now he sticks to it to ensure a healthy future.

You must be willing to do whatever it takes to accomplish *your* goal. Since you have purchased this book—you took action—I know good health really is a goal for you. You've already taken the first step toward it. Good for you!

YOUR SMART FITNESS GOAL

Let's talk about your fitness goal for a minute. What is yours? If you haven't really given it much thought, this chapter will guide you through an excellent process of determining what you really want and how to obtain it. I encourage you to disclose your goal to a person close to you. Somehow when we actually speak our goals verbally, especially to someone who can know whether we're pursuing them or not, we make a deeper commitment to those goals. And a loved one or close friend can be a great support system and accountability partner.

As you start thinking about your goal, check out the following criteria. Be sure your fitness goal is SMART:

Chart 3.1 | **SMART Goal-Planning Criteria**

• <u>Specific</u>	Gives us a target/direction to focus our energy and activity
• <u>Measurable</u>	Measures progress and know when we achieve the goal
• <u>Actionable</u>	Requires some kind of action (Required to achieve *anything*!)
• <u>Realistic</u>	Provides motivation through faith that we can/will achieve our goals
• <u>Timed</u>	Time specific. Accountability. Keeps us on track.

Get out a piece of paper and actually write down your goal with these elements in mind. Be *specific* with what you are trying to accomplish. The more details you can include, the more you will know what you are attempting to do and what will be required of you. Write down your motivation, too.

A client of mine named Karis wants to decrease her dress size from a 9 to a 7 for her wedding. (Her motivation is to look her best.) This is an excellent goal because it meets the SMART requirements. First, it is *specific*. If your goal is vague, you won't have focus for your energy.

Second, Karis's goal is *measurable*. I actually measured Karis's body so that we would have a starting point or benchmark to measure against. She could also try on a size 7 to determine if she had reached her goal. In either case, we have concrete ways to measure success. Keep this in mind for your fitness goal. Is it measurable?

Third, Karis's goal is *actionable*. She will have to work the cardio and weight-lifting programs I developed for her. I am only the trainer and coach. She will also need to watch her food/calorie intake in order to get where she wants to go. If she doesn't do the work, she won't achieve the goal. Action is required. Does your goal require you to take action? What will *you* need to do?

Fourth, Karis's goal is *realistic*. She used to be a size 7 and just got into some bad habits that caused her to gain a little weight. Combined with being unable to play soccer due to a knee injury, Karis went through a change in her body that she didn't like. Her body will remember, however, and with dedication and work, she will get there in a reasonable time frame. If, however, she were a size 13 and had always been a size 13, attempting to shrink her to a much smaller size would not be realistic—at least not right away. The better approach in that case would be to start off with a more reasonable, obtainable goal such as a size 9 or 10.

Make sure your goal is realistic, too. Avoid setting yourself up for failure. Life beats us up enough when we don't expect it. Don't put yourself in a situation where you may face more hardship, pain, frustration, and discouragement. Set goals that challenge you, but make sure they are actually attainable, as well. We all do better when we can celebrate a victory, even if it is a small one.

Fifth, Karis's goal is good because it is *timed*. She wants to get into a size 7 by her wedding day, which as of this writing was five months away. She is on her way to achieving her goal and will walk down the aisle with a big smile on her face!

Your goal needs to have a deadline, too. I have found that if people do not set a due date on their goals, they will never accomplish them. It is all too easy to put off and procrastinate when you do not sense urgency. A deadline creates a sense of pressure and creates the momentum we need to take steps toward the final goal. Give yourself a realistic time frame to achieve your goal, and you will have something to shoot for.

Be honest with your fitness goals as you write them out. Remember, the more specific, the greater your chances of success. Did you know that those who write out their goals are ten times more successful at achieving them than those who do not write out their goals? This exercise will help you define exactly what you want to accomplish. Then I'll show you *how* to do it based upon your personality.

OVERCOMING OBSTACLES

Great. You have written out your fitness goals. Now, what is going to prevent you from reaching them?

No, I'm not being negative—I'm being realistic. We are all given only twenty-four hours a day. In that day, we have to work, take care of the house and the cars, cook, clean, wash clothes, sleep, and spend time with family and friends (just to mention a few). A busy schedule is definitely an obstacle for most people. You must spell out your obstacles so you can know ahead of time what you may encounter along the way—the resistance you will face—and plan how to overcome them.

You might even be one of your own obstacles. Do you tend to put things off until the last minute? Why? Procrastination is on the top-ten list of time management traps and is responsible for more pain and disappointment than all other time traps combined.[1] Procrastination is the only time trap we impose upon ourselves. No one makes us procrastinate; we do it to ourselves out of fear of failure, fear of success, or any number of reasons. Those who procrastinate know they do it, but they may not always understand why. If you can create some leverage or motivation through this exercise, then you just might be able to overcome that bad habit!

Finances can be an obstacle, too. Is money going to hinder your attempt to get fit? If you don't have the funds to join a gym, you will have to be creative.

What I'm asking you to do is jot down anything you think may get in your way so that you can overcome them! So take a minute and list out your potential hazards. Go on. I'll wait…

Good to have you back. Keep that list handy as we go through the rest of this chapter.

RTP

Now I'm going to introduce you to a concept my husband and I have developed. We use it to teach, coach, and train. It is called *RTP*, or *Resources, Time, and People*. It is designed to help you see in advance where you are going and what challenges you may face. It prevents the "head-down-to the-grindstone-and-not-looking-up" syndrome. If we aren't careful, we can bump right into a brick wall. RTP will help you look further out in the future so that you may anticipate and respond proactively rather than reacting out of crisis.

Everything we do requires these three things: resources, time, and people. If we can outline in advance what we need to accomplish our goal, we will be more prepared and equipped for success.

A perfect example is hiking. I love hiking in the mountains, but I cannot just show up and hike. If I did, I could die. I could run out of water, get lost, injure myself, or encounter an array of hazards. I must know how long and how difficult the trail is and then determine what I will need in order to embark on my hike with confidence. My RTP for a typical hiking trip looks something like this:

Resources

- Hiking boots, socks, and stick
- Camelback full of water (depending on the length, more water)
- Hiking pack stocked with emergency gear (flares, first aid, etc.)
- Hat, sunglasses, sunscreen, and bug spray
- Trail map, walkie-talkies, and cell phone

- Gasoline in car
- Food

Time

- Driving time to and from
- Number of miles to hike
- Hours allotted to complete the hike

People

- A hiking buddy and me
- Someone not on the hike who knows where we are going and when we should return

The RTP system is perfect for thinking about what you'll need in order to reach your fitness goal, too. Draw out your own fitness RTP right now. A simple piece of paper with three columns will do. Will you need to purchase hand weights or actual weight-lifting machines? Will you need new shoes? Will you need to join a gym, or will you purchase your own cardio equipment? Will you need childcare?

Some of this you won't know now. We haven't talked about your specific fitness program, so you don't yet know what you'll need for it. Keep your RTP sheet handy because you will most likely add to it as we dig deeper into your style and determine a very specific program for you. For starters, though, I want you to have some idea of what you will need to reach your fitness goal and what obstacles you may face. This exercise can help determine what you can do to either prevent the obstacles or overcome them. No excuses now!

ENERGY GRAPH

Now that you have SMART fitness goals and RTP solutions outlined, the next step is to begin looking at your real-life schedule to determine how this new goal will fit in. For most of us, something else doesn't get taken off the plate when we add a new endeavor.

Take writing this book, for instance. I did not have the luxury of pulling the plug on my consulting, coaching, and training business (Concept One) in order to dedicate 100 percent of my time to writing. I needed to keep my regular income and keep the business running. Nor was I able or willing to quit all activities such as church, social events, and fitness classes. If I wanted to write a book and get it published, I had to squeeze my writing into my existing schedule. I was given a firm deadline date from my publisher, so I knew what I needed to do and by when. I then had to determine, on a monthly, weekly, and daily basis, how I would accomplish the goal.

Since I had the due date and a minimum word count, I was able to break that down to see how many words I needed to get written every month, week, and day. That worked for me.

Let's apply this to the number of pounds you want to lose. On the book, I broke down my total word-count number, which felt overwhelming at times, by dividing it by the number of days I had to write. You would divide your weight-loss goal by the number of pounds that are healthy to lose each week (1 to 3, depending upon your gender). I counted on only four writing days a week instead of five, just to allow for "crazy" days. For weight loss, you might give yourself extra time to take into account vacations and so forth. I then blocked out the appropriate amount of time each day to write that many words, based on my typing speed. In the same way, you can block out your workout days.

You face the same scenario as I did with your fitness goal: where will *you* squeeze it in?

An excellent tool I use for my clients and myself is an energy graph. An energy graph charts out your peak productive times of the day in order to capitalize on them. My best creative time is in the afternoon, so I would try to do all my other work in the mornings. Take a moment to draw out your energy cycle on the graph provided on page 37. Jot down when you're feeling especially energetic or particularly pooped. This will help you determine the best time of the day to work out.

Here's a tip: if you already enjoy fitness and are eager to do it, schedule your workout during a low energy time. Save your peak periods for those tasks you don't enjoy as much or that require more focus. Having more energy for these tasks will make them go faster and more efficiently. If, however, you dread exercising, then plan your fitness routine around your peak times, if possible. We do not live in a perfect world and cannot always do things when it is best for us, but knowing our energy cycle can help us use those bursts of energy to our advantage as much as possible.

Depending upon your FIT profile, you might also find that you have certain times of the day when you are able to tap into different traits more easily. I find that I am more creative in the afternoon. My energy increases as the day goes on. You might want to monitor a few "typical" days to help plot your graph more accurately. In the conclusion of this book you will find a journal page called "FIT Journal" for you to use for this purpose if you like. Make as many copies as you need.

Understanding your peak times and low times

Peak productivity times are the periods throughout the day when you are at your most energetic and get things done. By understanding when you are at your most productive levels, you can schedule certain events at those times. *Respect, protect,* and *direct* your energy levels and peak productivity times.

Using the chart below, draw a line that follows your peak productivity times throughout the day.

Chart 3.2 | **Energy Graph: Charting Your Daily Peak Productivity**

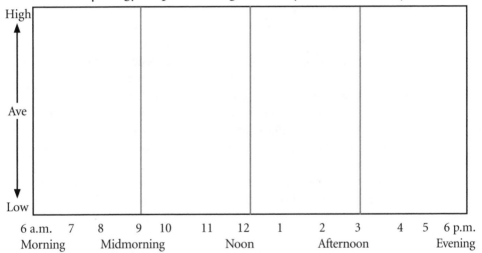

You probably already know whether you are a morning person or an evening person, but it can be quite insightful to visually see your other peak energy times of the day. Use this to help in scheduling not only your fitness program but all tasks you have to accomplish. You'll find yourself being more productive as you customize your day to your energy flow. In regards to fitness, it will certainly ensure that you have the energy to work out!

COMMITTING WITHOUT OVERCOMMITTING

No amount of physical energy alone, however, is enough to get you through your workout. You must also be mentally committed.

Many people are good at making and keeping commitments to other people. We all have work to accomplish and meetings to attend. Why is it that we keep appointments with business associates or attend our child's every T-ball game, but we have trouble honoring commitments we make to ourselves, such as working out?

For some, their personality style simply puts the focus on others first… always. If you are one of these people, let me be honest with you: if you are not taking care of yourself, you are not truly caring and loving those in your life. If you give and give but do not tend to your own needs, especially physical ones, you will actually end up hurting the ones you love. If your true motivation is to give to others, then start by taking care of yourself.

A great book to read on the subject is *Growing Weary Doing Good?* by Karla Worley.[2] In the book Karla shares her own story of how she always said yes and gave to everyone. She thought she was taking care of everyone by helping out at the church and school every chance she had—until the day she collapsed from exhaustion and illness. She was bedridden for months and could not lift a finger. She had time to reflect on what went wrong and realized she had allowed herself to get out of balance. And because she did not take care of herself, her family was suffering. She could not do one thing for her children, husband, church, or friends. She was helpless.

Don't let yourself fall apart. The best way to love others is to first love yourself.

One way of keeping yourself in balance is learning to say one small word: *no.* For such a small word, *no* can be extremely difficult for some people to say. Perhaps you were raised to always put others first or you have that temperament. In either case, learning to set boundaries will improve your emotional and mental health, not to mention freeing up time for your physical health.

Like anything new, it takes practice to say no. Evaluate each situation as it arises, and be honest about your feelings. Many times you may find yourself saying yes, but you really want to say no. This isn't fair to you or anyone else. Over time, resentment and bitterness will build up inside of you until one day you get angry and explode. People around you won't have a clue because you said yes! My best advice to you is to *say what you mean and mean what you say.*

Start off slow. If you are asked to do something but really don't have the time, try saying, "I can't help this time, but perhaps next time. Please try me again." It is still a no, but it is more cooperative. Or how about saying, "I can't do all of what you asked, but I could help with a small part." Again, it is a no to the full request but a yes to some part. Sometimes, you will just need to flat out say no. Know your limits.

A good sign of overcommitting to the point of mental and emotional stress is when you are constantly thinking of what you have left to do instead of living in the moment. You can't relax. You're edgy. You are short and impatient. Ouch. If you are already to this point, then I encourage you to set more definitive boundaries today! You are on the brink of burnout. Pick up my book *A Healthier, Happier You!: 101 Steps for Lessening Stress.*[3] I pray it will help bring balance back to your life.

■

SAY WHAT YOU MEAN AND
MEAN WHAT YOU SAY.

■

As you begin to say no when it is appropriate, you will free up time for you! Make "workout appointments," and then keep them. Treat yourself and your health just like any other important meeting, task, or person. Remember, you can't be anything for anyone when you burn out. In fact, avoiding burnout so you can continue serving others might be *your* motivation.

FINDING YOUR WHY

I have mentioned the importance of motivation already, but I will say it again: it truly is the key to reaching your fitness destination. You can set goals and manage your time more effectively in order to make room for working out. You can even make a commitment to yourself to change, but without a good reason why you're doing it, you will most likely fail. What is your *why*?

I have been active my entire life. When I was young, I worked out simply to burn off excess energy. I am one of those rare people who have more energy than they know what to do with, so I need the outlet to release it. As I got older, I began to use exercise as a stress buster. I would go to the gym to burn off my frustrations and anxiety from work. Today, I still work out for those same reasons, but my true motivator is to have a healthy mind, body, and soul.

Both of my parents died from cancer, as did many other relatives on both sides of my family. Because I firmly believe that cancer is a disease often caused by stress and a poor diet, I am doing my best to equip my body for a long, healthy life. One of the benefits I have enjoyed from living such an active lifestyle is that I've stayed toned and trim. I still fit in clothes that I wore in junior and senior high school! The only difference is that today I am actually more muscular than I was in my youth! Another benefit of being fit is that now I have even more energy…somebody stop me! I can accomplish everything I set out to do and still have energy left. My mental and emotional states are positive, and I rarely get sick.

I'll ask you again: what is your *why*? You might simply want to fit into a smaller size again and will feel better about yourself when you do. Or you may be like me and want to defy the odds of illness and be around a long time for loved ones. Whatever your reason, write it down. Better yet, memorize it. If you can associate your *why* with a visual, it will have more power to motivate you. I have pictures of my parents in my office. When I see them, I remember what an inactive, unhealthy life can do to you. I don't want to go there. I am choosing another path; I want good health and happiness.

The amazing thing about knowing your *why* is that it then helps you to prioritize your life. When something is truly important, you *will* find the time for it. Period. Most of us don't go weeks without eating, for instance. We can't live without it for very long because our body requires food to function. As a result, when our bodies need fuel, they tell us, "Hey, I'm hungry," and we eat. It is a priority. When I need to eat—I mean really need to refuel my body—I can't think of much else. The idea of food consumes my every thought until I take care of it. Then I am able to move on to other things.

Your priorities are the same way. They direct your years, months, weeks, and each day—your whole life. Your health should be one of your biggest priorities. Without it, all your other goals may become unattainable.

In order to keep your focus on your priority, write out the benefits you expect to enjoy from achieving your goal. If you need help, go back to the introduction and review the benefits of good health I have outlined. The more personal you can be, the better off you will be. You will own your goals, stay committed, and take the necessary action.

On page 254 I have provided a success contract for you to fill out. After you have read your specific FIT chapter, go ahead and write in your answers on that contract. One of the questions it asks is, "What will you do to celebrate when you achieve your goal?" I want you to spell out something meaningful for your celebration. Make it a big deal, because sticking to your fitness program and reaching your goal *is* a big deal. Living a healthy lifestyle is huge! Too often, we don't pause long enough to celebrate our victories. Take the time to tell yourself, "Good job, and way to go!" If you have something big like a weekend trip planned, it will also motivate you to stay on track. Many people respond well to a rewards system. Make it work to your advantage.

■

WHAT IS YOUR WHY?

■

Now that you have everything outlined for specific fitness SMART goals and have learned the value of RTP (spelling out what you need to accomplish your goal), I am going to share some fitness facts and proper techniques with you in the next section. The more you know, the better equipped you will be to succeed in your own program. My goal in that section is to ensure that you have a safe but effective workout that is fun! Let's do it!

BODY BEAUTIFUL

FITNESS FACTS

UNDERSTANDING YOUR PERSONALITY style is going to be crucial in establishing a fitness program that works *with* you, not *against* you. It will set you up for success, not failure. But in order to achieve any fitness goal, you must have some basic knowledge of how your body works.

Whether you're a seasoned veteran or a greenhorn when it comes to fitness, the information in this chapter will be extremely helpful for your new FIT program. I have taken some complex theories and brought them down to a practical level in order to make them quick and easy to understand and use, no matter what your style. My goal is to give you enough information to keep you safe, but not so much as to overwhelm you with details that aren't necessary for you to know. If you would like to gain a more in-depth knowledge of health and fitness, I suggest the book *Fitness and Health* by Brian J. Sharkey, PhD.[1]

THE THREE PILLARS OF FITNESS

To get fit you must address all three aspects of your health: cardiovascular capacity, muscle strength and endurance, and flexibility.

Your cardiovascular capacity is simply your ability to take in and process oxygen. This is why cardio exercise is so important. The greater the workload on your heart, the more efficient it becomes. If you get completely winded from an easy endeavor, it means your cardio capacity isn't very good. Your body isn't producing enough oxygen for the required work. Time to work on your cardiovascular fitness.

Muscle strength and endurance are the use of our muscular system. Muscle strength is the ability to handle heavy loads quickly, while muscle endurance is the ability to go the long haul. We need both. We need to be able to lift that piece of furniture, but we also need to be able to walk miles and miles at the mall. Our muscle health is directly related to our bone health, as you will soon learn.

Then we must not forget flexibility. Your ability to stretch out your muscles and allow your body to recover will determine how effective your fitness and overall well-being will be in the future. If your muscles are perpetually tight, you are more likely to incur injury.

Let's look more closely at each of these three pillars of fitness.

The heart of the matter

Research shows a direct correlation between cardio capacity and blood pressure.[2] The greater your capacity to process oxygen and use it, the lower your blood pressure will be because the heart doesn't have to work as hard to get what it needs. It will be finely tuned and operating at its maximum efficiency. When it has to struggle, it works harder and cannot produce enough oxygen to support the load on the body. This raises blood pressure. And since heart disease is associated with high blood pressure, this should inspire you to immediately increase your cardio activity.

Developing your cardio efficiency will also improve your circulation, which will ensure that blood gets to all parts of our bodies quickly and effectively. Many times, those with poor circulation have a weak heart. It isn't strong enough to pump blood properly. Exercise can change that!

We will address nutrition in chapter ten, but for now remember this simple rule: to lose weight, burn more calories than you eat. It's that simple. There is no miracle weight-loss cure, and trendy diets that promise quick weight loss are dangerous. Why are there so many "diets" out there? Because people keep gaining back the weight they lost on the last trendy diet! Think about it: if any of these diets worked, we would be a slim nation, not an obese one. No one would need another diet because the one they tried worked. But the hard truth is that the only thing that brings safe, long-lasting weight loss is old-fashioned *work*.

Calories are needed to produce energy for our bodies. But when we take in more calories than we need, our bodies store the excess as fat. Think of calories as fuel. You can't run your car on an empty tank—but neither can you put more fuel in the gas tank than it can hold. You want just the right amount of fuel. If your body has excess fuel (stored fat), you will want to decrease your fuel intake (calories) until you catch up. Allow your body to burn off what it has stored, and get in the habit of burning what comes in and not taking in extra amounts of fuel.

Heart health

Let me start off by saying that we need to exercise in order to live a healthy life and achieve the things we want in life. Perhaps it will help to explain the need for cardio exercise rather than just telling you it is good for you. Understanding how critical it is to your health may also make it more of a priority for you. So here goes.

Your heart is a fine piece of complicated machinery. Just like any piece of equipment, it must be used in order to operate efficiently. Take, for example, your car's engine. If you didn't start your car for months and it just sat there, the chances of it starting are pretty slim. Most likely, you wouldn't expect it to run without some maintenance first. And even if it did start right up, it would probably run roughly, which would also require some attention because all the mobile parts would be stiff or rusted.

In the same way, if your heart sits unused, it will eventually clog up. If it doesn't stop running altogether (heart attack), it will certainly chug along, causing all sorts of problems. Just like a car, you can't expect it to perform if you don't take care of it.

■

WE NEED TO EXERCISE IN ORDER TO LIVE A HEALTHY LIFE.

■

In order for your heart to be lubricated and kept clean, you must "turn your heart on" by working out to push it into a cardio zone (a level of exertion that is greater than normal activity). Remember the man I mentioned in chapter three who began cycling with me to reduce his cholesterol? Prior to taking my class, he had tried working out on his own. After three months, his cholesterol had gone up, not down! His doctor told him he wasn't working hard enough. That was when he came to see me, and I have been making him sweat ever since!

You need to work the engine to keep it clean. And the cleaner your heart is, the better it will run. Breathing in and out isn't enough because the heart was designed to do that. Breathing is just like a car parked in the garage. The heart needs workload forced upon it to make it pump harder and push blood throughout the body. It is for your own good health. That is why we must incorporate cardio exercise into our lifestyle. Without it, we are walking time bombs. Our engine could go dead…literally. But when your engine is clean and working at top performance, it is providing you with more oxygen, which will give your muscles more strength and your energy system a boost. This is why you will actually have *more* energy when you exercise.

One of the most discouraging things for me to see as a personal trainer is people at the gym dedicating the time to a healthy activity, like using a treadmill, yet not using it correctly or at the right intensity level to receive any health benefit. Perhaps you are one of these people. If so, I hope this information helps you know that you must change your workout in order to help your heart.

The Aerobics and Fitness Association of America (AFAA) has found that 80 percent of Americans do not get enough exercise on a weekly basis to receive any health benefit.[3] That means only 20 percent of Americans are exercising correctly, even though a lot more people are at the gym. It also means that 80 percent of those at the gym might as well be at home flicking their remote control because their cardio workout would be about the same as what they're getting at the gym. Does that alarm you? It does me. That's why I am providing this information to help you and to make a difference.

The heart needs to be challenged to remain strong. If you don't know how your body works, any time you spend in exercise may be wasted. Certainly, getting out and moving is good for you. But if you truly want to improve your cardio capacity and reduce your chances of heart disease, you must work the body hard enough.[4] This chapter will give you insight and information into cardio exercise so that you can work out properly and obtain the health benefits you desire. It will also discuss the necessity for weight-bearing exercise and stretching and how these will also help you reach your fitness goals. Knowledge is power!

EXERCISE THAT FITS

When I train clients or speak on wellness to groups, I use the FITS formula to explain the parameters of proper exercise. You may have seen something like it before or read about it in a health magazine, but I have customized it to accommodate *Finally FIT!* FITS stands for *frequency, intensity, time,* and *style.*

Frequency

We are talking here about how often you work out. The AFAA (from which I received my certifications and credentials) recommends that you engage in exercise three to five days a week.[5] Their research has proven that exercising a minimum of three days a week will maintain a certain level of health. If you're working out three days a week, you probably won't notice any serious changes to your outward appearance such as significant weight loss or muscle definition, but you should receive healthy benefits like reduced chances of heart disease and less illness. And you'll definitely feel better. If you haven't been working out much at all, know that any exercise is better than none.

■

MINIMALLY, WE NEED THREE DAYS
OF CARDIO EXERCISE EACH WEEK.

■

Not everyone wants to be a supermodel or muscle-bound weight lifter. Simply being healthy is an excellent goal for some. But if you do desire to actually change your body (that is, lose weight or build muscle mass), you'll need to increase your cardio exercise to five days a week. Athletes with challenging goals—to compete in races or tournaments, for instance—will work out five to seven days a week.

Now, I know that some of you may be wondering how in the world you are going to squeeze in three days of exercise in a week. Shooting for three days may be a big step for you. Don't be discouraged. Remember what I said about small, baby steps? Anything is better than nothing. I'm simply providing guidelines to manage your expectations. By starting with *anything*, you are already winning!

As I was writing this book I had just started working with a woman who wasn't exercising at all…not one single day. She is a wife and mother and runs her own business. When we sat down to review her goals, I explained that she would need to have three cardio exercise days and two weight days each week. She just about fell off her chair. "Yeah, right," she said. I proceeded to share with her some creative options for getting the job done quickly. She was already a member of Curves, so I suggested she go there three times a week. She will get her cardio and weight training in all at once…in only thirty minutes. She trains with me once a week to ensure she is making progress. I show her new moves for her routines and different ways to work her muscles. In just one month she has lost an inch in her waist, an inch in her buttocks, and a half inch in her legs. She is jazzed!

See, it can be done. Put your thinking cap on, and think outside the box.

Do you like walking outdoors? That could be a great way to get your cardio and weight exercise done at once. Research published in several health magazines has found hiking to be one of the most beneficial fitness activities out there. When you hike you are challenging your cardio system, but in most cases you are also providing resistance: with your backpack. Since hiking is usually done in hills or mountains, the incline pushes the entire body to work together. It's a great way to work out and enjoy God's creation.

The bottom line here is to ensure you are exercising enough times throughout the week to help your cardio ability (your heart) improve. For me, I do a minimum of four cardio days a week, but on average I get five to six in. I like being at the top of my game and able to handle with strength and endurance whatever comes my way.

Intensity

The *I* of FITS refers to how hard you are working when you exercise. I can't believe how many people I see at the gym talking up a storm while they are supposedly working out. They think that just because they are sweating they are working hard. Wrong! Sweat is not an indicator of intensity. It is our body's cooling device and way of evaporating moisture and toxins. You can even sweat standing still—ever been to Atlanta, Houston, or Orlando in the summer?

Let me give you a quick heads-up: if you can maintain a normal conversation while you are exercising, you aren't working hard enough. You need to increase your intensity. In fact, if you can work out and simultaneously read a book or magazine without feeling sick, you aren't working hard enough.

I know the trend is to maximize your time by reading while you exercise, but if you truly want to be healthy you will need to work at an intensity level that makes doing anything else impossible.

The harder you work, the heavier you breathe. The heavier you breathe, the more you will be trying to keep up…not talking or reading. You can start off by reading during your warm-up, but you shouldn't be able to continue to do so once you get into your "zone," your ideal intensity level for cardio health. Having an intensity level that is too low is probably one of the biggest mistakes people make when working out. They just aren't pushing themselves hard enough.

When I first met Virginia, she was cycling on her stationary bike in her home several times a week for thirty minutes at a time. But she wasn't losing any weight. She was frustrated and came to me for an evaluation. During our time together, I learned that she was reading really good books that required a lot of thought while she cycled. In order to stay focused on what she was reading, she was, by default, limiting her intensity level. If she got too winded, she couldn't concentrate on the words.

IF YOU CAN MAINTAIN A NORMAL CONVERSATION WHILE YOU ARE EXERCISING, YOU AREN'T WORKING HARD ENOUGH.

I informed her that she would need to increase her intensity, and if she really worked hard enough, she wouldn't be able to read at the same time. As she adjusted her workout, sure enough, she could no longer read past her warm-up. But she did start to see the results she was after. As of this writing, Virginia has lost close to 20 pounds.

Of course, the intensity of your workout is up to you. You can multitask—with little or no health benefits—or you can get serious, put the magazine and cell phone away, and do it right. If you are going to put the time in, make it count.

Time

The *T* in FITS refers to how long you work out.

Most of us have been taught that our cardio workouts should last twenty minutes. But new research indicates that we need at least thirty minutes of continuous exercise for it to be effective for our cardiovascular health.[6] And in 2003, the American Heart Association (AHA) released new data that suggests we actually require a full hour of exercise *each day* in order to receive health benefits for the heart.[7]

Note that the AHA counts "cumulative" exercise, which means activities over the course of the day. For example, if you take the stairs instead of the elevator and park in the farthest lot and walk in, it counts toward your one hour total for that day. But you must still have at least thirty minutes all at once at a high-intensity level to truly help your health. Everyday tasks such as walking, lifting, gardening, and sweeping are certainly good for the cumulative effect, but they aren't intense enough. You will need to ensure that you are balancing both high-intensity exercise and other activities to keep you mobile. Remember, though, to be creative. You can do it!

Most fitness classes are one hour in length to guarantee that you are getting a solid thirty minutes of true cardio exercise. When you take into account warm-up, cool down, and stretch, you are left with about thirty to forty minutes of actual exercise. Some people may need a little more time to get into their zone. Take this into account when you are running on the treadmill or cycling. Are you actually getting thirty minutes of high-level exercise, or are you just putting in your thirty minutes?

Style

The last component of the FITS formula is style, or how you actually exercise. The type of exercise you choose will determine what you achieve. Exercising through sports will produce different results from what you will get by using cardio machines. Fitness classes produce something different still.

Chapters five through eight will give you a much more in-depth explanation of what kind of workout style works best for your temperament. For now, know that the style of exercise you choose is an important element in your fitness equation. It will have the most influence on whether you stick to your program or not. You can dedicate the right number of days and actually work within your zone, but if you don't like what you are doing, you won't last thirty minutes.

Personally, I hate the treadmill. I count every second. Put me outside, though, and I enjoy the challenge of watching traffic, going up hills, and actually going someplace. On a treadmill, I hope to last twenty minutes. Outside, I can run forty minutes or more without giving it a second thought. It has nothing to do with the fact that I'm in good shape; I just don't like the treadmill.

Your attitude toward your workouts will have a significant impact, positive or negative, on your fitness program. You have to find something you enjoy. That's what *Finally FIT!* is all about. In the chapter relating to your specific temperament, I'll help you find the right style of exercise for you.

FINDING YOUR ZONE

I have already mentioned the importance of working out in your zone, your ideal intensity level. Since each of us is different, our zones will also be different. Each of us will have a different target to aim for based upon a variety of factors. Age, gender, and current level of fitness all affect your cardio capacity, and thus where your zone is. Alcohol, cigarettes, and any drugs (even prescription medicines) also affect your heart rate.

If you are embarking on a fitness program for the first time in your life, congratulations! Way to go! I strongly encourage you to seek the counsel of a physician before you start. Get a complete physical, and ask how any prescription drugs you take will alter your heart rate and how you should adapt. Even if you've exercised at some point in the past it might be a good idea to get an overall checkup before starting a new exercise program.

Your doctor will evaluate your health condition, check your cholesterol levels, and take your blood pressure. All of this is important to know. Knowing your blood pressure and cholesterol levels will give you a benchmark. After six months of sticking to your FIT plan, get these checked again. I can almost bet you will see encouraging results.

Note: If you are pregnant, you must get your OB/GYN's permission to exercise. You will receive great benefits from exercising during your pregnancy, such as a quicker recovery afterward, but you will need to lower your intensity and watch your range of motion. Seek professional guidance first.

Let's talk about how to find your zone. As a personal trainer, I was taught the model of "220 minus your age" to determine your maximum heart rate (MHR) in beats per minute, which would then be used to find your target zone.[8] It works like this: once you know your MHR (220 minus your age), you calculate your target or training heart rate (THR) by multiplying the MHR by 55 percent to 85 percent (target cardio zone range).

For example, let's say a thirty-six-year-old woman has a MHR of 184 (220–36=184). If she wanted to perform at the low end of her zone, she would multiply 184 by 55 percent, which equals 101 THR. She'd want to maintain a pulse rate of 101 beats/minute for thirty minutes. But if she wanted to work at the higher intensity level of her zone, she would multiply 184 by 85 percent, which equals 156 beats/minute. Her pulse rate would be much higher for her workout, which means she would get a better health benefit from her thirty minutes.

I don't know about you, but this is too cumbersome for me! For one, I am not good at math and cannot calculate this in my head, especially when I'm working out. I don't carry a calculator to the gym, either. Second, it doesn't really mean much to me. It's just numbers. Third, it's not always accurate. Someone in excellent condition will have a much lower heart rate and will need to push harder to obtain health benefits. Someone else, on the other hand, may use this formula but overexert himself because he is not in good condition.

You can certainly try the 220 minus your age formula and see how it works for you. Most gyms and fitness classes post the target heart rates on the wall somewhere. However, if you're having math anxiety right now, you can try a method I've developed. It is much simpler and is customized to your personal level of fitness. I encourage you to give my intensity chart a try.

INTENSITY CHART

The foundation for my intensity chart is something called the rate of perceived exhaustion (RPE) scale. The idea behind the RPE scale is that we have workout intensity levels ranging from 0 to 10.[9] I have modified this scale and have attached actual descriptions of how you should be feeling to help you know when you have achieved a certain intensity level in your workout.

Use this chart as a way to monitor your intensity, and you are sure to exercise at the proper level. It is easy to use and doesn't require any math. You simply monitor your breathing patterns.

Chart 4.1 | **Workout Intensity Chart**

Intensity Level	Description
1	Very light exercise—Breathing through nose. Easy to talk.
2	Light exercise—Breathing fuller through nose with deeper breaths.
3	Slightly moderate exercise—Breathing pattern begins to change. Deeper and less controlled.
4	Moderate exercise—Breathing through mouth begins. You can still speak, but not quite as easily.
5	Strong exercise—Labored but controlled breathing through the mouth. More difficult to talk now.
6	Hard exercise—Labored but controlled breathing. You must now take a breath every few words to maintain a conversation.
7	Very hard exercise—Labored, heavier breathing through mouth. "Comfortably uncomfortable."
8	Very, very hard exercise—Labored, heavier breathing. "Uncomfortable but doable." Talking is very limited and difficult.
9	Extremely hard exercise—Begin breathless stage. Talking is extremely difficult.
10	Maximum exercise—Complete breathlessness. No talking at all.

This chart works because it is *your* body you are monitoring, not some test subject who may not be the same age, gender, or physical shape as you. Level 4 for you won't be the same as for the next person—so it works for everyone.

Here's a sample workout based on a walk:

- Start off in your warm-up stage, which is level 1. Slowly increase your intensity so that at the end of ten minutes you're at level 5.

- At this point, walk up some hills or power up your pace to bring your intensity level up to a level 7 or 8. Walk at this pace for fifteen minutes.

- Here comes the kicker. Increase your intensity to a level 9, and stay there for five minutes.

- When you challenge your body to go to a higher level, you are increasing your body's capacity to process and utilize oxygen, which is the ultimate goal of cardio exercise. The more efficient your body is with oxygen, the healthier your heart!

- After five whole minutes at level 9, begin to slow down to bring your heart rate to a level 6. Allow a few minutes to taper off your intensity.

- Over the course of the next ten minutes, slowly cool yourself off, bringing yourself back down to a level 2.

- A good five-minute stretch at the end should get you back to level 1. You've done a fantastic cardio workout in only about forty-five minutes!

I use this scale when I teach fitness classes of all ages. The beauty of this system is that everyone is working at the same level, but it is for each person's physical condition, not mine. It also works well for groups with a variety of ages. As we get older, it doesn't take as much exertion for our heart rates to climb. Those in the "golden years" can still participate in group activities, but they are monitoring their heart rate for their age.

For example, when I tell my stationary cycle students in class that we are climbing up a hill that requires an 8.5-level effort, each person is gearing his bike up to *his* 8.5. One person's tension may be tighter than someone else's in the class in order for her to achieve her 8.5, but we are all working at the same level. We are all climbing the same hill!

This scale is also great because it takes into account how you feel. We are not robots, so our condition can vary from day to day. You might be fighting a cold or struggling with allergies. On those days you'll need to adjust your level accordingly because your body isn't as strong. Other days you might be feeling mighty fine and can increase your intensity and challenge your cardio capacity.

On a side note, if you are coming down with something, an accepted rule of thumb is that as long as you have no fever, working out at an adjusted level may be extremely helpful for pushing through the toxins more quickly.[10] Many times I have been able to fight off a sore throat and avoid the full-blown cold when I have exercised at the onset of the illness. If, however, you are running a temperature, lay off exercise until you are well. Your body has enough to combat without the strain of physical exertion.

If, after you exercise, you find that you take a very long time to cool down and recover, you definitely need to increase your cardio exercise throughout the week. (You have been cleared for this exercise by your doctor, right?) What your body is telling you is that it is not able to produce enough oxygen for the workload you have given it, and it isn't able to effectively utilize oxygen in your system. In other words, your heart is out of shape, and this is a very dangerous place to be! The good news is that you can change it right away by working out faithfully every day. Take baby steps.

If, on the other hand, you can attend a one-hour fitness class and never get your heart rate above level 5.0, you are probably in very good condition. It takes more effort for a well-conditioned body to be challenged. You will have to really push yourself and take the intensity far beyond most everyone else's to achieve the same effect.

One caution: some people don't push hard enough but still think they are trying their best to work out. Refer back to the chart, and make sure you are honoring the scale. Even professional athletes can get their heart rates to the higher levels. It just takes them more work to get there.

My clients have probably benefited more from understanding this intensity scale than from anything else I have offered them. People can't work hard enough if they simply do not know what a good workout is supposed to feel like. This scale will revolutionize your workout and make it more effective. If you are going to put in the time, you might as well do it right.

RESISTANCE TRAINING FOR HEALTHY MUSCLES

After cardio workouts, the second pillar of total fitness is resistance training. That's another way of saying weight lifting.

Many people are not interested in weight training. They have no desire to grow big muscles. And frankly, many people just don't like "pumping iron!" Most women I talk to hate sweating during the exercise and despise feeling sore afterward. I can relate. I was never a big weight-lifting fan—until I learned *why* it was so very important for me to incorporate it into my fitness program.

Let me share an illustration with you that should make it perfectly clear for you and hopefully change your perspective.

Have you ever seen a young tree with a very thin trunk? The landscaper stakes up the frail tree so that it can withstand the wind. Without the stakes, it is too thin to bear its own weight; a gust of wind would snap the poor thing in half. But with stakes the young tree is able to grow a deep root system to stabilize itself. In eight months to a year, the stakes are removed.

Even then, though, the tree is still too thin. It has the ability to hold itself up now (core muscles), but it is still unable to handle strong winds. It may resist the breeze, but if a strong gust blew, it would still snap. The tree, therefore, has to quickly put every bit of energy into growing a thicker trunk when the stakes are removed. As the wind blows and the tree grows, it begins to get thicker and stronger. Before long, it has a very thick and strong trunk that can withstand the most wicked winds.

WITHOUT WEIGHT-BEARING RESISTANCE, OUR BONES HAVE NO NEED TO GROW DENSE.

Our bones are like that tree. They were designed for normal movement, but they need to grow stronger. They grow stronger only when they're acted on by the muscles pulling on them. If our muscles are not being challenged, they aren't pulling on the bones—and without this pulling our bones have no need to grow dense and strong. In fact, they will become flat out frail and rigid.

That's how people of any age can step off a curb wrong and break an ankle. Their bones are weak! Osteoporosis is a result of unhealthy, weak bones. You can take all the calcium supplements available in the world, but if you do not have weight-bearing exercise in your life, your bones will be weak. Calcium is certainly necessary for our bone health, but *density* comes from resistance training. When we add resistance to our muscles and make them pull harder against the bones, the bones are forced to get thicker and dense.

It is as simple as that. If we don't use the muscles for resistance, they will not pull enough at the bones to make them healthy and strong. Weight-bearing exercise (weight lifting) is a matter of good health, not just body shape. You do it not to be buff but to have strong bones.

Researchers believe that 30 percent of the aging process cannot be controlled or altered.[11] Actually, that's pretty exciting news. This means we *do* have control over 70 percent of the aging process. Taking care of our bones is one thing we can and must do today in order to have a healthy tomorrow.

Walking, running, hiking, and any other activity that requires movement is not good enough for resistance training (unless you add wrist and ankle weights). They can serve as great cardio options, but they do not meet the criteria for muscle work. In order to gain bone density, you must have resistance against the muscles. You don't need to lift incredibly heavy weights, but you must lift something.

Swimming on land

Later, you will learn which approach to muscle strength and endurance works best for your temperament, but I would like to offer up a suggestion here that works for many people, especially women, who do not like weight-lifting machines. I have trained many women in this technique and use it in my SportsCircuit training class and my Forever Fit (seniors) class. And if you are one of those folks who were concerned about finding time to exercise, this is a great option for you.

All you need is a set of light hand weights that you can buy inexpensively from Wal-Mart. Women should start off with 5-pound weights, with the goal of increasing their resistance to 8 pounds. Men should be able to easily start off at 10-pound weights and move to 12 pounds rather quickly. I like to play music while I do this, but it is up to you. We're going swimming!

Stand nice and tall with your legs spread comfortably apart and your knees soft (not locked). Hold one weight in each hand. Now do a swimming stroke. You can use any stroke you like—front crawl, backstroke, breaststroke—and you'll get a good workout. The key is to use proper form: don't lock your elbows, don't swing or sway, do resist gravity on the downstroke, and remember to take full breaths. Go for twelve reps or rotations with each arm. When you are finished with one style of swim stroke, proceed to another.

Now you know why swimmers have great upper bodies: it's the resistance! With these swimming exercises you are working your shoulder rotation and mobility, your biceps, your triceps, and your deltoids (all of which you'll soon learn more about). The hand weights mimic the resistance of the water on your upper body.

The last segment is what I call the dive. Push the weights straight up over your head (shoulder press) and then bring them down to your side (using the back muscles). Keep your arms straight and pointed out to your side, just like you would in jumping jacks, but don't lock your elbows. Count to twelve. If you are game, repeat the entire routine a second or third time. This whole routine should only take about ten to twenty minutes, depending on how many sets you do. But in this short amount of time, you have worked your entire upper body.

When I travel, I bring hand weights with me just in case the hotel does not have a weight room. A woman from one of my workshops suggested water weights. These are empty plastic weights that you fill with water to the appropriate level or weight. When you are done, you drain them, which makes it much lighter to pack your weights when you travel. What an idea! I recently saw them advertised in an in-flight magazine, but I'm sure you can get them anywhere.

Regardless of what you have thought about weight-bearing exercise in the past, I hope you now know the importance of incorporating it into your weekly routine.

Resistance Training That FITS

Just as we did with cardio exercise, let's apply the FITS model to weight training. As you recall, FITS stands for frequency, intensity, time, and style.

Frequency

If all you are wanting is a maintenance program to keep your bones healthy, doing resistance training one to two times a week is plenty when combined with your three to five cardio exercise days. If you want to actually alter your body composition or shape, then you should add weight resistance to your routine two to three times a week. In either case, you need to allow forty-eight hours to recover between weight-training days.

We can exercise our hearts every day. In fact, it is healthy to use our hearts as much as possible in order to keep them clean. But you can't do that with weight lifting. The reason for that is found in what happens when we exercise our muscles. Resistance training actually tears our muscles down. Don't worry: you aren't injuring yourself. That's just how God designed muscles to grow. Exercise breaks down the tissue in the muscle so that it can be rebuilt, stronger. To grow, muscle tissues need to be broken into more pieces (multiplying) so that when they combine, you have more tissue than when you started.

That's why you get sore after you work out. There's some tearing down and building up going on. But it's a good kind of soreness, one that means your muscles and bones are getting stronger. You shouldn't be in severe pain after a workout. You may have some tenderness, but with a proper cool down and stretch, you shouldn't truly hurt. If at any time you begin to really hurt, *stop*. Pain is not the name of this game.

Intensity

When it comes to weight lifting, intensity is found in form. It's not so much how much weight you're lifting or even how many times you lift that counts. What matters is *how* you lift. You don't have to lift hundreds of pounds to get the results you seek, but you do need to lift properly. Ever see someone at the gym just belting out his reps (repetitions) at warp speed? He seems to be really strong, but he isn't as strong as he could be. In fact, if he actually slowed down his reps and lifted properly, he would most likely need to decrease his weights. His muscles would not be strong enough to handle the full load since he's only been working one phase of the muscle contraction process.

Another scenario is those who lock their joints when they lift. They can lift heavy amounts because they are putting most of the weight on their joint. Bones (and joints) are stronger than muscle. However, our joints wear out. If you lift like this, over time your joints will get overworked and cause pain. Making the muscles take the load of the lift takes proper form, but it also gives you the most bang for your buck.

No matter how much you are lifting or what you are lifting (hand weights or using a machine), to grow your muscles you must put them through both the concentric and eccentric movements.[12]

Concentric contraction simply means that as you lift, the muscle shortens. It is typically the "pull" that enables you to actually lift the weight. You are moving against gravity, overcoming it. The *eccentric* contraction is the muscle tension created when the muscle wants to go quickly with gravity, but you are resisting. In other words, it is typically the "release" of the lift. It is when you have to be most careful of not going too fast. You will want to let the weight down in a hurried manner, but the slower you release it, the more you are working the muscle. Your muscles need to be challenged in both movements or phases, not just the lift. So when you see someone pumping fast, he is concentrating only on his concentric lift, not his eccentric release.

Let's look at a bicep curl, which most people are familiar with. (Don't worry if this is all new to you: chapter five provides pictures, which speak a thousand words.) A bicep curl requires you to lift up and curl your arm. As you slowly bring your hand toward your chest, your muscle is in a concentric contraction. You can even see the bicep muscle tighten up and shorten.

Note: It is now, during the concentric contraction, when you should breathe out. Breathing out on the pull helps give you power by releasing oxygen into the muscle. Breathing also slows you down, helping you resist the temptation to quickly pull up.

Once you are ready to lower your arm back down toward your leg, begin to breathe in. Breathing in provides oxygen to the required part of your body. Basically, your bicep is sending a message to your brain saying, "Hey, we are working hard here! We need more oxygen for the muscle to perform." By concentrating on solid breathing techniques, you are ensuring that oxygen gets where it needs to go.

Now slowly release your arm down in your bicep curl, resisting the temptation to let go quickly. Gravity wants to pull your arm down quickly, but don't let it.

As you slowly move your arm in the eccentric phase, you are completing the concentric/eccentric cycle and thus building muscle in two phases: lift and lower, "pull and release." You repeat this process and count to your rep goal. (I'll explain reps in a minute.) The bottom line, in case you are still a bit foggy on the two phases, is that you are maximizing your workout by working the muscle twice as hard, getting results twice as fast. As long as you are going to lift weights, you might as well do it in the way that will give you the most bang for your buck!

Time

The third part of FITS for resistance training is *time*. Just as with cardio conditioning, here you must make sure you are getting the right amount of time in for your weight training. Unlike cardio, however, weight training has a variety of options to choose from, and you do not have to follow specific guidelines. You can develop a weight program that is right for your goals. That is where reps come into play.

A rep (short for *repetition*) is the number of times you perform the exercise. Your fitness goal will determine the number of reps you complete. Those who simply want to create healthy bones will use lighter weights and will benefit from twelve reps, two times, which equals two "sets." All of your reps, twelve in this case, equal a set. How many times you count to twelve is the number of sets you have completed. Someone who wants to build muscle mass and develop muscle definition will lift heavier weights for three sets of ten reps each. Again, it all depends upon what you want to accomplish and your FIT profile.

Personally, I like to get it done fast. I lift aggressively: two sets of fifteen reps each. This pushes me but gets my workout done in a shorter amount of time. You will receive more instruction in this area in the next chapter.

Style

Your temperament will greatly impact the style of weight resistance that will work best for you. (See the chapter on your specific FIT for ideas on this.) Here I will briefly compare two styles of weights for resistance training: handheld (free) weights and weight machines.

The greatest advantage to free weights is that they are easy to use. Anyone can initiate a resistance program with hand weights. Weight machines are more complicated and usually require someone showing you how to operate them. Handheld weights can be purchased and used at home, but to use weight machines you'll probably need to join a gym. Even in gyms you don't normally have to wait in line to use free weights, whereas during peak exercise hours weight machines may have a waiting list.

Free weights are actually more dangerous than weight machines. Weight machines assist you in regulating the pressure and force you to perform the exercise in a certain manner. You are on your own with free weights. In fact, with free weights you are required to use more of your core muscles to stabilize yourself than on a machine. This is both good and bad. If your posture isn't good when you lift, you could hurt your back. If you use good form, then you are building core muscle strength, and we all need more of that! In either case, it is wise to have a workout partner spot you. A spotter will be ready at any time to help you lift or let go. When you work out with someone, you are more likely to push yourself harder, too.

I want to introduce you to a concept called *working a muscle to fatigue*. Some schools of thought within the fitness community encourage working a muscle to complete *failure*, but I recommend working only to fatigue, unless you are entering a bodybuilding contest. Fatigue means your muscles are tired and just about worn out. You can finish your set, but it is a struggle. Failure means that your muscles cannot work anymore, but your partner helps you push. By the last part of your reps, your spotter ends up doing most of the work, but your muscles get additional tearing, which is what builds extra mass. I prefer muscle fatigue over muscle failure.

No matter what type of resistance program you select, you need to ensure that you are eating enough protein and drinking plenty of water (more nutrition information is available in chapter ten). Our muscles consist of 70 percent water and 30 percent protein,[13] so you can see how important it is to have these two elements in your diet. Eliminate these, and you are damaging your muscles.

STRETCHING THAT FITS

We've covered the first two pillars of fitness: cardiovascular exercise and weight-resistance training. Now it's time to look at the third pillar: stretching. Stretching is something we tend to forget in fitness programs, but it is paramount to our overall health and well-being. Let's take stretching through the FITS formula.

Frequency

Muscles require more blood during exercise, so the body sends it to whichever muscles are being recruited the most. You need your blood to be dispersed evenly once you have finished to prevent blood clots. Stretching is what allows your muscles to perform at their best the next time you work out. Therefore, you should integrate three to five days of stretching into your fitness program. This may sound overwhelming, but stretching doesn't take hours. In fact, you can stretch out in five to ten minutes. The best way to determine how often you should stretch is to simply stretch every time you do your cardio and muscle workouts.

Intensity

Go slow and work hard when you stretch. Be sure to breathe correctly.

For more on how to stretch, check your specific FIT chapter for ideas as well as the pictures under the "stretching" header in chapter five.

Time

You should stretch before and after each cardio exercise. You should also stretch before and after you lift weights. Before and after you do any active endeavor, you should stretch. Concentrate on stretching the muscles you know you will be using. Use the style of stretching that fits the program. Here are a few quick suggestions:

- If you will be cycling, warm up with easy, limbering movements. Cycle at a light resistance to start warming up the quads and hamstrings. Static stretch your upper body. Cool down by static stretching the quads, hamstrings, and upper body (more on these terms under "Style" below).

- If you will be playing tennis, warm up with static quad, hamstring, and inner/outer thigh stretches. Use limbering movements for the upper body (swinging the arms and rotating the shoulder). Cool down with static stretches for lower and upper body.

- If you will be playing basketball, static stretch your quads and hamstrings along with your back. Mirror your shooting, hook shots, and passing without the ball (limbering stretching). Cool down with static lower body, upper body, and back stretches.

- If you will be in an aerobics class, your warm-up should include both limbering and static stretches, especially if you are to perform high-power moves like kickboxing. Your cool down should start off with limbering moves until the heart rate declines slightly, then static stretch the lower and upper body as well as the back.

I highly recommend you also add at least one day a week when you stretch for thirty minutes solid. Pilates and yoga can suggest some excellent moves to add to your routine to keep it fresh.

The key to stretching is to "breathe through." Take deep breaths and allow the muscle to release and relax. Some stretches will feel warm, but they shouldn't hurt. Other times, your muscle might actually start to shake. Don't worry. You are just stretching deeply, and that is good! Over time you will find your flexibility increasing and your performance improving as a result of stretching.

Style

There are three types of stretching: ballistic, rhythmic limbering, and static.[14] Ballistic is the type of stretch where you bounce or "pulse" through it. Studies have shown that this type of stretch isn't safe for the general public and causes more harm than good.[15]

Rhythmic limbering is the kind of stretching most aerobic classes include in their warm-up stage. Rhythmic limbering is warming up the exact muscles you expect to utilize in a workout. You are performing the actual movements but at a lesser degree. For instance, if you were going to do a series of squats with weight resistance, a limbering warm-up stretch would be easy squats without the weights. By repeating this several times, you are giving the muscles a warning that they are going to be used. They will then remember the movement and be prepared for the additional weight.

A static stretch is one you hold for a few seconds, breathing through. A quad stretch is a perfect example. You stand there holding your foot so that your leg is curled behind you. You aren't bouncing or moving. You are simply stretching the quad muscles out by holding it for a few seconds and breathing. Stretching is important both before and after a workout.

I do not recommend ballistic stretching, so I will concentrate on rhythmic limbering and static stretches. Exercise, especially resistance training, contracts the muscles or makes them tight. Stretching helps elongate the muscles, allowing them to return to their original state. Ever notice when you work out that your muscles are firm? By using them, they contract and get hard. Without stretching, over time your muscles will actually shorten, and you will lose flexibility. In other words, they will remain hard and not release back, leaving you susceptible to injury.

Even if you don't mind losing flexibility, take into account that it is flexibility that prevents injury. The more mobile you are, the less likely you are to pull a muscle. Those who participate in sports are often guilty of not stretching before or after; thus they often incur injuries like pulled hamstrings. Stretching is preventative maintenance. It also helps cool your body down after a workout. If you stop cold turkey after your cardio routine, your blood can accumulate and pool, creating blood clots.[16] Stretching helps the blood flow back where it belongs.

CONCLUSION

I know I have given you a lot of information to absorb. You may find yourself referring back to this chapter and rereading some pages. You may want to do more research to get even greater detail. That's great! The more active your lifestyle becomes, the more this information will become second nature. It is like anything else: sometimes you don't know what you don't know, but once you know it, you know it!

Knowledge is power, but seeing is believing! Chapter five uses lots of photos to illustrate exercise form, pointing out what is correct and what to avoid. It will give more details on posture and utilizing your core muscles. You will learn how to determine how much weight you should be lifting as well as what type of program you might utilize.

Are you ready to take a look? Let's go!

FIVE

SEEING IS BELIEVING

LET'S PAUSE FOR just a moment to say, "Good job!" You are already on your way to a healthier you by reading *Finally FIT!* thus far.

In chapter four you learned some pillars of fitness: cardio exercise, muscle strength, and flexibility. You discovered that in order to live a healthy life, you must include all three in your weekly fitness regimen. Obviously, these areas are much more complex than how I have presented them, but you now have a good base and can begin to delve a little deeper into customizing a program that works for your temperament.

In this chapter, we get to the pictures. Here I show you proper and improper muscle-resistance training, some excellent floor exercises, and a few powerful core-stretching techniques, all of which will help you reach your specific goals. Refer to this chapter as often as you like.

EXERCISES FOR STRENGTHENING YOUR MUSCLES

Since a picture is worth a thousand words, let's start off with reviewing the major muscles of the human body. (That's me in the photos, by the way.)

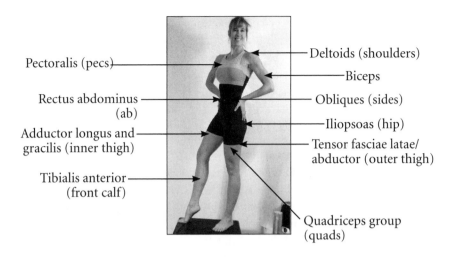

Pectoralis (pecs)

Rectus abdominus (ab)

Adductor longus and gracilis (inner thigh)

Tibialis anterior (front calf)

Deltoids (shoulders)

Biceps

Obliques (sides)

Iliopsoas (hip)

Tensor fasciae latae/ abductor (outer thigh)

Quadriceps group (quads)

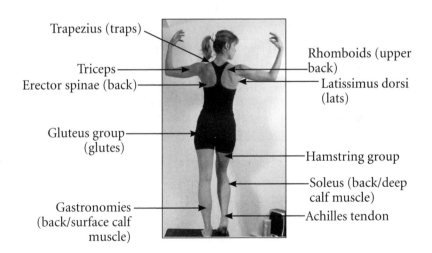

Trapezius (traps)

Triceps

Erector spinae (back)

Gluteus group (glutes)

Gastronomies (back/surface calf muscle)

Rhomboids (upper back)

Latissimus dorsi (lats)

Hamstring group

Soleus (back/deep calf muscle)

Achilles tendon

The human body is very complex. Some people spend years of their lives dedicated to studying it. For the sake of this book, however, we will keep it simple. We are focusing on the major muscles involved in living a healthy life. You don't need to worry about memorizing the names of the muscles, but I do want you to become familiar with the major muscle groups I have listed in Chart 5.1. You need to know what muscle you are working in order to concentrate on it.

Exercising opposing muscles

The most important thing to remember about muscle work is that you must also work the *opposing* muscle. Think of our bodies as being divided into the front and back sections (anterior and posterior). Each side has different muscles. For instance, if you lift weights that utilize your quads ("anterior" or front leg muscles), then you need to also lift weights that challenge the opposite muscles—in this case, your hamstrings ("posterior" or back leg muscles).

Often, people will forget this basic principle and injure themselves. For example, a runner who is building up his quads and forgets to work his hamstrings is more likely to pull a hamstring during a race. Why? His quads are overpowering his hamstrings and pulling on them. Because his hamstrings are weaker than his quads, they cannot sustain the tension and they snap.

In order to prevent injury and simply balance your body, be sure to work the following muscles equally:

Chart 5.1 | **Upper and Lower Body Opposing Muscles**

Primary Muscles (Anterior)	Opposing Muscles (Posterior)
UPPER BODY	
Pecs	Traps/Rhomboids
Biceps	Triceps
Abs	Erector spinae (back)
Obliques	Lats
LOWER BODY	
Hips	Glutes
Quads	Hamstrings
Tibialis anterior (front calf)	Gastrocnemius/soleus (back calf)

One of the best ways to ensure you work every muscle properly is to dedicate one workout day to your upper body only and another day to your lower body only. This method ensures that you have the time to work every primary body muscle and its opposing counterpart. Those who require a faster paced workout will want to do the entire body in one day. That's fine. Just keep in mind the importance of working not only the front of a muscle but also the backside.

I'll show you some great ways to work each muscle later in this chapter. I'll also give you a couple of options for each muscle so that you won't wear them out, create repetitive motion injury, or get bored.

Once you do become a committed exerciser, you will want to guard your body against overuse due to repetitive actions. People who continually perform the same exercise week after week are subjecting themselves to the possibility of repetitive damage. Make sure you change your workout occasionally to prevent injury. Do not do the same movement or motion every time. Try different ways of accomplishing the same thing.

Besides, the more variety you include in your workout, the less likely you will be to get bored. Boredom is the number one reason people drop out of fitness programs.[1] Prevent it by changing things up. When you keep your muscles guessing as to what will be expected of them, you are preventing your body from "hitting the wall"—a state in which you find yourself unable to improve performance. When you change it up, you will notice that every exercise requires different core muscles. They are assisting the primary muscles and must be worked as well.

Exercising your core muscles

Core muscles are harder to show you because they are attached deep within our body. They help us stand, sit, balance, and so much more. Your abs and erector spinae are two of the largest and most important core muscles we have, so these are the core muscles we will focus on in this book.

If these two muscles are weak, all of your other training will be affected, and you won't see much improvement elsewhere. These muscles must be strong in order to provide you with stability. In other words, you must be able to stand upright in order to work your other muscles such as your quads. If you can't even hold yourself up in proper alignment, you won't be able to lift any other weights effectively.

Most people have very weak core muscles and do not even know it. Research indicates that 80 percent of Americans suffer from back pain.[2] Are you one of them? Here is a great test for you to determine your core strength:

Get down on the floor and lie face down. Put your weight on your elbows and your toes, keeping a completely straight line from your toes to your head. How long can you hold this? If it is literally just seconds, then you have weak core muscles. If you can hold it for a minute or longer, then your core muscles are in decent shape. The longer you can sustain the position, the better. This is also a great core stretch to practice on a regular basis. See if you can extend the amount of time you stay up in position.

Here are some other ways to build core strength, which will improve your overall health and performance:

This core muscle exercise is working not only your abs and erector spinae (back), but it is also strengthening your glutes and legs. Start off by lying on your back with your arms to your side. Your knees are bent with your feet flat on the floor. Concentrate on pushing your abs through to the floor, through your back. Your back should be pressed against the floor and your abs flat and firm. The key to this exercise is to proceed slowly, with control.

Begin lifting your tailbone off the ground, and continue to lift one vertebrae at a time. Considering we have twenty-six vertebrae, this should take you at least thirty seconds. Once your shoulder blades are lifted off the ground, hold this "tabletop" position for a count of ten. Then slowly lower your body down in reverse, one vertebra at a time. You should feel your core muscles working hard to stabilize you. Your body will want to "plop" down on the ground. Don't let it! Resist. Breathe slowly and really concentrate. Repeat this several times for a superb core-strengthening exercise.

This exercise is not only excellent for building stronger core muscles, but also for stretching your shoulders and hamstrings. Start off sitting on the floor with your legs out in front of you, pressed against the floor. Stack up your spine nice and straight and begin to lean back, one vertebra at a time. As you lean back, maintain control; do not allow gravity to pull you down quickly. Once you are lying flat on your back, reach your arms up over your head to stretch your shoulders out. Take in a couple of breaths.

Now lift your head and look at your toes. Begin to bring your torso up, one vertebra at a time, reaching your arms forward. Stack your spine back up and reach for your toes; touch them if possible. Pause here for a moment and stretch out your hamstrings by grabbing on to your toes (but do not pull on them). Stack your spine back up and repeat this process several times.

Exercises to build core strength should be woven into your fitness program. If you are the type who needs a group environment to accomplish this, check out yoga, Pilates, or PiYo (combination of the two) classes at your local fitness club or gym. These classes will challenge you and make you sweat! They are excellent for your core strength as well as your flexibility. Kickboxing is a great cardio exercise that works your core muscles, too, because you need strong abs and back in order to kick properly. I would not recommend kickboxing for beginning fitness enthusiasts, however.

Specific weight-training goals

Hopefully by now you have outlined some goals for yourself. Do not forget to include your weight-lifting program. What are you trying to accomplish? What is your desired outcome? Here are some guidelines to help you formulate your specific program:

Chart 5.2 | Weight-Training Program Guidelines

OBJECTIVE	REPS/SETS	WEIGHTS USED
Healthy muscles and bones	12 reps/2 sets	Lighter weights
Maintenance program	12 reps/2 sets	Lighter weights
Tone and define muscles	10 reps/3 sets	Medium weights
Reduce body fat	10 reps/3 sets	Medium weights
FAST option for toning or reducing body fat	15 reps/2 sets	Medium weights
Increase muscle mass	8 reps/3 sets	Heavy weights

Finding your maximum lift potential

In order to find the right weight for your workout, you will need to determine your maximum lift potential or one-rep maximum (1RM) for each exercise. If at all possible, you should have someone help you with this process. The first time takes the longest, but once you have established your benchmark, you are ready to take off.

Let's use a bench press as an example to illustrate the 1RM concept. In a bench press you lie flat on your back, usually on a special bench, and press a bar up from your chest and then lower it back down. You will need to repeat this process (the process of finding your maximum lift potential, that is) for each muscle or exercise.

Have your partner put on 75 percent of your total body weight to see if you can lift it. You should be able to push out one and only one rep. If you can, take this weight and multiply it by 50 to 65 percent, and you have your starting weight. If you cannot lift 75 percent of your body weight, lower it slightly and continue to try to lift until you can push out one bench press. Then multiply *that* weight by 50 to 65 percent to find your starting weight. Remember, you are trying to push out only one, and it will be difficult to do. This process will enable you to find your 50 to 65 percent range that you will use to set up your lifting program reps and sets.

A partner is important, especially for exercises like the bench press, because you are lifting heavy weights to find your range. Do not try this alone. If you do, you could find yourself in trouble.

Let's say a 136-pound woman is trying to find her maximum lift potential (her one-rep maximum or 1RM). Seventy-five percent of 136 pounds is 102 pounds. With a spotter, she should be able to struggle through one lift of this weight. If so, this weight—102 pounds—is her rep maximum (1RM). Her start weight should be 50 to 65 percent of her 1RM. If she is a beginner, she'd go with 50 percent, which is 51 pounds (102 x 50 percent). This should be a good place to start with a bench press. If she has worked out before, she could go with 60 to 65 percent of her 1RM, which would be in the neighborhood of 61 to 66 pounds.

Don't feel bad if you are unable to lift within these ranges at first. If your muscles have not been worked before, they will be fairly weak. The exciting news is that our bodies respond quickly. Before you know it, you will be getting stronger and healthier.

To find your 1RM for other muscle movements such as your legs, shoulders, and back, simply lift as much as you possibly can. Add on more weights until you can't lift it through, and this will determine your maximum lift potential. Mark down your numbers, and you will have a good starting point.

CAUTION: During any exercise, whether cardiovascular or weight lifting, if you experience pain, *stop!* Your body is telling you something. It is better to listen up front than to experience an injury that will prevent you from exercising for a longer period of time. Pain is often an indicator of too much, too soon. If you feel pain when working your heart, simply reduce your impact, lower your arms, or walk in place. With weight lifting, lower your weights until you eventually build yourself up to a heavier weight.

This doesn't mean you should never feel anything. If you are embarking on a new fitness program, you *will* feel it. You will experience soreness and muscle fatigue. If you follow the guidelines in this book, however, such discomfort should be minimal.

I mentioned earlier that I highly suggest you seek the counsel of a physician before you start your new program. I can't emphasize this enough, especially if you are overweight and have been living a sedentary lifestyle. If you are pregnant or have a family history of heart disease, you definitely need to get a checkup and overall physical before you begin. Better to be safe than sorry!

Maximizing muscle work

OK, you are probably eager to apply some of what you have learned, but before I show you actual movements for each of the major muscle groups, let me give you a few quick pointers on how to maximize your muscle work.

First, lifting weights is not a race. You are not competing against the clock; you are striving for proper form. Concentrate on slow concentric and eccentric movements. Breathe in through your nose on the eccentric portion of the lift (the slow release or drop of the weight), and exhale through pursed lips on the concentric phase (the lift), which is when you need the additional oxygen assistance.

Breathing correctly will be crucial to your performance. Don't underestimate its importance. In rare cases, injury can occur to the heart when a person holds his or her breath while lifting weights.[3] Don't risk it; breathe!

Remember to move slowly in order to gain muscle strength evenly. The faster you lift, the more momentum you are utilizing, which means the muscle isn't working as hard.

SPECIFIC MUSCLE EXERCISES

Let's put some of this information into practice, starting with your arms.

Biceps

As you may recall, your biceps are anterior (front) upper arm muscles. They are easy to isolate and work with using hand weights, weighted bars, or weight machines. I prefer the hand weights and the bar, partially because some people experience wrist pain while using the bicep machine. If you prefer using machines, however, follow the instructions on the bicep machine. The tips and suggestions I have outlined here for form and safety will also apply to the machines. These pictures are for using handheld weights.

Since each arm is working independently, you may need a lower weight than you could lift with a bar. For instance, if you can curl 35 pounds with a bar (using both hands), try 15-pound hand weights. Don't be afraid to try out several weights to see what fits you best. You're not trying to impress anybody.

With a weight in each hand, stand with your feet shoulder-width apart. Keep your knees soft, never locking them. Start off with your hands at your side with soft elbows, again never locking the joints. You will keep your arms close to your body during this exercise. They should rub against your sides as you slowly lift one arm at a time.

Bring the hammer in your right hand up toward your chest and breathe out, leaving the left hand down by your leg. As you slowly lower your right hand, take a breath in. Once your right arm is down at your side, lift the left arm up, repeating the same process. A rep includes one right arm curl and one left arm curl.

Bicep curls with a bar provide a different angle and typically allow you to lift a little heavier weight. Your starting position is the same as above, and so is your breathing pattern. Breathe in as you curl the bar toward your chest, and breathe out as you lower it. Remember: do not lock your knee or elbow joints. Make sure your hands aren't too far apart on the bar. Keep them fairly close together. I like the curved bars that have the hand areas already marked because that makes it easier to watch your hand position.

INCORRECT FORM

CAUTION: In either option of working your biceps, be sure to stabilize your back. Do not swing forward or back, as I'm doing in this picture. If you require your body to sway in order to lift the curl, you have too much weight. Reduce the weight on the bar, and concentrate on proper, safe form. The purpose of these exercises is to isolate and work your biceps, not strain your lower back. If you see people at the gym swaying like a rocking horse to curl their weights, they are endangering themselves and not working their biceps to their full capacity. You're probably tired of hearing me say it, but if you are going to put the effort into exercising, why not make it safe and effective?

Triceps

The opposing muscle or posterior muscle of the biceps is the triceps. These muscles don't get worked too often, but they are certainly the cause of great frustration for many people, women in particular. These are the muscles that, when out of shape, jiggle under our arms. The good news is that the triceps don't take long to respond to exercise.

Since the triceps aren't worked as often as other muscles throughout the normal course of a day, they will not be as strong initially. Start off with a lower weight than what you used for your biceps—and use only one handheld weight (grasped in both hands). If you were lifting 15 pounds per arm for your biceps, start off with a 10- or 12-pound single weight for triceps.

With your legs shoulder-width apart, hold the weight over your head with both hands, keeping your arms in close and elbows tucked in toward each other. The top of the weight should be facing the ceiling.

You'll know you're doing it right if you are almost giving yourself a back scratch. Let the weight almost touch the back of your neck before you begin to lift it back up to the starting position. Breathe in as you lift up, and exhale as you lower the weight. Protect your back, and avoid rocking forward or backward. Keep your posture upright. No slouching or leaning. And hold on to the weight firmly so it doesn't slip out and perhaps hit your head.

The same weight used for the above option can be used for this one except that you will have a weight in each hand. Start off with your feet shoulder-width apart, and then bend forward from your hip, keeping your back nice and flat. You are hinging at the hip like this so you can take your arms back and keep them flat and even. The key to this exercise is pushing through the elbow and not moving the entire arm. Remember, you are concentrating on just the triceps. Start with your arms bent as you inhale.

As you push out through your elbows, breathe out. Use both arms at the same time, and keep your head even with your back, not looking up or down, to prevent strain on the neck. Keep the movement slow and controlled. Repeat.

CAUTION: Again, the key to this exercise is hinging from the elbow, forcing the triceps to take the brunt of the workload. Your shoulders and upper arm should remain stable. Remain slightly bent at the hip, but keep your back and neck straight.

INCORRECT FORM

Shoulders

Your shoulder muscles and deltoids are closely related, but I have included exercises to isolate each and make sure they are both strengthened. Just as the muscles of your back are comprised of several sections, so are the muscles in your shoulders. As with your triceps, your shoulders may be a bit weaker than other muscles, especially if you are a woman or have experienced any rotator cuff injuries.

To start, try the same weight you lifted with your triceps (10 or 12 pounds, for example). This time, however, you will use a solid bar, not handheld weights. Most health clubs will have a shoulder press machine that uses either a solid bar or two hand grips. Either way works the same muscle. Your feet should be roughly shoulder-width apart. Bring the bar all the way up over your head (but do not lock your elbows). This is your starting point. As you take a breath in, lower the bar until it is even with your chin or your arms are in a straight line elbow to elbow, whichever comes first.

Exhale through your mouth as you push the bar back up over your head. Your movements should be slow and controlled. Again, do not lock your elbows. Repeat until you've done all your reps.

I like to call this shoulder exercise "pouring water" because that word picture helps people maintain proper form as they perform the exercise. You will use hand weights this time (same weight as triceps or 10 to 12 pounds, for example). Start off with your legs shoulder-width apart and hinge from your hip (bend from the waist). Bend your arms at the elbow to a 90-degree angle and bring them together in front of your body. Breathe in, then raise your arms up in one, solid motion.

Keeping your arms at a 90-degree angle, raise them up to each side and bring them to an even plane. Keep your head even with your back, which should be neutral or flat. As you lift, exhale and slowly rotate your wrists with the hand weights to simulate pouring water, as if you're emptying two pitchers. This ensures proper movement of the shoulder and prevents injury.

INCORRECT FORM

CAUTION: Be careful not to lift your arms too high, as this can cause you to strain your upper back and neck. Focus on keeping your upper arms in alignment with your upper back. Your elbows should never be higher than your shoulders. Do not look up or down. Concentrate on keeping your head aligned with your back. Rotate your wrists and pour the water out on the concentric lift (against gravity).

Deltoids

The shoulder muscles work closely with the deltoids, but it is a good idea to also emphasize just the deltoids in order to protect the shoulders, making them stronger and preventing injury.

Start with your feet shoulder-width apart and your knees relaxed. (Are you seeing a trend here yet?) The single hand weights you used for your triceps and shoulders should be sufficient, but you be the judge. If you can push out twelve reps and perform three sets without breathing hard or getting muscle fatigue, you aren't lifting enough. You certainly don't want so much weight that you can barely lift your first set, but do be honest with yourself. You will know when you need to increase your weight. Remember, you are exercising for *your* health and attempting to reach *your* goals, no one else's.

Hold the weights so they rest on your thighs. Your knuckles should be pointing forward, away from your body. When you lift up, your knuckles will point at the ceiling and your palms will be facing the floor. Your arms should be straight and firm, but do not lock your elbows. Locking your elbows will seem to give you more strength, but you are actually using your elbow joint to lift, not your muscles. This kind of movement is dangerous to a joint and can cause pain and injury.

Breathe out, and lift your right arm straight in front of your body. Bring your arm up until it is parallel with the floor. Inhale as you lower your right arm and exhale as you lift your left arm up. One rep consists of both a right- and left-arm lift. I suggest you lift only one arm at a time to prevent you from breaking form and hurting your back.

This exercise is similar to the front lift, but here you are lifting the handheld weights out to your side. The same principles apply: do not lock your elbows or your knees, and place your feet shoulder-width apart. Your starting position is with your arms resting by your side with your palms facing the sides of your body. Make sure you are standing tall and pressing your shoulders down.

Slowly lift the right arm up first, bringing it to an even plane straight across from your shoulders. Exhale on the lift, and inhale as you lower your right arm down, resisting gravity. Quickly breathe in and then out as you lift your left arm to the same position. A rep consists of one right- and one left-arm lift. Maintain your erect position throughout your reps and sets.

If at any time you experience pain, *stop.* You can always decrease your weight until your shoulders build up strength.

INCORRECT FORM

In order to protect your back, make sure you don't arch your back or sway. If you must move your body and sway, then you have too much weight. Reduce your weight, and practice safe, effective form. Do not lock your elbows or knees, and keep your hands facing down.

Latissimus dorsi and trapezius

Your lats and traps are the posterior (back) muscles complementing your pecs. Many lifters fail to work them effectively and can, therefore, experience back pain when working other parts of their bodies.

In my opinion, the best way to work your lats and traps is with a machine. The first exercise is called the "pull down." You will need to adjust the seat so that the bar is just out of your reach, requiring you to lift up off the seat a little to grab it. The wider your grip, the more you will engage your lats. The closer in, the harder your traps will work. They are both getting a workout with the pull down, but you can change what muscle is being emphasized by the width of your grip. You will need to set the weight on the machine by placing the pin in the appropriate hole.

Using the example of the 136-pound woman, 50 pounds should be a reasonable place to start. Lift what is appropriate for you. Remember to determine your 1RM for every exercise.

Reach for the bar and pull it down in front of your body. Exhale on the pull, and inhale when it is going back up. Use slow and controlled movements. Resist the urge to let the bar swiftly accelerate up to its original position.

Note that these photos show me in two different positions relative to the machine. Either way works fine.

When you pull the bar down, concentrate on squeezing your lats and traps together, toward your spine. Keep the bar even with your chest, holding it just a second before you let it slowly return upward. Lift your head slightly to watch the bar, and pull again. Do as many reps and sets as your fitness goals dictate.

Another option to work the muscles a little differently is to pull the bar behind your head. Be careful not to bang your neck. Ladies, if your hair is pulled up or in a ponytail, it might get in the way.

Do not arch your back or lean and sway. Your torso should be stable, forcing the lats and traps to perform all the work. The same rule applies for the row pull (below). Keep your back steady.

INCORRECT FORM

I really like the row machine because it mimics a real-life sport. Sit far enough back on the seat (or the floor, depending upon your equipment) so that your legs are extended but your knees are not locked. Set the machine at the same weight as you used for the pull down. Depending upon your bicep strength, you may be able to pull more laterally than you can vertically. Play around with it until you find just the right weight. Remember, you want to be challenged but not overworked to the point of strain or injury. Reach for the handle, and pull it toward your body. The key here is to allow the elbows to push past your anterior and toward your posterior. In other words, you are again squeezing your lats and traps toward your spine.

As you let go, you will move slightly forward to allow the handle to retract but not to its original position. Do not sway or arch the back. Sit up nice and tall with a stable torso.

Pecs

Most people are familiar with the pec muscles. Any person who is serious about lifting will usually have protruding pecs—like Arnold Schwarzenegger. It is much easier for men than women to build these muscles up. Testosterone works in men's favor, and they also have larger muscle strands to begin with.

Although machines exist to work the pecs in a butterfly motion (squeezing two pieces of board together in front of you), I prefer barbells. The butterfly machines are known to be rough on rotator cuffs, and many people experience pain and even injury in the butterfly movement. The machines require such care for proper executions that I'm not even going to tell you how to use them. I would much rather show you a similar routine without the hassle.

Start off lying supine (on your back) on a bench. Have a barbell in each hand. Use barbells of roughly the same weight you used for your bicep hammer curls. Your arms will each be at a 90-degree angle, even with your chest. Your wrists will be facing each other. At this stage, you make the letter *U*.

Breathe out as you push your arms up. Keep those elbows relaxed, and do not lock them. Instead, make the pecs work and squeeze them at the top, forming the letter *A*. (By *A*, I mean that you are forming a triangle with your chest as the base and your arms as the two sides.) If your arms form the letter *U*, you probably didn't bring your hands together. I like to have the weights touch so that I'm sure I form the *A*. Also, make sure you are extending your arms out far enough—without locking the elbows, of course. Slowly lower your arms back to the starting position (the *U*), but do not let your elbows dip below your chest line. Keep a nice even line with your arms and chest.

Another way to work the pecs is a good, old-fashioned bench press like the one we used in our 1RM example. If you have been in the military, you will be quite familiar with these puppies. You should be able to press the same weight you did with your bicep bar curl. Again, lie supine on a bench, preferably one that is simply horizontal, not elevated on one side. Bend your knees. The starting position for the bench press is the same as the previous exercise. Your arms are at a 90-degree angle by each side, even with your chest. Make sure your wrists are facing away from your face and that your hands are evenly spaced on the bar. Breathe out as you push up.

Do not lock your elbows, but instead force the pecs to squeeze at the top. Breathe in as you lower the bar down, no further than aligned with your chest. Repeat.

INCORRECT FORM

Be sure to keep your back pressed down against the bench. If your back arches, you probably have too much weight. Lower your weight, and concentrate on using your abs to keep your back pressed to the bench. Avoid locking your elbows. When your elbows lock, the joints—not your muscles—are taking the brunt of the lift. Keep your arms softly curved and force the pecs to do the work.

Quads/hamstrings

Your quads are large muscles in your legs that should easily be able to handle 65 percent of your 1RM total. In fact, you might try upwards of 80 percent of your total body weight. Remember, though, that you are working out for *your* health goals, not mine, so pick a weight that is in accordance with your plan.

The leg extension machine is a great way to work your quads. Your seat should be set to allow you to curl back far enough to create tension or resistance as you lift up. If you are too far forward, you will feel a pinch on your hamstrings. If you are too far back, your knees will feel strained. Spend a few minutes to adjust the settings properly.

Use the handgrips, and lift your legs as you exhale. Do not lock your knees, but focus on bringing your toes up to almost full range of motion. Your focus should be on a strong leg extension without strain on the knee. Push through the tops of your feet. Inhale as you slowly lower your legs back to the starting position. By moving with slow, controlled movements you are once again working both the concentric (lift) and eccentric (lower) phases of your muscles—twice the bang for your buck! If you are lifting a proper weight, your third set of reps will burn your quads and make you sweat. I literally hop out of this machine when I am done because my quads have had enough.

If you work your quads, you will want to work your hamstrings, too, because they are opposing muscles. The leg curl is a good hamstring exercise.

By the way, both the quads and hamstrings have several muscles that make up the group. For simplicity purposes, we have grouped them together since they are all worked at the same time. If you would like to learn the names of all the muscles, I recommend you consult a good book on human anatomy.

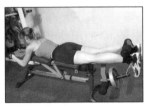

With the leg curl, it is important to once again adjust your seat properly. Make sure you are seated far enough back to support your hamstrings and not pinch them. With this machine, you actually start with your legs out and your hip bones pressed against the seat. The emphasis here is to squeeze at the bottom. Fold your legs in and breathe out as you curl your legs back. Hold on to the handgrips.

Next, squeeze your legs and force your heels back toward your glutes. Breathe in as you allow your legs to slowly go back up to the starting position. Repeat. Remember to avoid locking your knees. Control your movements to get the most out of this exercise.

Glutes

As with your legs, your glutes are made up of many muscles. We will concentrate on the whole glute group and not isolate each muscle. Trust me, they will all get a good workout.

Do you remember *Buns of Steel*, the popular exercise video that came out in the late 1980s and 1990s? Well, that woman was on to something. It is basic and elementary, but often it is the simplest exercises that are the most effective. That is certainly the case with lunges.

The key to lunges is your posture. If you think of a pole coming in through your head that goes through your spine and out your knee, you will align yourself properly. Make sure your feet are far enough apart that you are pushing your back knee down, not your front knee forward. Keep one hand on your front knee to remind you that it shouldn't be moving.

Breathe out as you press your back knee through toward the floor, but don't touch the ground. Keeping your posture straight and your head forward, bring that back knee up to the starting position as you breathe in. One rep involves lowering your right leg and then your left. You may choose to do all your right leg first and then your left. Just ensure that you balance both legs as you seek to meet your fitness reps and sets goals.

If you would like to intensify this exercise add hand weights of, say, 15 pounds or a weighted bar. This creates more resistance for your muscles to work against.

Another great basic exercise for your glutes is the squat. A squat is a very natural movement—like sitting down onto a chair. And just like sitting down, we don't squat all the way to the floor in this exercise. Many injuries occur from squats performed too deeply, putting too much pressure on the knee joints. Even if you don't feel the pain as you perform the exercise improperly, you could still be causing long-term damage on the joints.

In a squat, you actually start by standing up nice and tall, with soft knees. Your legs should be shoulder-width apart with your feet facing forward. Your back should remain stable throughout the entire exercise, and your head should continue facing forward.

Breathe out as you push through your glute as if you were trying to reach a chair with your rear to sit down.

Again, your knees should not move forward; rather, your glute should move backward. Push your arms out in front of you as you squat and bring them in as you stand back up, taking a breath in. Repeat. You can also add hand weights to this exercise.

INCORRECT FORM

Our knees get enough abuse. We do not need to add any additional strain or stress on them. Do not put the weight on your knees by leaning forward. Make your glutes and leg muscles perform the work. Keep your back straight and do not lean over. This will help prevent the tendency to push your front knee forward.

Outer/inner thigh

Many athletic people forget to work their inner and outer thighs, but thighs are important for hip strength and mobility. The technical name for the outer thigh muscle is the *abductor* muscle, and the inner thigh muscle is the *adductor* muscle. Think of it this way: to be abducted means to be taken away. Your outer thigh is moving your leg away from your body while your inner thigh is bringing it back in.

The easiest and quickest ways to work both of these muscles are with a machine designed to strengthen these specific muscles or on the floor. Since the machines at the gym have clear instructions on how to use them, I will concentrate on explaining the floor exercises that work these muscles.

Lie down on your side. Align your body so that you are in a straight line. Tuck your glute in and use a hand in front on the floor for stability if you need to. With your feet facing forward, begin to slowly lift your leg.

Breathe out as you lift your leg up as high as you can. Concentrate on controlling the movements. You will feel this in your outer thigh and hip area. Breathe in as you slowly lower your leg back to the starting position. After your reps with this leg, switch to the other leg.

If you want to make this exercise more of a challenge, add ankle weights for additional resistance.

The opposing muscle for the outer thigh is the inner thigh. This time, start off with your top leg curled around in front of you. Grab your ankle with your hand for support, maintaining that same alignment on your hip. Your foot of the lower leg is facing forward.

Exhale as you push your lower leg up toward the ceiling, again raising it as high as you can. Don't be discour-

aged if you can't lift it very high off the ground. These muscles don't get worked very often and may be weak. If, however, you find it easy to lift, add the weight of your other leg as additional resistance. Maintain straight alignment with your feet facing forward.

Calves

Although we utilize our calf muscles each time we take a step, it is good to give them a little extra attention now and then. An easy way to focus on your calves is to do calf raises. All you need is the floor. A step of some kind would increase the movement and require a little more lift and balance.

The key here is to squeeze your calf muscles at the top, contracting them before you lower your heel back down. If you use the step, the lower your heel goes below the step, the deeper the stretch for the foot and calf, but the more difficult it will be to balance. If you can press your heel deep, it is a great move to enhance your flexibility, especially with your Achilles tendon.

Breathe out as you raise your heels and squeeze your calves, and inhale as you lower your heels and release the calves. Again, you can increase the intensity by adding additional resistance via hand or ankle weights. (Note: never run with ankle weights on.)

Abdominal muscle (ab)/obliques

Contrary to popular belief, we only have one abdominal muscle.[4] We see "abs" all the time, but that's actually inaccurate. I've used "ab" in this section. We also have our obliques, which are the side muscles or "love handles" of our bodies. We can, however, work different areas of the muscle such as the upper or lower portion.

Possibly everyone has heard, seen, or performed the ab "crunch," but I like what I call the "leanback" because it forces you to work against gravity. It is a much slower and more controlled move, working the upper portion of your abs really hard.

With this exercise, you actually start by sitting up straight. Stack your spine, and put your arms out in front of you like Frankenstein (reaching forward). As you lean back, take a big breath in. Just when the small of your back touches the ground and gravity wants to pull you down, sit back up slowly and exhale, pushing out through pursed lips.

  Stack back up and repeat. You should feel the strain on your ab because it is resisting gravity and pulling you back up. These are killer! Concentrate on quality not quantity here. Focus on keeping your ab tight.

You can incorporate your obliques into this move by holding the lean-back position and rotating or twisting your waist before you slowly move back up into the stacked position. Say good-bye to those love handles with this move!

To work the lower portion of your ab, lie supine (on your back) on a mat, with your knees bent and your feet flat on the floor. Lift your shoulder blades off the ground, keeping your chin off your chest and looking up at the ceiling. The easiest way to monitor your form is to pretend that you have an apple under your chin. It should prevent your chin from ever touching your chest, and it will force your head to look up.

 With this sit-up, you are not bouncing or pulsing. You are simply contracting your ab and keeping it contracted. Your shoulder blades should never touch the ground, and your ab is helping press through your back on the floor. Tap your knees with your hands, continuing to look up at the ceiling. Remember, your chin should never touch your chest. Keep that imaginary apple under your chin at all times. Reach a little further if you can, and feel the burn!

Do as many as you can without losing the contraction. As soon as your stomach "pooches" out (pooching is when you can't keep your ab held in), back off and rest. If you continue to press on, you will end up working deeper muscles that will end up pushing out your fatty tissue further. Instead of having a "six pack," you will have a stomach pack.

INCORRECT FORM

Remember to keep your chin off your chest. If you don't, you will put unnecessary strain on your neck. We want the ab to do the work, not your neck.

Erector spinae (back muscles)

Many people forget that the back is full of muscles, all of which need to be strengthened. As I mentioned before, an alarming 80 percent of all Americans suffer from back pain,[5] so it is important to work your erector spinae.

You don't have to use heavy weights or machines to get an effective workout. Lie prone (facedown) on the floor with your arms stretched out over your head and your legs straight out behind you.

Keep looking down at the floor, and at the same time lift your *right* arm and your *left* leg to a comfortable height. Hold it for just a second, and then switch to your left arm and right leg. Hold again for a second. Switch and continue to repeat, breathing slowly and with control.

If you want to challenge yourself further and work deeper back muscles, take both your arms together and place your forehead on your hands. Again, keep looking down at the floor. Lift your arms, head, and both your legs at the same time. This requires more concentration and work.

A great back strengthening exercise that stretches out your ab at the same time is what is known as the cobra. Lie prone (facedown) on your mat with your legs straight out behind you. Lean up on your elbows and look up. You should feel the use of your back and a stretch deep through your ab.

To make it more difficult, push up onto your hands, continuing to look up. If you have had serious back pain in the past or injury to your back, I do not suggest you try this move, at least not without counsel from your doctor. Start off with the beginning cobra and work your way up.

Floor work

Your muscle workout isn't complete without some additional floor work to challenge certain parts of your body.

I'm a big fan of push-ups! They have been around forever, and nothing works your entire body like a push-up. I like to offer people three different levels of push-ups to match their level of fitness. For the first level, position yourself on all fours (hands and knees). Keep your torso straight and firm.

The point here is to work the upper body (pecs, shoulders, and triceps), so lower down, bending your elbows. Breathe in as you lower yourself close to the floor. Exhale as you push your body back up.

For a level two push-up, everything above applies, but you extend your knees farther out behind you. Concentrate on lowering and lifting slowly, forcing your muscles to work.

You will feel your core muscles and muscles in your ab and back working hard to keep your torso in place. That's what makes this a great floor exercise. It is working nearly your entire body all at once. For those who want something quick and powerful, this is your exercise.

To take it to the third level, straighten your legs and point your toes. Keep your body as straight as possible. Avoid raising your glute up toward the ceiling. How many can you do with great form?

Most people are familiar with this type of push-up, but they haven't done what I call the triceps push-up.

For this exercise, you will sit with your arms behind you. Make sure your hands are facing in toward your bottom. Bend your knees and have them away from your seat, just enough to create a "tabletop" with your torso.

The key here is to make the triceps—not your torso or legs—push your body up. Keep your torso flat like a tabletop. Exhale as you lift up and inhale as you lower, never letting your bottom touch the ground. Remember, your triceps are doing the work, not your torso. Repeat as many as you can. You will want to stretch out when you are done.

STRETCHING

Now that we've looked at cardio fitness and weight-resistance training, we need to talk about the third pillar of complete fitness: stretching.

Entire books have been dedicated to the topic of stretching. It's something we all need more of in our lives. Stretching is what prevents injury and enables our muscles to perform for us once again at their optimum.

In this section I will show you two series of stretches, one for your legs and one for your arms. Together, these series will stretch out just about every muscle in your body in a matter of minutes. They are very effective stretches that, if you commit to doing them on a regular basis, will improve your overall flexibility and mobility. I'll start off with your legs.

Leg stretch series

Bend one leg and bring that foot in toward your groin area. Extend the opposite leg out as far away from the other leg as you can manage. Keep it pressed on the floor. Reach for your foot but do not pull on your foot. You may grab it, but don't pull. Give your hamstring and calf a good stretch by breathing in and out slowly. For each of these stretches, hold the stretch for a count of twenty seconds.

Next, take the leg that was stretched out and twist it behind your butt. I know this is starting to sound like yoga, but it is very simple. Trust me. Keep your bent leg and foot in the same position. Twist your torso away from the leg you just placed behind you. This is an excellent stretch for your quad, inner thigh, erector spinae, and oblique.

Keeping the bent leg and foot in the same position, now take the leg behind you and bring it around over the bent leg. This move can feel a bit like a pretzel and does require some balance, but I know you can do it! Concentrate and breathe. Give yourself a hug with the opposite arm. If your right leg is twisted around your left leg, hug yourself with your left arm. This stretches your glute and outer thigh.

In the last step of the leg series, move the same leg you have been switching to cross over your other leg. Walk your bottom as close to your heels as possible, and sit up nice and tall. The closer your chest is to your leg, the deeper the stretch. This is awesome for your hips and glutes. Believe it or not, tight hips can cause back pain. When you lose mobility here, it affects your walking. This in turn tweaks your back muscles.

Do this stretching series for both legs.

Arm stretch series

We will need to also stretch out your arms. For this series sit Indian style if you can, or in any position that is comfortable for you.

Sitting up nice and tall, move your arms behind you and grab your hands together. Your arms should be just about straight, but don't lock your elbows. Raise your arms up as high as you can go but keep your head looking forward. This stretches out your shoulders and deltoids. Keep breathing deeply for at least twenty seconds.

Now, curve your spine and bring your arms forward, looking down. Press your wrists out away from your body. This will stretch your lats, rhomboids, and upper back. Remember to breathe as you hold this stretch for at least twenty seconds.

Check your posture and make sure you are sitting up nice and tall again. Spread your arms wide. Bring your left arm across the front to the other side. With your thumbs facing the floor, bring your right arm over and push your left elbow to extend the stretch. Hold it here and breathe for twenty seconds. This will stretch out your triceps and outer deltoids. Switch arms and reverse the stretch. Hold again for twenty seconds, breathing all the while.

 The last arm stretch in this series will get your triceps and shoulders. Sitting nice and tall again, bring one arm back over your shoulder as if giving yourself a pat on the back. Your other hand will grab your elbow and push it back as if to help it reach further down your back. Keep your head looking forward to reduce strain on the neck. Hold it there for twenty seconds, breathing deeply. Switch arms, and you are done!

HIT THE SHOWERS

What do you think? A lot of information, I know. But don't panic: you won't do every one of these exercises in one day's workout. What I have attempted to do is give you some options. Plenty more exist, but these will give you an outstanding beginning. As you begin to customize your program according to your FIT profile, refer back to these photos and descriptions to help you, just as if I were there with you.

How exactly do you customize your program? The following section will outline recommendations for your particular personality or temperament. Select the chapter that corresponds to your FIT profile, and let's get rolling!

WORKING OUT WITH STYLE

SIX | # JUST DO IT— MAKING FITNESS **FAST**

BEING A FAST person myself, I know that if this is your temperament you probably jumped right to this chapter because you want to know what this book can do for you. So I will get right to the point and tell you that this chapter will help you make fitness FAST!

Since you are a mover and shaker, you will appreciate this approach of getting exercise done and over with so that you can enjoy benefits such as more energy, better health, and improved stamina. All these fruits of a healthy life will ensure you are successful in all that you do—and that's the bottom line, isn't it?

This chapter will customize an exercise program that will fit into your busy life without boring you.

MAKE BEING FIT A GOAL, AND JUST DO IT.

I do encourage you to read chapter one and take the FIT Assessment. I also highly recommend that you look over chapter two. Why? Because:

1. You will learn basic principles about the different personality styles, which will make you more effective in dealing with other people.

2. You will discover what your particular FIT (Fitness Individuality Trait) really means and how it can influence your entire life for the better.

3. You will have the chance to work through your goals and objectives to ensure you reach your target, and I know you like to win!

This chapter builds on that foundation. Here you will now learn how your specific personality style influences your fitness routine: what you do, how you do it, with whom you do it, how long you will do it, and so forth. *This chapter is the key to reaching your health and fitness goals* that you set in chapter three. The more you understand yourself, the better equipped you will be to succeed, not just with your fitness routine but also in your relationships with others, personally and professionally.

WHY SHOULD YOU GET FIT?

If you are like me, you will want to make being fit a goal and just do it! You are probably a competitive person who likes to set and achieve challenging goals. But even though we FAST types are go-getters, we still need to live a healthy lifestyle. The difference with us is that we must decide we want it. So let me ask you some questions:

1. Do you want to achieve great things?
2. Do you want to be successful?
3. Do you want to be at the top of your game?

OR

1. Do you want to miss the mark?
2. Do you want to fail?
3. Do you want to be a has-been?

The choice is yours. If you identify with the first set of questions, then you will need good health to get there. Period. You know it; you just have to admit it. I know it can be tough for us FAST people to acknowledge our humanness, but why ignore the rules when we can make them work to our advantage? Maximize your potential by being fit.

Someone else (significant other, family member, boss, doctor—or me, for that matter) telling you to go get fit won't work for you. Why? Because you have to be in the driver's seat. You need to be in control of your own destiny. You have the power to do anything you *choose* to do, but you must first make the choice. Are you brave enough to take on the challenge? I bet you are. But you will still want to get something out of it. Here's what I can promise:

- Increased energy that will allow you to accomplish more
- Mental alertness that will keep you at the top of your game
- A toned body, which will improve the impression you give to others
- Better rest that will help prevent illness and keep you in the game longer
- Eating right, which will keep your body running like a finely tuned machine
- Fitness, which will allow you to make more money

In chapter three I gave a lot of other reasons why you should exercise, but you need to find your own motivation. If you happened to rush past chapter three, you might consider going back to formulate your strategy to maximize your chances of success. Remember the old saying that we never plan to fail but always will if we fail to plan.

■

***ALL THE SUCCESS OF THIS WORLD DOESN'T MATTER
IF YOU DON'T HAVE YOUR HEALTH.***

■

For those extreme FAST FITs who can't think of one good reason why they should slow down and waste their time exercising, here's a story that might change your mind. It will take just a second.

In November 2002 my husband and I attended a coaching conference in Seattle. We had recently joined this coaching organization and were eager to hear the president speak on new trends and strategies in the industry. We were very impressed with his business success. He'd started his company as a one-man show and had built it up to a coaching empire, certifying people like us all across the globe. As he spoke, he shared about all the sacrifices he had made in order to grow his business. He worked well into the wee hours of the morning most days, traveled extensively, and didn't have time for exercise, friends, or relationships. Balance was not in his vocabulary. He was rich, well known, and successful. He did what it took and challenged us to do the same.

Yet something was missing, and he knew it. He had gained significant weight due to his intense travel schedule, and he lacked companionship. He decided to make a change to improve the quality of his life. He began to watch what he ate, he started exercising a bit, and he purchased a dog for a pet. Unfortunately, he waited too long for his life-changing decision. In January of 2003 he died of a massive heart attack. He was forty-three.

All the success of this world doesn't matter if you don't have your health. We FAST folks can sometimes think we are above these natural laws, but they apply to every one of us.

If those laws haven't caught up with you yet, they will. Take control and be the one in charge. As I mentioned before, you have the ability to manage 70 percent of the aging process, which means only 30 percent cannot be altered and will be what it will be. Decide today to determine where you will go in the future, how you will get there, and what your health will be like tomorrow. Take the health challenge.

THE FAST PROFILE

What does being FAST really mean? It means you are a fast-paced individual who prefers *doing things* rather than being with people. You are outgoing, but you do not need the social scene to feel fulfilled. In fact, big parties aren't your thing unless you work the room, make a few key contacts, and then book it home. You tend to be very ambitious, driven, and goal oriented. You are competitive with yourself and others. You love a good challenge.

You normally don't like rules and feel they don't apply to you. You'll work within them if it works to your advantage; otherwise, you'll throw them out the window. You'll ask for forgiveness rather than permission. You focus on results and achievement. You do not often show your feelings or emotions (unless it is frustration, impatience, or anger), and you like to be in charge. You can be very objective and fair, but you set your sights high.

Your motto is "My way or the highway." You are certainly open to other people's opinions, but they are usually wrong. If someone presents an idea to you, you will think about it and decide if you like it or not.

Right now, your view of fitness is most likely one of the following:

1. I compete in sporting events because I like the challenge.
2. I have specific fitness goals and work toward achieving them quickly.
3. I believe exercise takes too much time, so I do not engage in it.

In any case, your fast-paced, results-oriented attitude is affecting how you approach fitness. You desire a program that is active, varied, and challenging.

How to quickly identify someone with your style

You can spot another FAST person by observing his or her pace. FAST folks talk and walk with purpose and power. In fact, you can probably hear a FAST person coming with each pound of his or her foot. FAST people usually dress for success. They typically wear power suits and strong colors. They won't have flashy accessories, but what they wear will be classy, like an expensive watch.

Chances are, they drive a sports car or a very high-end luxury automobile that portrays their status of success. They are usually the ones driving at warp speed on the freeway because they have places to go, people to see, and things to do! They tend to be impatient, especially when they want something right now, which is most of the time. Their office may or may not be neat, depending upon their needs. If neatness will help them accomplish their goals more efficiently, then they will keep things orderly. If they feel it isn't crucial, things will be in disarray.

Whatever they do, FAST people will do it (or not) because they have *chosen* to. Their personal objectives dictate which areas of their lives they give attention to. You probably won't see a lot of cute knickknacks or family pictures in their office—unless they have *decided* to decorate that way or found that it would be to their advantage. Otherwise it will probably be stark and barren. You may, however, see awards, plaques, and pictures of pinnacle moments.

Famous people with FAST profiles:

- Rudolph Giuliani
- Hillary Clinton
- Dr. Laura

Just because these folks are FAST doesn't mean they cannot slow down or that they aren't interested in people. Remember that we can temporarily adapt our temperaments to respond to the needs of the moment. FAST people simply feel more comfortable doing things this way, but they do utilize the other areas to function.

■

JESUS BECAME EXACTLY WHAT HE NEEDED, WHEN HE NEEDED IT.

■

Often when I am training people on the concepts of personality styles, somebody asks me what temperament Jesus was. The answer is easy: He was all four. Jesus became exactly what He needed, when He needed it. He is the perfect example of how every one of us should be striving to balance and blend with people. We each have our strengths, but we must be careful not to live just there. We must attempt to improve all areas of our complex being. The more balanced you are, the more versatile you will be, and the more versatile you are, the greater the chance of success in all areas of your life.

Your many strengths

As a FAST person, you bring to any group or situation the ability to make quick decisions. People look to you for guidance and leadership simply because you aren't afraid to take on the challenge. You display courage and confidence, which attracts people to you. You have the ability to see the big picture and often cast the vision.

In most cases, when you set your mind on something, it happens, no matter what it takes. You don't mind burning the midnight oil or going the extra mile if you have set the objective and have the target in sight. You are very results oriented. Unlike others, for you the more difficult the task is, the more motivated you are to succeed. FAST people can easily become workaholics.

You are driven and tend to enjoy taking on a variety of projects at once. You have vast amounts of energy, which enables you to multitask well. Because you don't wear your feelings on your sleeve, you are able to confront "touchy" situations more objectively. You have no difficulty handling problems—in fact, you typically turn these challenges into opportunities. You don't mind debates or tension and can stand your ground on issues, usually keeping people and personal aspects out of it. Although FAST people will hold a myriad of positions within a group, they often make great leaders.

How to conquer challenges

FAST folks can get a bad reputation because some of us—the extreme FAST folks—can be harsh and unkind, even brutal. But remember, *any* person's strengths pushed to an unhealthy extreme will result in a negative consequence. All FAST people do not have to be steamrollers. You can decide to soften up your edges. People respond better to sugar than to lemon juice.

Because of your fast-paced approach to life, however, you may not slow down enough to truly listen to others. Even though you'd rather be focusing on tasks, you still need people to accomplish your goals. And you do care about people; you just show it differently than others do. You may do things for others to show your appreciation. But sometimes people—especially FUN or FRIENDLY people—need more than that. Take the time to slow down and learn about the people in your life. What do they need? Try using words of encouragement that work for them.

Your ability to make quick decisions is certainly a plus, but I caution you to slow down at times and give serious thought to those situations requiring a bit more detail. If you find yourself having to fix or redo things because you decided too quickly, try pairing yourself up with a FACTUAL person who will help you look at the details. These people are amazing at seeing obstacles along the way, preventing you from wasting valuable time, effort, and money. They aren't being negative when they find a problem in your plan; they are just attempting to avoid any unnecessary turbulence.

LEARN TO SLOW DOWN AND LISTEN TO OTHERS.

Instead of leading people, you may have a tendency to boss them around. Although some personalities will seem to tolerate this for a period of time, they are actually building up resentment and bitterness toward you. I've heard countless stories about overbearing FAST men married to soft, sensitive FRIENDLY women. The husband is led to believe that everything is just fine. He tells her what to do, and she does it. Then one day he comes home to an empty house, discovering that his wife has taken the kids and is filing for divorce. What happened?

What happened was that the wife didn't feel she was able to share her feelings with her FAST husband, so she stuffed them away—until she finally exploded. Who is to blame? Both parties failed to understand the other and didn't take the time to learn how their temperament affected the other. Take the time.

Some of the other profiles might be afraid of you due to your directness and ability to confront. Do not permit yourself to take advantage of this fear and abuse relationships. Rather, understand how people perceive you and attempt to adapt your communication style to the environment or particular person with whom you are speaking. When you do, everyone wins: you get what you want, and the other person feels respected.

Because you can easily leave emotions out of the equation, you can come across as cold and uncaring. FAST people tend to fear being taken advantage of or being seen as weak. Often, their curtness is a protective wall. Let your barriers down once in a while and let people in. Life is too short to not have intimacy with at least a few people. It can get lonely being the leader.

Have you seen the movie *Saving Private Ryan*? A powerful scene for me was when Tom Hanks' character, after pulling everyone through a major crisis, finally breaks down all alone. He was required to carry the load of his platoon and lead them through a horrific war and dangerous assignment. Having no one to share with, he cried to himself. I agree with his statement that problems should "flow up and not down," but we all need someone to turn to. Don't isolate yourself. Even a hero needs a hug now and then.

How to beat stress

Although FAST people thrive under pressure, they can become quite hostile when faced with extreme duress or stress, especially when their goals are threatened or they feel someone is taking advantage of them. Remember when I said that any strength pushed to an extreme is a weakness? Every profile has a negative side, and it usually rears its ugly head when we are stressed. Look for these warning signs if you are a FAST person.

- Are you getting impatient over everything?
- Are you agitated and angry over little things?
- Is everything and everyone frustrating you?
- Are you suddenly more direct, abrupt, pushy, and assertive?
- Are you getting mean?

■

FAST PEOPLE NEED TO DO SOMETHING
IN ORDER TO RECOVER FROM STRESS.

■

When this happens, take a deep breath and decide to "visit" one of the other temperaments. This is where you need to choose to exercise attributes that are not in your normal way of behaving. For instance, when I am stressed I will often slow my pace and go to the opposite extreme, being extra kind (visiting the FRIENDLY profile) so that I can keep from biting someone's head off.

A great way for you to recover from stressful situations is to engage in physical activity. FAST people need to *do* something to recover from stress. If you don't do something positive, the stress will cause you to do something negative. The choice is yours, but I have just the solution for you in this chapter, so keep reading. When you damage relationships, everyone loses—including you.

RELATING TO THE OTHER PERSONALITY STYLES

The communication style of FAST people is usually very direct and abrupt. You don't beat around the bush; you get right to the point. Because you are a bottom-line kind of person, you expect others to be the same way. Although this communication style can be a strength, be aware that not everyone is like you.

Other FAST people

When talking with other FAST folks, be yourself! They will appreciate you getting right to the point. No need to break the ice or socialize with them. Because you are both strong personalities, be careful not to push too hard or be too forceful. Use words and phrases that would work for you. Most FAST people do not like being told what to do. They prefer options and deciding for themselves, so be sure to offer a number of suggestions that are results oriented and challenging.

Note that FAST people may have difficulty building strong relationships with other FAST types. Why? Because both of them will want to be in the driver's seat of the relationship. Most often, FAST people will get along best with FRIENDLY folks who are willing to support them...if they can learn how to communicate in a warmer manner.

Relating to FUN people

When interacting with FUN people, you need to make yourself stop and listen! Be a bit more patient and informal. Socialize and show enthusiasm. Don't go into great detail about anything, or you will lose their interest. If you need to get an answer, gently guide them back on track. Don't be forceful or demanding, and don't embarrass them. FUN people need to feel accepted and included, so make a concerted effort to let them know they are "OK."

Relating to FRIENDLY people

When communicating with FRIENDLY people, slow down! Don't interrupt their thinking, even if they seem to take a while to respond. Give them the time they need to formulate their thoughts. Be sensitive to their opinions and feelings.

A friendly, soft approach that affirms them works best. If you are too forceful with your communication, they will retreat, withdraw, and shut down. The problem is that you will probably not notice it because they will not say anything to you. Don't assume silence is acceptance. Be in tune to their body posture, facial expressions, and "temperature."

Relating to FACTUAL people

When engaging with FACTUAL people, focus on the facts. Again, you will want to slow down and allow them time to process. In fact, you may need to give them additional time to think things over before they respond. Don't be disorganized or aggressive with them. Systematically present your idea. No need to be too friendly; they are more concerned with receiving correct data. These folks are analytical and structured, so don't make a lot of sudden changes. Steady as she goes!

THE ULTIMATE WORKOUT PLAN FOR THE FAST PROFILE

Now that you have gained a basic understanding of yourself and how to interact with others, let's get down to the meat and potatoes of this book: working out with style—your style! We will take all this information and relate it to how you will approach your cardio exercise, weight training, stretching, and even nutrition.

Remember, how you are wired *does* affect everything. Your FIT profile, as it relates to fitness, is what makes this book unique. You will now have the opportunity to customize a program—a lifestyle—based on who you are as an individual. No more one-size-fits-all approach, and no more failure. Success and good health are in your future. Ready to revolutionize your exercise?

How to raise your energy level

Greater cardio capacity equals higher energy levels. Most FAST profiles are busy people with full schedules. Squeezing in cardio exercise isn't usually a priority. If you have attempted to work out in the past but failed, chances are you didn't view it as a challenge and understand how it can help you win the game. Or you simply moved on to another goal. FAST folks can tend to be so goal oriented that they don't always stick to things for the long term. Fitness is indeed a long-term goal—it's a life quest. The good news is that you can make sub-goals that will continually challenge you and keep things exciting and fresh.

Finding time for exercise can be a challenge, but you like challenges! Make it a competition with yourself to get your three to five days of cardio exercise in every week, and remember what your personal goal is and why you are doing this. What can good health do for you? Stay focused on these reasons and chart your course for success, one day at a time. You will get there. You will enjoy the benefits of cardio exercise, which is more energy to conquer the world.

For you, working out with *variety* will be important to keep it fresh and exciting. If you get bored, you will quit. I know you aren't a quitter, so whenever possible vary your workout. Do more than one thing per session. For example, run prior to lifting weights. This way you are killing two birds with one stone—and you've kept it interesting by changing gears halfway through. Stretch afterward, and you have a grand slam! Or try kicking a heavy bag between your weight-lifting sets. This keeps your heart rate in your target zone throughout the entire workout.

■

MAKE IT A COMPETITION WITH YOURSELF TO GET
YOUR THREE TO FIVE DAYS OF CARDIO EXERCISE IN EVERY WEEK.

■

You may find yourself getting bored with thirty minutes on the same cardio machine. If this happens, run for 10 minutes, cycle for 10 minutes, and use the elliptical machine for 10 minutes.

An elliptical machine is similar to a treadmill in that you are jogging or running, but it doesn't have the same impact on your joints. On an elliptical you are almost gliding, as if you were cross-country skiing. And since the machine uses your arms too, it makes it more interactive than the basic treadmill. This changes it up and prevents you from getting sick of the same thing.

Personally, I run. I choose running simply because I like the results of it. But I get bored very easily, and I hate the treadmill. I can run outside, but I have found that I enjoy triathlons much more. My competitive nature likes the challenge, and just when I am about to get bored with one leg, I'm on to the next. It is a fast-paced type of exercise. You might want to give it a try.

Setting your fitness goals in advance and committing to them for a six-week period will help keep you on track. Review chapter three, and utilize the information for goal setting and achieving. The quicker you decide to treat your health as if it is as important as any business deal, meeting, or project, the better off you will be.

In fact, let's pause just a second and see what kind of shape you are really in. Take the following measurements:

Waist-to-hip ratio
Waist measurement = _____(WM)
Hip measurement = _____(HM)
WM _____ divided by HM _____ = _____Ratio

If you are a man and the ratio is greater than .95, you are in the high-fat category, you have greater risk for heart attack, and you need to lose weight. If you are a woman and the ratio is greater than .85, you are in the high-fat category, you have greater risk for heart attack, and you need to lose weight.

Even if your measurements are acceptable (i.e. less than the numbers outlined), you must continually include cardio exercise in your routine in order to prevent future health problems.

Note that being extremely thin because you just don't eat isn't a healthy option, either. I have known too many "skinny-as-a-rail" types who have died young because their body couldn't go on. They pushed it to the limits, never providing fuel or conducting maintenance. You can be thin and your heart still be "sick," your muscles weak, and your bones extremely frail.

Schedule your exercise time on your calendar just as you would any other appointment. However, do not block out the portion of your day that is normally your peak productivity time. Remember your energy graph? Instead, find a "lull" or "dead zone" that you can fill up with something useful—like exercising! That way you don't feel as if you sacrificed something else for exercise. FAST types don't want to miss opportunities.

THE PERFECT CARDIO PROGRAM FOR FAST PEOPLE

On the following pages there are some cardio programs that are likely to be a good match for your FIT profile. Each one of them is well suited for FAST folks. The *intensity* column refers back to the Workout Intensity Chart on page 54. Try these programs, then adapt them as you see fit. The bottom line is to JUST DO IT!

Chart 6.1 | **FAST Cardio Programs**

Exercise	Frequency	Intensity	Time	Tips for Your Style
Running: fast; can be done anywhere; competitive	3–5 times a week	Level 8–9½ (Visit 9 and 9½, but try to keep the majority of your run at an 8.)	20–30 min.	Compete with yourself! How far can you go in thirty minutes? Monitor the distance, and try to improve it each time. Want even more of a workout? Increase the incline.
Indoor cycling: competitive; challenging; fast and effective	3 times a week	Level 8–9½ (Visit 9 and 9½, but try to keep the majority of your exercise at an 8.)	1 hour	Most classes are one hour in length. Challenge yourself with heavier gears each time. Aim for breathless!
Swimming: quick and effective; you decide when; challenging	3–5 times a week	Level 8–8½ (Visit 8½, but try to keep the majority of your swim at an 8.)	20–30 min.	Dive in, swim your laps, and get out. It's a fast, effective workout. Time yourself, and try to shave off seconds each time. Increase the number of laps as you improve.
Kicking bag: aggressive, quick, and easy	3 times a week	Level 8–8½ (Visit 8½, but try to keep the majority of your time at an 8.)	20–30 min.	A fast and furious workout. Make sure to wrap your hands and concentrate on proper form and technique to prevent injury. Most heavy bags come with instructions and guidelines.

111

Chart 6.1 | **FAST Cardio Programs (continued)**

Exercise	Frequency	Intensity	Time	Tips for Your Style
Jump rope: intense, fast, highly effective, and no wait!	3–5 times a week	Level 8½ (Try to keep the majority of your jumping at an 8½.)	20 min.	This is not for wimps. Ever watch a boxer really jump? Speed is the key. Keep moving. Change your jumping stance to prevent boredom: alternate legs, jack, kick forward, curl back.
Elliptical machine: like running without impact	3–5 times a week	Level 8–8½ (Visit 8½, but try to keep the majority of your run at an 8.)	20–30 min.	Don't allow yourself to fall into the trap of moving slow on this machine. In order to get the max out of this piece of equipment, you have to monitor your heart rate. Make sure you are at the level 8 minimally. Do whatever it takes to stay between 8 and 8½ for a majority of your workout, but don't forget to visit that 9 and 9½ to challenge your cardio system.
Team sports activities: competitive	1–3 times a week	Level 8 (Sports are more up and down, so try to keep moving whenever possible.)	1 hour or more	Depending upon the sport, your cardio workout may not be as intense as you'd get doing something else, but you will stay active longer and you won't be bored. Keys here are to make sure you warm up and try to keep yourself at an even pace.

Exercise	Frequency	Intensity	Time	Tips for Your Style
Solo sports activities	1–3 times a week	Level 8 (Sports are more up and down, so try to keep moving whenever possible.)	1 hour or more	Make sure you are doing the right things in the days and weeks leading up to your selected outdoor activity. For instance, if you plan to ski, work your quads several weeks before, and then give them a rest a couple of days prior to your trip. Weekend warriors incur injury because they do not do anything else throughout the week. Blend these activities with other workouts to ensure an effective and safe workout. The more prepared you are for the activity, the harder you can push it.
Extreme sports and/or competitive races	1–3 times a month	Level 8–10 (With most being high intensity, you shouldn't have problems getting a good workout!)	1 hour or more	You are an adventurer. Extreme sports were created for you (and the FUN profiles). The sky is the limit here as far as options that give you thrills and chills. Face a new fear each month! Sign up for a challenging race that will require your maximum effort.

Notes

- *Running* is a great form of cardio exercise, because it doesn't take much to get your heart rate up and receive immediate benefits. If your knees and back are in good shape, I suggest running for the FAST folks. Whether it is on a treadmill or outside, you can get a lot of bang for your buck in thirty minutes. Monitor your heart rate, or use the pacer on the treadmill to ensure you are working at the right level. Try registering for 5K and 10K races that will force you to practice, prepare, and compete. Anytime you can race against someone else, the more likely you will be to take it a bit more seriously.

- *Indoor cycling* is a phenomenal way to burn a lot of calories. A typical one-hour class can burn 600 to 900 calories. Most classes have formats that warm you up, work you hard, and cool you down at the end. It's down and dirty for the FAST types.

- *Swimming* can be done on your lunch hour. Within thirty minutes, you can improve your cardiovascular system without any strain to your joints. Swimming is easy on the body but requires focus and determination, which is right up your alley. Again, you can enter competitive events or just strive to meet your own goals.

- *Kicking bag.* Want a great way to release tension? Kick something…a bag. Punching and kicking properly on a heavy, weighted bag for thirty minutes will make you wonder who beat up whom! It's an effective way to "kick" the couch potato habit and "punch" through to good health.

- *Jumping rope* is for the super-FAST person who doesn't even have thirty minutes. In just fifteen to twenty minutes, you can get your entire cardio workout when you jump rope nonstop at level 8½. A jump rope is light enough to travel and can be used virtually anywhere. Be prepared to sweat!

- *Elliptical machine* is an alternative to the treadmill that is easier on the knees and back. When you get the arms involved, it becomes quite a challenging workout. Again, setting goals and attempting to improve your stride will keep you focused.

- *Sports activities* (basketball, volleyball, baseball, softball, tennis, and the like). Whether you play with a group of friends or join official leagues, sports activities are an excellent way to use your aggression and competitive spirit while getting a workout. Not all sports are created equal, though, so do not limit your entire cardio routine to just sports. Weave in some of the other suggestions as well. Organized teams require more of a commitment and guarantee that you will attend since you are paying to play.

- *Outdoor sports* (climbing, hiking, cycling, mountain biking, skiing, snowshoeing, water skiing, and the like). Your adventurous spirit will enjoy anything outside that is challenging. You are competing with yourself and taking on the elements. It's your cup of tea! Remember, though, that not all outdoor sports can sustain your heart rate in the right zone, so mix it up with other alternatives.

- *Extreme sports and competitive races.* From skydiving to bungee jumping to dirt bike riding, an array of extreme sport activities exists for you to conquer. They often require stamina, endurance, and the ability to face fear. All this excitement and challenge is right up your alley. Just know that some give you an extremely intense workout while others are more fun than anything. Don't sacrifice your other cardio options if you're entering races or doing extreme sports. Rather, weave these into your monthly program.

Remember, the more you can combine things, the quicker your workout will be. Jumping rope, for instance, can be woven into just about any program. Creatively craft a solution to meet your needs.

Cardio success log

On page 117 is a cardio success log for you to use to track your progress. I encourage you to use it—especially if you have trouble getting your cardio workout in each week. This will act as somewhat of an accountability partner or success record. Some people love cardio and get plenty of activity in each week. If, however, you struggle with cardio activities, log your attempts so that you begin to create an accountability record and also make it more of a challenge to improve from week to week. It will take only a second or two.

On the log, "mode" refers to how you worked out. Examples are listed above. I recommend you make copies of this form and use it as needed. Others may prefer to log their cardio exercise in their day planner. Do whatever works for you! I know filling out forms isn't your favorite thing to do, but this *will* help you reach your goals.

Chart 6.2 | **FAST Cardio Success Log**

DAY/DATE	CARDIO MODE	TIME	STRETCHES	NOTES
Monday				
Tuesday				
Wednesday				
Thursday				
Friday				
Saturday				
Sunday				
Monday				
Tuesday				
Wednesday				
Thursday				
Friday				
Saturday				
Sunday				
Monday				
Tuesday				
Wednesday				
Thursday				
Friday				
Saturday				
Sunday				
Monday				
Tuesday				
Wednesday				
Thursday				
Friday				
Saturday				
Sunday				

THE PERFECT WEIGHT-LIFTING PROGRAM FOR FAST PEOPLE

Your specific fitness goals will ultimately determine which weight-lifting program is best suited for you, but since you are a FAST person, I would highly recommend a down and dirty approach. Meaning you get after it and get out. Keep moving from one machine to the next. This is called the "superset" method because you don't rest between sets or machines.

Laddering

Another approach is what is called *laddering*. Laddering works like this: you start off with the heaviest weight you can lift. (Remember to do one rep maximum in order to determine your max weight, and do as many reps as you can.) You then reduce the weight by approximately 10 percent and lift as long as you can at this weight. At that point, reduce by 10 percent again, lifting as long as you can once more. You continue this process until your muscles cannot lift any longer or you are without any weight, whichever comes first. The advantages to laddering are that it's quick and you don't need a lifting buddy since you are reducing your weight as you go.

■

I HIGHLY RECOMMEND A DOWN AND DIRTY APPROACH.
GET IN AND GET OUT!

■

Most likely, you won't be as interested in free weights unless you want to compete. They take more time and effort. The machines are usually quick and effective. Work your entire body at one time to reduce the number of days you need to hit the gym. You can also work another muscle between your sets to keep it fast paced. Here are a couple of examples:

Chart 6.3 | Opposing Muscles Workout Model

Muscle	Machine	Opposing Muscle	Machine
Biceps	Curl	Triceps	Dips
Lats	Row pull	Pecs	Bench press

For example, if you're working your biceps on a curl machine, you might intersperse a triceps set on the dips machine between biceps sets. You might do one set biceps, one set triceps, one set biceps, one set triceps, and so forth.

If your place of employment has a weight-lifting facility, use it during the lunch hour. Allow yourself a few minutes to change clothes, about twenty-five minutes to get your sets in, and then you'll have the rest of the time to eat and change back. It will be FAST, but you like that! It will all be over in a flash.

A home gym can be convenient, but it can also cause you to let the time get away. As a FAST person, to maximize a home gym you must schedule time for your workout and protect that block of time. At home it is too easy to be distracted with other things. If you opt for a home gym routine, get your workout out of the way first thing in the morning before you head off to work. Better yet, hire a personal trainer to come to your home gym and help you work out effectively and efficiently.

Health clubs and fitness centers provide the best equipment options and have the most variety of machines, but they may be crowded and have lines in front of popular machines. Instead of waiting, just move on to another muscle and machine. If you can at least group all of your upper body exercises together and the lower body together, you will work everything to fatigue, which is what you're shooting for. When we can, it is much better to work all the upper body muscles together and all the lower body muscles together, meaning don't weave in a leg extension in between your biceps curls if you can help it.

Earlier I mentioned the *laddering* technique to work your muscles to fatigue (or to failure if you have a workout partner). This method is ideal for your fast pace. You aren't counting and completing sets. You are simply working until you can't work any longer and then reducing your weight by 10 percent.

For example, if you start out with a 100-pound bench press (your 1RM), you would do as many presses as you could at 100 pounds. If it is only one, then it is one. You then reduce the weight by 10 percent to 90 pounds. Press out as many at 90 pounds as you can. When you can't do any more, reduce it by 10 percent once again. Repeat this process until (1) you are completely fatigued and can't press any more at any weight, or (2) you have no weight left. Move on to the next muscle group, and do the same thing.

Each muscle is different, and you will be able to do a variety of counts. The counts don't matter...just get the workload in. Laddering is fast and effective.

If your budget permits, you will probably achieve great success working with a personal trainer. This way you have a financial investment along with a time commitment, and that will keep you motivated. This person will constantly challenge you, work you hard, and keep you on track.

One other method to try for your FAST profile would be circuit training. These classes incorporate cardio fitness with resistance training. They usually run one hour. You get everything done in one shot—BAM! The best-known program for women is *Curves*, but many health clubs have similar programs that are not gender specific. It's a great, fast, and fun workout!

Weight-lifting victory log

On the following page is a weight-lifting victory log for you to record your progress. I suggest you make ample copies of this and begin using it for whatever program you select.

Log your seat settings and weight so you can refer to them each time. You don't want to waste your time trying to figure out what you did previously. Record it, and build from there. I know you hate using forms because they take so much time, but these will not take long, and they will help you reach your target. Do whatever it takes.

The "mode" would be how you actually worked that muscle. For instance, "leg press" might be the mode for your quads and "15-pound barbells" could be your mode for biceps. Don't forget to change up the mode every now and then to challenge the muscle and prevent boredom.

Chart 6.4 | FAST Weight-Lifting Victory Log

Muscle	Mode	Seat/Settings	Weight/Reps #1	Weight/Reps #2	Weight/Reps #3	Notes
Quads						
Hamstrings						
Glutes						
Calves						
Inner thigh						
Outer thigh						
Biceps						
Triceps						
Shoulders						
Deltoids						
Pecs						
Lats/rhomboids						
Erector spinae						
Ab						
Obliques						
Stretch						

The Perfect Stretching Program for FAST People

Take a look at the stretches I have outlined in chapter five. These will be quick and easy for you, but they get the job done. Make sure to do both your upper and lower body. Add in a "cat" stretch for your back, which means you are on all fours (elbows and knees). Push your spine up toward the ceiling, which creates an arched spine. Breathe in, and then lower your back until it forms a curve in the other direction. Repeat this several times.

■

Stretching prevents injuries and keeps you in the game.

■

If you are actively involved in sports or outdoor recreation, I suggest you add a quad stretch (bring the heel of your foot up behind to your glute and push out through your knee) and a hamstring stretch (put one leg out in front of you with your heel on the floor and toe up; the other leg is bent at the knee, and you lean on your quad with your hand as you press your chest toward your quad). If you have trouble with your Achilles tendon, be sure to stretch your calves out (dorsiflexion, which is lifting your toes up, and plantarflexion, which points your toes downward).

Let me enforce the importance of stretching. As a FAST person, you will want to shave time off your workout by skimping on the stretching. Don't do it! You will pay the price with injury, and you will not be able to compete with yourself or anyone else. You will not reach any of your goals if you incur injury.

Stretching prevents injury by first preparing muscles for the workload (that is, stretching before the workout) and then by elongating those muscles that have been worked or contracted (during the workout). It also gets blood flowing back to the proper areas of the body, preventing the blood from pooling, which can cause clots. Stretching allows your body to perform at its best the next time you ask it to do so. It's plain and simple. You need to stretch, and that is the bottom line.

I recently attended an advanced personal trainer workshop certification program. Over the course of two days, we were to learn new techniques and strategies for helping our clients succeed with their health and fitness goals. During the practical application portion of the workshop, the facilitator had us do very advanced moves without first warming up or stretching. On top of that, she asked us to add heavy weights and move beyond our normal range of motion. I knew better but thought, *One time won't hurt me.* HA! I could barely walk for four days, and on the fifth day my left quad snapped completely between my hip and knee. It took months for my leg to recover completely.

Don't kid yourself. You may be a superman when it comes to performing at work, but you are not superhuman. The laws of being human apply to us all, even those of us who are FAST individuals in really good shape. Don't let your stubbornness get the best of you. Be safe, or miss out.

PUTTING IT ALL TOGETHER: YOUR ULTIMATE FAST WORKOUT PROGRAM

This is where the rubber meets the road. Now I would like you to actually spell out your weekly program. In this chapter I have provided an array of ideas and options for you to consider. Although I may understand your unique FIT profile, I still have not had the privilege of meeting you face-to-face. I do not know your personal schedule or the challenges you face. I am only the coach, guiding and directing you. Only you can determine what will ultimately work best for you, and only you can take the action to accomplish your goals.

To help get you started I've provided an example of one person's weekly schedule:

Chart 6.5 | **FAST Weekly Workout Schedule (Todd)**

Day	Activity	Location	Time	Notes
Monday	Indoor cycling	Fitness Club USA	1 hour	6:30 to 7:30 p.m./stretch
Tuesday	Weight lifting	With personal trainer	1 hour	7:30 a.m./entire body/stretch
Wednesday	Indoor cycling	Fitness Club USA	1 hour	6:30 to 7:30 p.m./stretch
Thursday	Run	Outside	30 min.	7:30 a.m./ stretch
Friday	Weight lifting	With personal trainer	1 hour	4:30 p.m./entire body/stretch
Weekend	Off			Maybe play basketball, rock climb, or hike

Todd wants results! He represents a man in his early forties whose goal is to lose 30 pounds and strengthen his muscular system. He has no desire to be a "muscleman," but he does want to improve his overall health and conditioning in order to increase his energy and abilities to perform.

Todd doesn't like to wait in lines at the gym and isn't into the whole "social gym rat" scene, so he opted to work with a personal trainer twice a week. He is willing to make the financial commitment to work with a PT in order to get the results he is seeking without a lot of hassle.

Todd has fitness goals, but he doesn't want to waste any time. He wants a fitness class where he can come in, work out hard, and get out quickly. Indoor cycling has proven to be a very effective outlet for him. Each person in the class cycles at his or her own pace and in pursuit of his of her own fitness goals. Cycling is also easy on the knees, and since Todd has had knee surgery, it was a perfect fit for him.

You will notice that Todd has three days a week of cardio exercise on top of his weight-lifting and weekend sports activities. He is strength training and stretching during the week to prevent "weekend warrior" injuries. Todd is on his way to quickly meeting his goals.

How about you?

Make copies of the following blank schedule, and start filling in the blanks with what you believe will work best for you. Set yourself up for success with programs that work for your FIT. Remember to stretch before and after exercise each time. Try to include at least three days of cardio exercise.

Chart 6.6 | **FAST Weekly Workout Schedule**

Day	Activity	Location	Time	Notes
Monday				
Tuesday				
Wednesday				
Thursday				
Friday				
Saturday				
Sunday				

Commit to trying this for a week or two. Then evaluate whether this worked for you or not. If it did, stick to it "like ugly on an ape" for six weeks. After that time, change it up a bit to prevent boredom.

You can use this and just abide by it each week, or you can do what I do and add these to your calendar. Include them in your reoccurring appointments, and respect those times like anything else. You may want to print up more of these sheets and follow it each week. Do whatever works best for you. Just make sure you get your cardio exercise in if you want to win the game.

KEYS TO YOUR SUCCESS

Below is a summary of things to do or not do in order to ensure that you are successful with your new FAST fitness program:

- Commit to six weeks per program in order to obtain results.

- Change it up after six weeks to prevent boredom and to maximize what's working and minimize what isn't.

- Block out time on your calendar for your workouts; protect and honor that time.

- Don't schedule your workout during peak performance times; FAST people will want to achieve great things during this time and will most likely not want to sacrifice this time for exercise. Again, set yourself up for success.

- Stay focused and keep moving, never allowing your form to suffer.

- Alternate muscle groups, and weave in other options (such as push-ups or sit-ups) when you can.

- Don't do too much too soon; you don't want to burn yourself out.

- Avoid peak hours at gym and health clubs, or work at home if you have the discipline.

- If you can afford it, join an elite country club with a gym so you won't have to wait and the equipment will be better. (Those places are also great for networking!)

- Remind yourself why you are working out; keep your goals handy.

- Keep your goals current; as soon as you conquer one, create new ones.

- Compete to win—not just the game but the real prize: good health.

Congratulations, you now have your own FAST fitness program, personalized to your temperament. I know you're eager to get busy, but don't skip chapter ten, which addresses nutrition, especially if losing weight is one of your goals. Chapter eleven will challenge you to commit to be fit (success contract) and will help you start implementing your plan immediately. All right, what are you waiting for? Get to it! Jump to chapter ten—FAST.

SEVEN | ARE WE HAVING FUN YET?— MAKING FITNESS FUN

I LOVE THE commercial for the Discovery Channel in which the little boy is scraping his sock-feet on the carpet, unbeknownst to his grandpa's cat sitting on a chair in front of him. With a somewhat devilish look in the boy's eyes, he creeps up and slowly stretches his finger toward the cat, who is still snug as a bug in a rug. The boy can hardly contain his excitement over what might happen. When his finger makes contact, the cat leaps off the chair, meowing from the huge spark radiating from the boy's finger. The boy's eyes are gigantic—he is amazed at his power. He has discovered electrical forces.

You're like that little boy, aren't you? You are inquisitive, and you love new and innovative things. That's what characterizes people of the FUN temperament type.

I hope you read chapter one. I know some FUN folks may jump right to chapter five, "Seeing Is Believing," because it has pictures. Others may jump right here, being eager to learn about themselves. But at the very least I hope you take the FIT Assessment in chapter one so that you know your temperament. (Besides, it's a fun assessment!) The FIT (Fitness Individuality Traits) Assessment determines your particular style.

In this chapter we will build on that foundation. Here you will learn how your specific personality style can and should determine your fitness routine—what you do, how you do it, who you do it with, and how long you will do it. *This chapter is the key to making fitness enjoyable and interactive for you.*

The more you understand yourself, the better equipped you will be to live a healthy life, including improving relationships with others, personally and professionally. Being fit will allow you to enjoy life to the fullest, continuing to discover new things and new ways to serve God.

If you relate most with the FUN profile, let me show you what an unhealthy life feels like:

BEFORE

Now, let me show you what a healthy life feels like:

AFTER

It's not a matter of letting your belly hang out (before) and then sucking it in (after). It's a matter of making a positive change that will enable you to have the most fun possible doing whatever you like to do.

■

BEING FIT ALLOWS YOU TO
ENJOY LIFE TO THE FULLEST!

■

You are the type of person who likes to be with people. It's no surprise, then, that when it comes to working out, you'll want to do that with other people, too. In order to live a healthy lifestyle, FUN folks will want to join groups of energetic people who enjoy working out. It is important for you to fit in somewhere and know you are accepted. You need interaction with people in order to get where you want to go. You are persuasive and make friends easily.

Details are not your strong suit, though, so I'm pleased to see that you have made it this far through the book. Since health and fitness are such hot topics and you will want to be prepared to talk about them intelligently with your friends and associates, make sure you read chapters one through five. When you can draw on that information in conversation, people will be amazed at how smart you sound!

Make an effort to set some goals for yourself, too. You probably get frustrated and discouraged because you don't always finish what you start. This book is the perfect opportunity to start fresh by beginning to achieve goals, not just set them. Want to continue to "be young and have fun"? Then you'd better get healthy!

Here's a prayer to help you:

> *Dear Lord, so far today, I've done all right. I haven't gossiped, haven't lost my temper, haven't been greedy, grumpy, nasty, selfish, or overindulgent. I'm very thankful for that. But in a few minutes, God, I'm going to get out of bed, and from here on, I'm probably going to need a lot more help! Amen.*

We laugh, but the reality is that when it comes to fitness we must take action and do something. It doesn't have to be perfect or full blown, but taking some steps toward a healthier life is better than taking no steps at all. Don't set your bar so high that you can't clear it. Set yourself up to win and feel good about yourself.

WHY SHOULD YOU GET FIT?

It's very important for FUN types to keep in mind the *why* behind their fitness goals. This will help you stick to the program. In chapter three I gave a lot of reasons why you should exercise, but you need to find your own motivation. Perhaps you're afraid that if you don't get in shape, you'll lose the respect of a peer or a loved one. Usually, the more you have to lose the more likely you will stick to something. If you happened to rush past chapter three, consider going back and thinking of *why* you want to embark on a fitness program. Even if your goal is simply to be with people and have a good time, knowing your motivation will help you stick to it.

Let's get an early start on FUN fitness. Take a look at the following activities to see how they help you burn calories:

Chart 7.1 | FUN Activity vs. Calories Burned

Activity	Calories Burned
Apple polishing	25
Getting around to it	50
Passing the buck	75
Beating around the bush	100
Putting out fires	250
Backstabbing	300
Jumping to conclusions	500
Running around in a circle	700
Climbing the ladder of success	850

Well, perhaps they don't help us all that much, but it does remain true that the more calories you burn, the more energy you will have. And the more energy you have, the more fun you can have! Life is too short to miss out on it or be excluded because you can't keep up. Join the fitness craze, and create a new, healthier you!

THE FUN PROFILE

If I were talking about a FUN person I'd say—not AOL's "You've got mail," but—"You've got style!" FUN folks are definitely not short on personality. Watch Bill Cosby, and you will always be smiling or laughing. He is so personable and entertaining. That's what FUN people are like.

What does being FUN really mean? It means you are a fast-paced individual who loves being with people. You are outgoing and social. You don't mind talking and sharing stories. Most likely, you get a kick out of large groups in which everyone is talking at the same time and building off one another. You tend to be very inspiring and motivational due to your high-energy personality. You are usually positive and can persuade people because you immediately establish rapport.

You normally have trouble with rules because you are inquisitive. You aren't quite sure you agree with why the rule exists, so you will explore to find out. For example, when you were a child and your mom said, "Don't touch the stove because it is hot," you probably thought to yourself, "Well, how hot is hot?" and proceeded to stick your hand in the flame or on the burner to find out. Ouch!

You tend to have to learn things on your own. My father-in-law says, "A wise man learns from his mistakes, yet a wiser man learns from the mistakes of others." You are probably not in the wisest category, but you will have more adventures and stories (and burns) than others! There you go, discovering again. ☺

You are curious and love asking questions. You are interested in everything. New products, trendy services, and the latest and greatest tech gadgets fascinate you. You are a whirl of mental activity, and you rarely completely shut down. Can you say, "Energizer Bunny"? You keep going, and going, and going…

You strive to fit in and be accepted in groups. You can get emotional if your feelings are hurt. You are a passionate person. When you are up, you are flying high; when you are down, you have a black cloud looming over your head. Regardless of your mood, you have difficulty masking it—everyone knows how you feel. You don't like to be ignored or ridiculed, especially in public.

Your motto is "If it ain't fun, why do it?" I mean, life is too short, am I right? Eat dessert first! It stands to reason, then, that doing repetitive tasks is not your bag. You prefer short-term engagements and projects that involve creative energy and people. You can be easily influenced by popular opinions, which can cause you to be too impulsive at times. You are flexible and enthusiastic, but your lack of structure and detail can prevent you from moving ahead.

Right now, your view of fitness is most likely one of the following:

- If there is a group of people participating in something fun, I'm there!
- I am really good at working out for a while, but then I get bored and quit.
- I do not think fitness is fun, so I do not do anything.

In any case, your fast pace and people-oriented attitude will affect how you approach fitness. Whether you realize it or not, you desire a fun way of working out that allows you to interact with others. Fun exercise, fun people, and a fun variety of workout modes are the keys for FUN folks finding long-term success in a fitness program.

Chances are that you have failed at previous attempts of getting in shape— probably because you tried that "one-size-fits-all" approach. It didn't work for you, did it? This time, use your gift of inquisitiveness and try a variety of things with different people to keep you engaged. This book will give you all sorts of fun and exciting ways to get and stay fit.

How to quickly identify someone with your style

I can hear it now, "LUUUUUUUUUUCY!" You remember how Ricky Ricardo would scream at the top of his lungs in a stern voice on *I Love Lucy*, don't you? You knew she had stuck her hand in some fire in an attempt to see just how hot it was. She was always up to something. She was definitely a FUN type.

You can spot another FUN person by listening. FUN folks talk, talk, and talk! Did Lucy ever shut up? They are not quiet or shy. In fact, you can probably hear a FUN person laughing up a storm several offices down at work. They usually have the latest joke to share or an exciting story to tell from their weekend. FUN people are not afraid to try new things and typically wear trendy clothes that are bright and colorful. In some cases, they will actually get quite flashy outfits since they aren't nervous about being noticed. In fact, they love strangers coming up and talking to them because they are potential new friends!

I once saw a famous country music singer at the Los Angeles Airport. She was dressed in neon lime green with hot pink accents. Talk about a FUN person! Everyone was staring at her, and she ate it up. FUN folks can never have enough friends or people to converse with.

If FUN people can afford it, they'll usually be driving a flashy automobile that is the latest hip ride in town. It won't be white—no, it has to be a bold color. They are usually the drivers who go really fast for a while and then all of a sudden slow down to a crawl in the left lane. Chances are that they got involved in some really juicy conversation and lost their focus on driving. They probably have no clue that anyone else is on the road with them, and when they do, they will just smile at the other drivers. My husband (a notorious FUN person) called me from the road one night. He was twenty miles past our exit. He'd gotten so involved in listening to a radio program that he'd zoned out and lost track of where he was driving. Oops! He had a good time despite the forty-five-minute error.

FUN individuals normally have a short attention span unless you have truly captured their interest. (Hey, I'm talking to you! Focus. Are you listening now? OK, good.) Although they really want to listen to you, they are more excited about sharing *their* thoughts with you. They can have difficulty focusing on your words because they are formulating their next sentence.

If you see an office that looks like a bomb has gone off in it, it's most likely the office of a FUN person. Keeping things orderly and clean isn't fun, so why bother? As long as they feel they have some sort of system that works for them, it isn't a priority.

During a time management training session I attended in Atlanta, a CEO presented his time management system to me. It was a three-ring binder bulging with papers. It had no rhyme or reason to it, but he'd written down everything and anything in there. It seemed to work for him, but it gave me hives!

If things start to get too out of control, FUN people will work on organizing themselves until their office is spotless. FUN folks really don't have an in-between mode. They have the "high acceleration" gear (pedal to the metal) and the parking brake. Their office will be fun to sit in, as they will have all sorts of neat pictures on the wall along with every award, certificate, and plaque they have received. They are proud of their accomplishments and want others to know. Usually, they will have some really cool gadgets and stress toys that help them stay on track—or at least make being unproductive fun!

Besides Lucy and Bill Cosby, other famous people with FUN profiles are:

- Jim Carrey
- Robin Williams
- Bill Clinton

Just because these folks are FUN doesn't mean they cannot be quiet or concentrate on details. On the contrary, they can be quite controlled when they want to be. FUN folks are amazing influencers and motivators. Remember that we can temporarily adapt our temperaments to respond to the needs of the moment. FUN people simply feel more comfortable doing things this way, but they do utilize the other areas to function.

Often when I am training people on the concepts of personality styles, somebody asks me what temperament Jesus was. The answer is easy: He was all four. Jesus became exactly what He needed, when He needed it. He is the perfect example of how every one of us should be striving to balance and blend with people. We each have our strengths, but we must be careful not to live just there. We must attempt to improve all areas of our complex being. The more balanced you are, the more versatile you will be, and the more versatile you are, the greater the chance of success in all areas of your life.

YOU GO!

Your many strengths

You've heard the age-old story about the tortoise and the hare? Both animals decide they will race to the finish line to see who gets there first. The hare, chuckling to himself because he knows he will win due to his speed, darts off when the gun is fired. The tortoise, on the other hand, slowly makes one small move after another. The hare gets distracted and off course, and before you know it, the tortoise wins the race by taking just one safe step at a time. A FUN person says, "Hogwash with that! At least the hare had fun getting there and saw a bit of the world!"

As a FUN person, you bring optimism and positive energy to any group, whether it is professional or personal. People are inspired by your outgoing, personable, warm approach. You are indeed fun to be around. You have the gift of making people laugh.

You are probably great at starting projects and new ventures. You can easily pour yourself into activities, sharing your excitement with others along the way. You are at your best when you are working through others, influencing and inspiring them to contribute their best to the team. You are motivational. Your creativity often lends itself to providing new and innovative ways of accomplishing goals. You don't do things as they have always been done. You have no problem blazing your own trail.

You are talkative and in touch with your feelings. You have vast amounts of energy, which attracts others to you. You are flexible and work well in unstructured environments. You are most likely popular with many groups of people and juggle a number of relationships. Although FUN people will hold any of a variety of positions, they can make awesome performers, salespeople, and politicians.

WARNING, WARNING…

How to conquer challenges

I know you typically don't like to hear about limitations or what you can't do because it isn't much fun, but FUN folks can get in trouble by talking too much and not listening enough. "Huh?" you say. They are great storytellers, but any person's strengths pushed to an extreme will cause a negative consequence. Just look at Lucille Ball again. She found herself in some pretty tight spots that caused stress and pain to those she loved.

Just because you are a FUN person doesn't mean you have to dominate conversations and shut others out. On the contrary, FUN folks can be active listeners by reminding themselves that they would want to be heard. How would you feel being talked over, interrupted, and ignored all the time? Concentrating on the other person's feelings and relating with him or her can help a FUN person listen first and speak second.

The older I have gotten, the more I have noticed that successful people do more listening than talking. The more insecure or uncertain about themselves people are, the more they talk. This isn't to say that all talking is bad, but it really is amazing how much respect you can gain by saying less and listening more. People admire and appreciate good listeners. Hey, you like trying new things—so give this a shot some time. Shhh, be very, very quiet. ☺

Asking questions is also another effective way of taking the emphasis off of you and placing it upon the other person. Ultimately, this will build stronger relationships and make you an even more likeable person!

Because you tend to express your feelings, you can sometimes let go inappropriately. Even though it is a vital aspect of your makeup, remember that timing is everything. Be careful as to when, where, and with whom you share your feelings. Also realize that everyone is not like you. Many people keep their feelings inside and don't particularly care to know your feelings, either. You may think, *Surely, they want to know this or that,* but the reality is that they probably don't care—at least not yet. Instead of forcing yourself on others, try warming up to them first. Before you know it, they will be asking you to tell them the very thing you were going to share. Everyone wins. Cool, huh? It is called influence, and FUN folks can be masters of it.

Your ability to persuade people is truly a gift. You could sell a block of ice to an Eskimo! If you are passionate about something and excited about its potential, you will get other people fired up about it, too. Just be cautious not to overdo it or push too hard. Used car salesmen get a bad rap for being over the top. Basically, they are FUN people who went too far. Too much of a good thing is still too much. Tone it down, and tune it down for your audiences. Unless they are all FUN folks, in which case you can have at it and have a blast! Party on.

TALKING ABOUT SOMETHING ISN'T DOING IT. TAKE ACTION!

If you find yourself having to apologize for being late or not completing tasks on time, it's probably because you are getting stuck in your creative element and not paying enough attention to details. As I mentioned before, procrastination is one of the top five time traps. It is responsible for more heartache and disappointment than any other time trap. It is also the trap FUN people fall into most often.

Although you pour yourself into the project at the beginning, you can lose interest quickly and move on to something else, never finishing what you started. This is not only dangerous, it is also destructive to you, your career, your goals, and your relationships. You are never short on ideas, but you also must follow through on those to generate actual accomplishments. Talking about something isn't doing it. Take action!

Make a commitment to finish. I have coached FUN individuals in this area before, and I always find that having an accountability partner helps them.

Another way to beat procrastination is to understand what you are putting at risk if you fail to perform or follow through. With every unfinished project you are losing respect, and you will continue to do so until you live up to your word. If you want to be respected and liked, I suggest you do what you said you would do—when you said you would do it. An entire organization was formed to help men be promise keepers, not promise breakers. Trust is so easily broken and takes a very long time to rebuild. Think things through, and you won't blow it.

FUN folks are eager to help, but they can easily overcommit themselves. By saying yes to everyone, they think they are being friendly. On the contrary, they will be upsetting people and frustrating them when they fail to do as they promised. Better to say, "Sorry, I can't do that" and keep the relationship intact than say yes and drop the ball, possibly losing the friendship.

Practice the principle of setting boundaries and honoring them. As you get in the habit of being more honest with yourself and others, you will increase your authenticity and gain more credibility with others—not to mention reduce your stress.

How to beat stress

Ever feel like you are living in a bad sitcom? FUN individuals often live in the "crisis" mode of life, putting out one fire after another. They end up being very reactionary instead of proactive, which makes them susceptible to getting burned. It may make for a funny story later, but it's definitely not fun while it's happening.

In order to recover from stress, you need social interaction. If circumstances prevent you from getting together with others and force you into isolation, you can get too emotional. If you do not manage your stress, your emotions will become outbursts. Remember when I said that any strength pushed to an extreme is a weakness? Every profile has a negative side, and it usually rears its ugly head when we are stressed. Male FUN folks tend to have more difficulty in acknowledging their needs. They may not take the time to manage their stress, and this puts them at a higher risk of heart disease and other stress-related illnesses as a result. Look for these warning signs if you are a FUN person:

- Are you talking faster and more often?
- Are you interrupting more and listening less?
- Is everything bugging you and rubbing you wrong?
- Are you becoming overly sensitive?
- Are you getting too emotional?

When this happens, get out and do something with someone. When things get tough, the tough...go shopping, or whatever works for you. While other people may need peace and quiet to recharge your batteries, you need excitement, energy, and people. Do something that will make you happy and fill your tank:

- Catch an entertaining movie.
- Go bowling with a friend.
- Go roller skating or ice skating.
- Go dancing.
- Sing your heart out at karaoke night.
- Have a costume party.
- Play charades.

Whatever you do, just have fun!

Another great way to manage your stress and at the same time move toward better health is to attend a fitness class. You will get to see other people, experience vast amounts of high energy, listen to fun music, and generate movement.

FUN people need some sort of social activity to recover their energy. If you don't give yourself a social outlet, the stress will build up negative emotions that will explode without warning. In order to protect your relationships and remain in good standing with people, managing your stress is paramount. Your FIT program can be one excellent way of doing just that.

RELATING TO THE OTHER PERSONALITY STYLES

Your communication style is informal, friendly, and most of all fun. Why get straight to the point when telling a story is more exciting? Have I ever told you the one about the…? Because you are a very talkative person, you often don't notice how quiet others are being. You are so enthusiastic and energetic you can talk for long periods and lose track of time.

When my husband and I take road trips, he can talk literally for hours without hearing one peep from me. One thought leads him to another and yet another. Before long, he has forgotten what he started talking about. I can usually bring him right back on track—that is, if my ears aren't swollen shut! Although "sharing" is one of your strengths, be aware that not everyone is like you.

Relating to FAST people

When talking with FAST people, be direct and to the point. They will appreciate you getting right to the bottom line. No need to break the ice or socialize with FAST folks. Use words and phrases that are results oriented and that answer the question, "What is in it for me?", which is foremost on their mind.

Most FAST people do not like being told what to do. They prefer options and deciding for themselves. Instead of dictating demands, offer suggestions that are results oriented and challenging. If you have details or stories to share, simply ask, "May I share this with you?" That way you get their permission and their undivided attention. You both win.

Other FUN people

When interacting with FUN people, just be yourself! You are speaking with other folks who love a good story. Laughing it up with this group is what it is all about. Details will not be the focal point, so if you do need to get an answer about something, gently guide them back on track. This may be difficult for you since you enjoy a good conversation, but you will know how to motivate others to respond since you are an influencer! Other FUN types make great friends to get out with.

Relating to FRIENDLY people

When communicating with FRIENDLY people, slow down. Don't interrupt them, even if they seem to take a while to respond. Give them the time they need to formulate their thoughts. For a FUN person it may seem like an eternity, and you have so much to say, but be sensitive to their thoughts and feelings.

A friendly, soft approach that affirms them works the best. If you are too verbal with your communication, they will retreat and shut down. The problem is that you will probably not notice. Don't assume that silence is acceptance and admiration of your verbal skills. Be in tune to their body posture, facial expressions, and "temperature." Remember, they love people like you, but they show it in a quieter manner. FUN people enjoy companionship with FRIENDLY people.

Relating to FACTUAL people

When engaging with a FACTUAL individual, give 'em "just the facts, ma'am." Picture in your mind Sergeant Joe Friday, and you have a pretty good idea what you are dealing with—your opposite.

Again, you will want to slow down and allow these folks time to process. In fact, you may need to give them additional time to think things over before they respond. Don't be disorganized or too personal. Try to present your idea systematically. They want you to stick to business and are more concerned with receiving correct data than hearing your latest fish story. These folks are analytical and structured, so don't make a lot of sudden changes. Steady as she goes! These people are your complete opposite and will require the most effort to relate with, but you need them in your life. That's a fact, Jack (or Jill)!

THE ULTIMATE WORKOUT PLAN FOR THE FUN PROFILE

Now that you have gained a basic understanding of yourself and how to interact with others, let's get down to the meat and potatoes of this book: working out with style—your style! We will take all this information and relate it to how you will approach your cardio exercise, weight training, stretching, and even nutrition.

Remember, how you are wired *does* affect everything. Your FIT profile, as it relates to fitness, is what makes this book unique. You will now have the opportunity to customize a program—a lifestyle—based on who you are as an individual. No more one-size-fits-all approach, and no more failure. Success and good health are in your future. Ready to revolutionize your exercise?

How to raise your energy level

"Wa-hoo!" The most wonderful thing about FUN profiles is that they are social people with lots of energy. Bouncing is what Tiggers (and FUN people) do best. Well, bouncing and talking. ☺ Your energy isn't always focused and consistent, however, so keeping a regular exercise program will take some creativity and discipline.

You've heard "Ready, aim, fire!" before, right? Well, FUN people are more like "Fire, aim, ready!" You are eager to get going but don't always have your target set. In order to keep your eye on the fitness target, you need to make it fun to work out, and you need to include other people. Answering the question "Who is involved?" will be important to you and will help you stay on track one day at a time.

■

SHORT, OBTAINABLE, BITE-SIZED
GOALS WILL WORK BEST FOR YOU.

■

Variety will be important to keep your workouts fresh and exciting. Don't set yourself up to fail by creating a stagnant fitness schedule or one that doesn't fit your energy cycle. Since FUN people are always eager to please, you may *say* you will get up at the crack of dawn to exercise with a friend, but unless you are a morning person you won't do it. It will cease to be fun, and at that point you will lose your focus.

Be sure your program coincides with your energy cycle, and change the program up often. You will enjoy exercising more if you do it during times when your energy is fairly high, but reserve your highest peaks of energy for important tasks that must get done in order to remain on target and focused. Try new classes and weight machines that accomplish the same thing. This way, you won't get bored and give up.

Short, obtainable, bite-size goals will work best for you. Don't try to swallow the entire elephant in one bite! Break it into smaller chunks and chew it up one piece at a time. Review chapter three and utilize the information for goal setting and achieving. What will you gain by being more healthy and fit? Who will you meet as a result of getting out more? It is "in" to be fit, so get on the healthy train today!

Let's pause for just a second and see what kind of shape you are really in. The following measurements will take only a minute:

Waist-to-hip ratio

Waist measurement = _____ (WM)

Hip measurement = _____ (HM)

WM _____ divided by HM _____ = _____Ratio

If you are a man and the ratio is greater than .95, you are in the high-fat category, you have greater risk for heart attack, and you need to lose weight. If you are a woman and the ratio is greater than .85, you are in the high-fat category, you have greater risk for heart attack, and you need to lose weight.

This is just a reference, a starting place. Don't wig out if you're over the limit! And don't be complacent if your measurements are acceptable (that is, your ratio is less than these numbers), because you must continually include cardio exercise into your routine in order to prevent future health problems.

You don't want to end up like so many overweight people I see at the store who are completely out of breath and sweating because they got out of their car and walked in the store. I was at the movies recently, and a lady could barely walk up the steps to her seat, which she really didn't fit in. She breathed heavily for the entire movie, which was over two hours long. She never did recover from the strain. She's a walking time bomb.

I know FUN people like to have a flexible schedule, but you need to make time for your exercise program just as you would any other social appointment. In fact, consider it yet another social outlet. When you arrive a few minutes early to class, you get to talk with others. Try working out at the end of your day when you are stressed. Socializing is a great outlet and recovery for you. Combining it with exercise is a win-win proposition!

THE PERFECT CARDIO PROGRAM FOR FUN PEOPLE

On the following pages there are potential energizing programs for your FIT style. They involve people, are high energy, present a challenge, and should be fun. The *intensity* column refers back to the Workout Intensity Chart on page 54. Try these programs, and adapt them as you see fit. Act young, and have fun. ☺

Chart 7.2 | FUN Cardio Programs

Exercise	Frequency	Intensity	Time	Tips for Your Style
Group aerobic classes: *group* is a key word, people!	3–5 times a week	Level 8–9½ (Most of your class will be at level 8, but try to take it up to the 9 and 9½ for a visit.)	1 hour	Try to attend classes regularly so that you get to know other participants. It's more fun doing it with people you know! Plan to arrive a little early and stay a little late for talk time.
Running club: key word is *club*. A group of people with the same interest as you.	3 times a week	Level 8–9½ (You will get into a runner's groove, which will be your 8 or 8½. Sprint to your 9 and 9½ for a quick visit.)	20–30 min.	Join a group of runners who pick different paths or trails each time. You'll bond with each other and enjoy nature.
Indoor cycling: a class setting with lots of whooping it up to motivate and inspire each other.	3 times a week	Level 8–9½ (Your teacher will take you to the higher levels to visit, but you have to do the work by putting on enough gear.)	1 hour	Cycling is much more fun in a group than on a stationary bike alone. Besides, you get to use your imagination and go to exotic locations!
Cardio kickboxing: another great class opportunity, and you can kick some butt!	3 times a week	Level 8–8½ (By nature of kickboxing, it will bring you to 8 and 8½ easily with short bursts of 9 and 9½.)	1 hour	Kickboxing is even more interactive than aerobics classes. Many times you are partnered up with someone to practice punching or kicking. Besides, it's popular right now!
Sports activities: fun times with fun people!	1–3 times a week	Level 8 (Interval but you should be in a good zone)	1 hour or more	A great way to make friends, do a sport you love, and get exercise in all at the same time. Just make sure you are getting other cardio exercise in throughout the week.

Chart 7.2 | FUN Cardio Programs (continued)

Exercise	Frequency	Intensity	Time	Tips for Your Style
Outdoor sports: fun in the sun!	1–3 times a week	Level 8 (Again, more up and down, so try to get a good amount of time in at your level 8.)	1 hour or more	Make sure you are doing the right things in the days and weeks leading up to your selected outdoor activity. For instance, if you plan to ski, work your quads several weeks ahead of time and then rest a couple of days prior to your trip. Weekend warriors incur injury because they do not do anything else throughout the week. Blend these activities with other workouts to ensure an effective and safe workout. The more prepared you are for the activity, the more fun it will be.
Hiking club: hooking up with a group of people outside. It doesn't get any better!	1–3 times a week	Level 8 (Depending upon your trail, you will be forced to work at your level 9 or 9½ for a stint. Remember, altitude will increase the intensity.)	1 hour or more	Again, another way to get outside with people. Research shows that hiking is one of the best activities for overall good health, strength, and endurance. Join this fierce group and hike!
Extreme sports: yeah, baby!	1–3 times a month	Level 8–10 (By their nature, you will be working at higher intensity.)	1 hour or more	You are an adventurer. Extreme sports were created for you (and the FAST profiles). Try something new each month—just be careful.

Notes

- *Group aerobic classes* are the perfect way for you to work out and socialize. By their nature, people gather early before class starts and can catch up. Everyone encourages each other by hooting and hollering. You will have so much fun at times you may even forget you are working out!

- *Running* is a great form of cardio exercise because it doesn't take much to get your heart rate up and receive immediate benefits. If your knees and back are in good shape, running in a club can be great fun. Monitor your heart rate or use the pacer on the treadmill to ensure you are working at the right intensity level. Your group may sign up for 5K and 10K races that will force you to channel your energies and focus a bit, but you'll do it together.

- *Indoor cycling* is a phenomenal way to burn a lot of calories. A typical one-hour class can burn 600 to 900 calories. Most classes have formats that warm you up, work you hard, and cool you down at the end. The music pounds so loud you think your ears will bleed. It's awesome! ☺

- *Cardio kickboxing*. Talk about an intense yet extremely exciting way to work out frustrations and get your cardio exercise, cardio kickboxing is ever-changing and always unique. Learn new moves that will make you look cool. These classes will introduce you to a lot of people.

- *Sports activities* (basketball, volleyball, baseball, softball, tennis, and the like). This is a superb way to get a group of friends together. Not all sports are created equal, though, so do not limit your entire cardio routine to just sports. Weave in some of the other suggestions, as well. Organized teams require more of a commitment and guarantee that you will attend since you are paying to play. Don't join if you don't intend to stick it out. Pick-up games might be a better alternative for you. That way you have variety!

- *Outdoor sports* (climbing, hiking, cycling, mountain biking, skiing, snowshoeing, water skiing, and the like). Your adventurous spirit will enjoy anything outside that is new, exciting, or trendy. You are usually game for anything, and trying new sports prevents boredom. Again, not all outdoor sports can sustain your heart rate in the right zone, so mix it up with other cardio alternatives.

- *Hiking club.* Just like any other club, in a hiking club you'll meet up with others and hike different sites each time. Someone coordinates and plans the entire event, so you just have to show up! It's a phenomenal workout that offers gorgeous scenery and the opportunity to gab away…until you reach high altitude, anyway.

- *Extreme sports.* From skydiving to bungee jumping to dirt bike riding, an array of extreme sport activities exists for your entertainment. They often require stamina, endurance, and the ability to face fear. All this excitement is right up your alley. Just know that some extreme sports offer an extremely intense workout, while others are more fun than anything. Don't sacrifice your other cardio options, but weave these into your monthly program.

Cardio success log

On the following page is a success log to track your progress. I encourage you to use it—especially if you have trouble getting your cardio workout in each week. This will act as somewhat of an accountability partner or success record. Some people love cardio and get plenty of activity in each week. If, however, you struggle with cardio activities, jot down your attempts so that you begin to create a "social outlet" calendar.

On the log, "mode" refers to how you worked out. Examples are listed above. I recommend you make copies of this form and use it as needed. Others may prefer to log their cardio exercise in their PDA. Do whatever works for you!

Chart 7.3 | **FUN Cardio Success Log**

DAY/DATE	CARDIO MODE	TIME	STRETCHES	NOTES
Monday				
Tuesday				
Wednesday				
Thursday				
Friday				
Saturday				
Sunday				
Monday				
Tuesday				
Wednesday				
Thursday				
Friday				
Saturday				
Sunday				
Monday				
Tuesday				
Wednesday				
Thursday				
Friday				
Saturday				
Sunday				
Monday				
Tuesday				
Wednesday				
Thursday				
Friday				
Saturday				
Sunday				

The Perfect Weight-Lifting Program for FUN People

Unless you are the Six Million Dollar Man or the Bionic Woman, you need weight-bearing exercise to stay strong. Remember, our bone health is based on the amount of resistance we place on our muscles. And if we want to remain strong and able to keep dancing, we must work our muscles. I know, too bad you can't just eat some spinach and "be all that you yam."

Resistance training doesn't have to be boring, though. Since you are a FUN person, I'm guessing you will most likely enjoy a group environment for muscle conditioning. For you, I highly recommend the Body Pump or REP Reebok programs. The music kicks and the energy is high. During the course of one hour, you will move from one muscle to another, working your entire body by the end of class. It's awesome! (NOTE: Most health clubs and fitness centers require advance registration. You will need to plan ahead and sign up early to get in to these popular classes.)

Another idea for you is to have a workout buddy. The two of you would keep moving from one machine to the next. This is called the "superset" method because you don't rest between sets or machines. Because FUN folks tend to get bored easily, you will like the variety and pace of doing supersets with a partner.

Most likely, you won't be as interested in free weights unless you want to compete. Free weights take a lot more time, effort, and commitment. Weight machines are usually quicker and allow conversation time while one partner works out and the other watches. Work your entire body at one time to reduce the number of days you need to hit the gym. If your place of employment has a weight-lifting facility, use it during the lunch hour with a co-worker. Grab a quick bite to eat after your workout, and you have maximized your time *and* gotten to know someone better!

I would not recommend a home gym for you. These can be convenient, but you must dedicate the time and protect it. You may even have some great equipment in the garage or spare room right now, but you don't use it. It is too easy for FUN people to be distracted with other things. Health clubs and fitness centers provide the best equipment options and have the most variety of machines—and they provide you with a social outlet.

If you want to use that equipment you invested in, hire a personal trainer to work with you. This way, you are accountable to someone and you will set a specific time to hook up. A personal trainer will keep your workout fresh, exciting, and challenging. You will enjoy the process much more having someone with you than if you attempt to lift on your own.

Another group alternative for your FUN profile would be a circuit training class or program. These classes incorporate cardio fitness with resistance training and usually run one hour. You get everything done in one shot…BAM! The best-known program for women is *Curves*, but many health clubs have similar programs that are not gender specific. It's a great fast and fun workout!

Weight-lifting victory log

On the following page is another success log for you to record your progress in weight lifting. I suggest you make ample copies of this and begin using it for whatever program you select. Log your seat settings and weight so that you can refer to them each time. Don't waste time trying to figure out what you did previously. Record it and build from there.

On this log, the "mode" refers to how you actually worked that muscle. For instance, "leg press" might be the mode for your quads and "15-pound barbells" could be your mode for biceps. Don't forget to change up the mode every now and then to challenge the muscle and prevent boredom.

Chart 7.4 | FUN Weight-Lifting Victory Log

Muscle	Mode	Seat/Settings	Weight/Reps #1	Weight/Reps #2	Weight/Reps #3	Notes
Quads						
Hamstrings						
Glutes						
Calves						
Inner thigh						
Outer thigh						
Biceps						
Triceps						
Shoulders						
Deltoids						
Pecs						
Lats/rhomboids						
Erector spinae						
Ab						
Obliques						
Stretch						

THE PERFECT STRETCHING PROGRAM FOR FUN PEOPLE

A great commercial came out last year on the radio. You hear a woman putting on a yoga videotape. You hear her take a deep breath in as she follows the instructions given. "Take one leg and wrap it around your neck," the voice says. You hear her groan. "Take the other leg and wrap it behind your neck as you take your arms and…" The instructions go on, but the poor woman has gotten stuck. "HELP!" she cries. The announcer then says, "There are better ways to relax." No kidding!

Flexibility is very important to overall good health. I encourage you to take a look at the stretches I have outlined in chapter five. Stretching provides a great opportunity to gab with your workout friends. Make sure to stretch both your upper and lower body. Add in a "cat" stretch for your back, which means you are on all fours (elbows and knees). Push your spine up toward the ceiling, which creates an arched spine. Breathe in, and then lower your back until it forms a curve. Repeat this several times.

If you are actively involved in sports or outdoor recreation, I suggest you add a quad stretch (bring the heel of your foot up behind to your glute and push out through your knee) and a hamstring stretch (put one leg out in front of you with your heel on the floor and toe up; the other leg is bent at the knee, and you lean on your quad with your hand as you press your chest toward your quad). If you have trouble with your Achilles tendon, be sure to stretch your calves out (dorsiflexion, which is lifting your toes up, and plantarflexion, which points your toes downward).

I recently attended an advanced personal trainer workshop certification program. Over the course of two days, we were to learn new techniques and strategies for helping our clients succeed with their health and fitness goals. During the practical application portion of the workshop, the facilitator had us do very advanced moves without first warming up or stretching.

On top of that, she asked us to add heavy weights and move beyond our normal range of motion. I knew better but thought, *One time won't hurt me.* Ha! I could barely walk for four days, and on the fifth day my left quad snapped completely between my hip and knee. It took months for my leg to recover completely. You can easily avoid such pain by stretching properly.

As a FUN person, you may get wrapped up in other things or derailed in conversation, but don't skip your stretching. You can talk and stretch at the same time—I know you can. ☺ Stretching before and after exercise prevents injury by elongating muscles that have been worked or contracted. It also gets blood flowing back to the proper areas of the body, preventing the blood from pooling, which can cause clots. Stretching allows your body to perform at its best the next time you ask it to do so. It's plain and simple: we all need to stretch.

PUTTING IT ALL TOGETHER:
YOUR ULTIMATE FUN WORKOUT PROGRAM

This is where the rubber meets the road. Now I would like you to actually spell out your weekly program. In this chapter I have provided an array of ideas and options for you to consider. Although I may understand your unique FIT profile, I still have not had the privilege of meeting you face-to-face. I do not know your personal schedule or the challenges you face. I am only the coach, guiding and directing you.

To help get you started I've provided an example of one person's weekly schedule:

Chart 7.5 | FUN Weekly Workout Schedule (Jennifer)

Day	Activity	Location	Time	Notes
Monday	Indoor cycling	Fitness Club USA	1 hour	6:30 to 7:30 p.m./stretch
Tuesday	Body Pump	Fitness Club USA	1 hour	5:30 to 6:30 p.m./stretch
Wednesday	Cardio kickboxing	Fitness Club USA	1 hour	4:30 to 5:30 p.m./stretch
Thursday	Weight lifting	Personal trainer	30 min.	7:00 to 8:00 a.m./stretch
Friday	Indoor cycling	Fitness Club USA	1 hour	8:00 to 9:00 a.m./stretch
Saturday	Running club	Local area	1 hour	9:00 to 10:00 a.m./stretch
Sunday	Off			Play—what do you like to do?

Jennifer represents an enthusiastic woman in her early forties whose goal is to lose 30 pounds and strengthen her muscular system. She has no desire to be a "hardbody," but she does want to improve her overall health and conditioning and fit into that really awesome new outfit.

Jennifer doesn't like to wait in lines at the gym and is easily distracted when left to her own devices. Therefore, she opts for the group classes where she can hook up with friends and stay focused. She is also willing to make the financial commitment to work with a personal trainer one time a week to ensure she is weight training properly.

Jennifer enjoys fitness classes that are popular and fun. She likes to forget that she is really working out. She loves cardio kickboxing for this reason, and indoor cycling has proven to be a very effective outlet for her both socially and physically. Cycling is easy on the knees, and since she has had knee surgery, it was a perfect fit for her.

You will notice that Jennifer has four days a week of cardio exercise, and she is strength training twice a week. With this schedule, Jennifer is on her way to slimming down and reaching her goals—and having a blast along the way.

How about you?

Here's a blank weekly schedule for you to use. Make copies, and start filling in the blanks with what you believe will work best for you. Set yourself up for success with programs that work for your FIT. Remember to stretch before and after exercise each time. Try to include at least three days of cardio exercise.

Chart 7.6 | FUN Weekly Workout Schedule

Day	Activity	Location	Time	Notes
Monday				
Tuesday				
Wednesday				
Thursday				
Friday			.	
Saturday				
Sunday				

KEYS TO YOUR SUCCESS

Below is a summary of things to do or not do in order to ensure that you are successful with your new FUN fitness program:

- Commit to three to six months of working out.
- Change up how you work out often to prevent boredom.
- View your exercise time as a social outlet also.
- Join groups whenever possible.
- If on your own, avoid peak hours at the gym to minimize distractions.
- If you can afford it, hire a personal trainer.
- Remind yourself why you are working out; keep your goals handy.

- Use exercise as a way to make new friends.
- Don't quit. Stay with it!

Congratulations, you now have your own FUN fitness program, personalized to your temperament. I know you're eager to start having fun, but don't skip chapter ten, which addresses nutrition, especially if losing weight is one of your goals. Chapter eleven will challenge you to commit to be fit (success contract) and will help you start implementing your plan immediately. It also provides some stories from people just like you that might help you. All right, now; what are you waiting for? Bounce on over to chapter ten, and get on the health kick! Everyone else is doing it.

EIGHT

TOGETHER WE CAN DO IT— MAKING FITNESS **FRIENDLY**

I HOPE YOU know you really do deserve a happy and healthy life. When you read chapter one, you learned basic principles about the different personality styles and how each of us is created uniquely. You also took a FIT (Fitness Individuality Traits) Assessment to determine your particular style.

In this chapter we will build on that foundation. Here you will learn how your specific personality style can and should influence your fitness routine—what you do, how you do it, whom you do it with, and how long you will do it. *This chapter is the key to making fitness a part of your everyday lifestyle so that you may continue to help others.*

> Life is crazy with its twists and turns.
> It can sting you like a bee and really burn.
> Life brings to us challenges and obstacles to overcome.
> It is stressful and overwhelming to some.
> Stress can turn to illness in an attempt to defeat.
> That is why your stress you must beat.
> If you don't take charge of your life, no one else will.
> You must be prepared, for the climb's uphill.
> Luck is preparation meeting opportunity in your life.
> The more prepared you are, the less strife.
> Do whatever it takes to manage well.
> Your final outcome, only time will tell.
> But you will become a healthier you.
> You will be less stressful no matter what you do.

You deserve a happier life, don't you know?
Let love, joy, and peace be what you show.
Balanced living is what it is all about.
You were intended for much more, have no doubt.
Don't settle for less and accept that stress.
Don't assume that your life will always be a mess.
Do whatever you need to do.
You're the only you!
May God bless you as you make different choices.
May you always hear only uplifting and encouraging voices.
May you be strong when times are tough.
May you know that what you have is already enough.
May good health be your goal.
May you have it right with God and your soul.

—LORRAINE BOSSÉ-SMITH
JUNE 2003

The more you understand yourself, the better equipped you will be to live a healthy life, including improving relationships with others, personally and professionally. Being fit will allow you to enjoy relationships longer, give you the energy to help and support others more, and give you more opportunities to serve God.

If you relate most with the FRIENDLY profile, let me share with you what a healthier life can do for you. Although at first you feel as if you are adding just one more thing to your schedule, having a fitness regimen will actually create a more stable lifestyle for you. You will have consistent energy and strength to help and support others while building stronger relationships.

■

BEING HEALTHY WILL CREATE A MORE STABLE LIFESTYLE.

■

You are the type of person who likes one-on-one relationships. In order to move toward a healthy lifestyle, you will want to find a buddy or partner to embark with you on your new fitness journey. It is important for you to create a predictable pattern in order to have stability in your life. But give yourself some time to adjust to your new routine. Slowly make steps to incorporate fitness into your current lifestyle. Before you know it, you will have a friendly environment that provides you with good health!

You are a sincere and patient person. Thank you for reading this book thus far. I hope it has helped you understand the importance of striving for a healthier life.

You're also someone who typically takes care of others first. That's why it is important to recognize the benefit of being good to yourself. Make sure you read chapter ten, which addresses nutrition. Because you are so compassionate and take on many people's burdens, you may use food as a comfort tool for healing.

You have probably become frustrated and discouraged in the past because you have tried to exercise or lose weight but just haven't seen the results. Chances are that you find it easier to focus on other people's needs rather than your own. Well, this book is the perfect opportunity for you to acknowledge the need to start taking care of yourself so you can continue to give to others, which I know is important to you.

WHY SHOULD YOU GET FIT?

To realize the value of a sister,
Ask someone who doesn't have one.
To realize the value of ten years,
Ask a newly divorced couple.
To realize the value of one year,
Ask a student who has failed an exam.
To realize the value of one month,
Ask a mother who has given birth prematurely.
To realize the value of one hour,
Ask the lovers who are waiting to meet.
To realize the value of one second,
Ask a person who has just survived an accident.
Time waits for no one. Treasure every moment you have.

—AUTHOR UNKNOWN

I would add this to it, "To realize the value of your health, just lose it."

You see, you can't be anything or do anything for anyone if you don't have your health. Everything will come to a screeching halt. You need to start taking some steps toward a healthier life today. Small steps are better than none at all. Don't take on too much too soon, or you might stress yourself out. The purpose of adding a fitness program to your life is to improve it, not make it worse. Start off slowly, and you will begin to feel good about yourself. The better you feel, the more you will be able to do for others. Make sure you have that buddy, friend, or partner to encourage you along the way. Support will be critical to your success.

And keep your focus on why you are exercising. Go back to chapter three if you have to. In that chapter I gave a lot of reasons why you should exercise, but you need to find your *own* motivation. Do you want to be married to your spouse for many more years? Do you want to see your daughter graduate from college? Do you want to hold your first grandbaby in your arms? Do you want to continue to teach and mold children until you retire? Whatever your desire, you will need good health to do it.

One woman I knew had those very dreams. She lived a simple life and just wanted to love her children and grandchildren. She envisioned sewing special clothes for them, participating in monumental events such as graduations, weddings, and births, and growing old to watch everyone's individual successes, cheering them on. She was so concerned with others that she failed to monitor her own health until later in life.

As her headaches increased and her muscle strength decreased, she continued to do for others. She shared with no one her pain because she was more concerned about others. She wanted to give because she found such joy in it. When she could not avoid the symptoms any longer and was rushed to the hospital, they found a brain tumor. If the tumor would have been found months earlier, the doctors might have been able to operate, but they could do nothing for her at that point.

That woman was my mother. She died just five and a half months after being diagnosed with a malignant brain tumor. She was the most loving, giving, and supportive person I have ever met, but she is gone now. She can no longer bless people and enrich their lives, at least here on earth. She will always hold a special place in all of our hearts. But she lost her dreams, and we lost an incredible person.

Don't make the same mistake.

The **FRIENDLY** Profile

Now, what does being FRIENDLY really mean? It means you are a calm, peaceful, slower-paced individual who loves helping others. You are more on the reserved side, but you love one-on-one relationships with people. You are a good listener and very sincere. You may not speak as often as the FUN folks. But when you do, you mean it.

You probably don't like large groups, especially if the attention is on you. You prefer an environment where everyone is working as a team, and you would rather be behind the scenes supporting the cause. You leave the big speeches and presentations to others when you can. You bring stability to any group, professional or personal. People can count on you to stay the course. You are a reliable friend.

You appreciate rules and structure as they provide stability. You support proven, traditional methods that have shown results in the past. You aren't always game for change, especially change for change's sake. You prefer to maintain the status quo when possible. For example, when someone at work comes up with a "great" idea and new way of doing things, you are hesitant to accept it right off the bat. In fact, you may disagree immediately before you have given it much thought. You usually need time to think about it and warm up to it. You may not even want to try new things if you are accustomed to your own way. You usually need encouragement to venture out and try new things.

You seek peace and harmony, and you desire a friendly environment. Because you are so easygoing, you have the ability to be very diplomatic. You want everyone to feel welcomed and included. You are a cooperative person, but you often mask your feelings, keeping them to yourself. The more you stuff, the more quiet you get until suddenly, you completely withdraw. These are the times in your life where you can overeat, oversleep, or overindulge as a way to cope. You don't like conflict or strife, but clamming up creates stress for you and others. No one knows how you really feel, and this creates division.

Your motto is "Together we can accomplish more." You would much rather work with a team to accomplish company objectives than fly solo. You may not always be gung-ho or quick to start projects, but you are great at finishing what you have been given. You are loyal, trustworthy, and steadfast.

When it comes to fitness, FRIENDLY people typically have one of the following opinions:

- I'm uncomfortable going to large gyms with lots of people.
- I think about working out but never seem to get started.
- With all my commitments to others I do not have time to exercise.

In any case, your slower pace and people-oriented attitude are affecting how you approach fitness. You desire a FRIENDLY way of working out that allows you to be with others. A workout buddy will be important for your success.

How to quickly identify someone with your style

You can usually spot other FRIENDLY people by their warm, soft smiles. You won't hear them talking much, but their kind mannerisms make you feel comfortable right away. FRIENDLY people are quiet and shy, so you won't see them in the spotlight or up on stage unless they have to be. You will have to look behind the scenes to capture them supporting others.

FRIENDLY folks are the ones who listen to the FUN people's stories. They genuinely care and want people to feel accepted and loved. FRIENDLY people typically don't like to try new things, preferring to stay with what has proven to work for them in the past. Normally, they will wear soft colors and comfortable clothes. They usually aren't into the latest fashion trend. They like to wear whatever makes them feel good. They will wear jewelry, but it won't be flashy or gaudy. They like the traditional, conservative look. They prefer smaller, more intimate groups of people and will try to avoid large gatherings when possible. FRIENDLY folks believe in quality of friends, not necessarily quantity.

Chances are you drive a family car, station wagon, or minivan. Your vehicle is probably white or some unobtrusive color. You are a cautious driver who believes in maintaining a steady speed. You abide by the speed limit and other highway laws most of the time. On occasion, you may be found going slow in the left lane, frustrating the FAST people who are always in a hurry. FRIENDLY individuals are patient and know they will get there when they get there.

The typical FRIENDLY person's office will most likely be warm and inviting with lots of pictures of family and friends. They like structure, but they may not have time to be as organized as they would like because they are constantly looking out for others. They will feel torn between making their office or home the way they want and spending time with people. More often than not, they opt to be with people rather than doing things like straightening up.

■

JESUS BECAME EXACTLY WHAT HE NEEDED, WHEN HE NEEDED IT.

■

Remember the biblical story about Martha and Mary? FRIENDLY people relate with Mary. They enjoy the company of people and care less about running around making things perfect. If you aren't familiar with the story, look at Luke 10:38–42. Martha was a whirlwind of activity, preparing food for her special guests. Mary, on the other hand, decided to be with her guests. Martha was irritated with Mary and confronted Jesus, saying, "I've done all this work, and she is just sitting there at your feet." Jesus replied, "She has chosen wisely." The moral of the story is that the dirty dishes would be there the next day. Jesus was only going to be there for the evening. Choose wisely.

If things start to get too out of control, FRIENDLY folks will begin to do less and less. They will find themselves slowly getting down to the point of complete withdrawal and isolation. They will retreat so far back that they abandon all that is important to them.

People with FRIENDLY profiles are:

- Nancy Reagan
- Jimmy Carter
- Fred Rogers (of *Mister Rogers' Neighborhood* fame)

Other people often think they can just walk all over FRIENDLY folks because they're not likely to speak out or fight for their rights. But you don't have to get abused. Remember that we can temporarily adapt our temperaments to respond to the needs of the moment. FRIENDLY people simply feel more comfortable doing things this way—with humility and quietness—but they can and do utilize the other areas to function.

Often when I am training people on the concepts of personality styles, somebody asks me what temperament Jesus was. The answer is easy: He was all four. Jesus became exactly what He needed, when He needed it. He is the perfect example of how every one of us should be striving to balance and blend with people. We each have our strengths, but we must be careful not to live just there. We must attempt to improve all areas of our complex being. The more balanced you are, the more peace and harmony you will have. This will provide a stable and predictable environment for you, and that will mean less stress!

Your many strengths

As a FRIENDLY person, you bring a steadfast presence to any team. You are loyal and supportive of others, whether it is professional or personal. People appreciate your soft-spoken demeanor, your kindness, and your genuine desire to help out. You are indeed a person to be trusted. You have the gift of supporting and helping others.

You don't usually like to get started on new projects, but once you do, you *will* finish it. You especially like working in a team setting where you can really contribute. You are most comfortable when you know what is expected of you, have done it before, and feel appreciated for your role. Your patience and understanding of others are an example for all.

You aren't very talkative and tend to hide your emotions unless pushed to your limit. You listen more than you talk, but you still need encouragement. You don't rush things and can almost be inflexible at times when changes are made quickly without explanation. Although people of your

FIT will hold a myriad of positions, they can make wonderful teachers, counselors, nurses, and homemakers.

CAUTION, CAUTION...

How to conquer challenges

FRIENDLY folks can be overly sensitive and can get in trouble by bottling their feelings inside when they feel hurt or betrayed. Have you ever been really upset at someone but never said a word? If so, you may have felt it boiling up inside of you—until that one day when you snapped. I know a very steady, even-tempered man who stuffs everything until the day he finally explodes. All those times of being silent and submissive are erased by the verbal outbursts and attacks toward those he loves.

In contrast, FAST and FUN people are quite expressive. Their timing might not always be appropriate, but they do get things off their chests. You could use some of that yourself.

Be sure to address your feelings and concerns right away. If you don't, you will find yourself avoiding people and retreating. This is when a FRIENDLY person becomes standoffish. You don't say anything bad, but you don't say anything nice, either. And you run the risk of blowing up and hurting the ones you love. I know you hate conflict, but it is a part of life. If dealt with early on, most conflicts can be resolved quickly and without any pain. The longer a dispute goes unresolved, the worse it gets—and the worse you will feel. Remember, any person's strengths pushed to an extreme will cause a negative consequence.

FRIENDLY individuals tend to allow others to walk all over them. This happens because they don't set any boundaries. You might say you don't care how others treat you, and in doing so you can appear unselfish and spiritually mature. But it's neither honest nor fair to others if you really do care. This leads to resentment and bitterness for both parties and creates division. FRIENDLY folks need to learn how to say no when they need to and not feel guilty about it.

They also need to learn when to say yes. When under stress, they may turn away from the very people they care about. Recently a friend of mine who is going through a horrible divorce stopped answering her phone or returning messages. She was so stressed she withdrew from everyone who cared about her. Rather than having the support and love of friends, she found herself alone and isolated to the point where she fell into a deep depression. Because she let it go so far, she wasn't even able to care for her son. She let him down, and she didn't allow her friends to give back.

There's a happy ending to this story. This woman read my first book and realized she wasn't where she needed to be spiritually. I encouraged her to see *The Passion of the Christ*, and she (and her son) accepted Christ!

Giving people must remember to allow others to give to them sometimes, because relationships matter. Don't lose sight of that. The better you are at setting your boundaries, the more time you will have for the things that matter most to you—like caring for your friends and letting them love you in return.

Because you tend to put others first, you may sacrifice your own desires and needs. For a short while, you won't mind. You may even feel good about helping others. But eventually you will start to get tired of it, even resentful. Even though it is a vital aspect of your makeup to care for others, please remember to take care of yourself. Be sure to take time to do things for you. You must refill your own cup if you want to fill other people's cups.

If you don't protect some time for yourself, you may find yourself sleeping more and more. It is a coping mechanism for you. If it's not sleep you turn to, you may use food to try to soothe your weary soul. Try being proactive by doing things along the way that will help recharge your batteries. Don't wait until it is too late. When you take care of yourself, you will have the energy to give to others. Everyone wins.

As long as you aren't stressed, you are very reliable. You bring great comfort to others simply because they can count on you. If you say you will help, you will. But if you do not manage your stress, you can become forgetful, missing important dates, appointments, and details. All of a sudden, you may find yourself never getting around to anything you had hoped to do, which creates stress and instability for you. Pages 166–167 have for stress management tips that will work for you.

Normally, though, you have the ability to create harmony and peace. You can get along with everyone. You usually don't have any "beefs" with anyone. As long as you have clear direction, you work steadily toward the goal and you get there. When changes are made, you can often become a little resentful and stubborn. Try asking questions first to understand the change before you decide you don't like it. Remember that the team wins when all members are on board and doing their job. Don't avoid changes, either. This is called procrastination and can cause you intense pain, frustration, and disappointment.

If you find yourself having to apologize for not following through on things, you have probably overcommitted yourself. You will need to briefly tap into the FAST temperament in order to set clearer, more defined boundaries. You don't want to let people down, and that requires saying no sometimes. Trying to please everyone all the time will set you up for failure and broken relationships.

FRIENDLY people often have trouble prioritizing things. Their heart is in the right place, but they try to be in ten locations at once. Narrow your focus and concentrate on quality, not quantity. Although you pour yourself into relationships, you can lose yourself. Before you know it, you don't even know what it is *you* like to do. FRIENDLY people are the ones who give to their spouse, raise their kids, volunteer at church, attend committee meetings, and help out the neighbors. But one day, they collapse in tears. They are done. They haven't nourished their own soul. Everyone else is important, and so are you. I have coached individuals in this area before, and I have found that it really helps when FRIENDLY folks have an accountability partner.

A great book to read if you haven't already is *Boundaries* by Drs. Cloud and Townsend.[1] It will change your life for the better. It changed mine.

It is this self-sacrificing cycle that can cause huge amounts of stress for a FRIENDLY person. Though you are seeking peace, harmony, and stability, you can actually end up obtaining the opposite if you are not careful.

How to beat stress

FRIENDLY people need time for undirected activity, a time when they don't have to *be* anything for anyone. If they don't take this time, they can get moody, critical, and unsociable. If they do not manage their stress, their emotions will drain them to the point of exhaustion, requiring more and more sleep. Remember when I said that any strength pushed to an extreme is a weakness? Every profile has a negative side, and it usually rears its ugly head when we are stressed.

Look for these warning signs if you are a FRIENDLY person:

- Are you finding yourself easily offended?
- Are you experiencing more fear than normal?
- Are you becoming more inflexible and stubborn?
- Are you getting picky, rigid, and negative?
- Are you not responding to friends and family?
- Are you missing important events or details?
- Are you retreating, withdrawing, and/or sleeping more?

When this happens, stop everything and do something for yourself. In my book *A Healthier, Happier You: 101 Steps for Lessening Stress*, I provide wonderful ideas for taking care of yourself. Pick up a copy the next time you are out. You are bound to find something that works for you. Perhaps a hot bubble bath will soothe your nerves, or maybe reading a great novel will take your mind off of things. Just do something for yourself to ease your stress so that you can be yourself again. Seek some peace and quiet in order to recharge your batteries.

One way to proactively manage your stress and also move toward better health is to exercise. Exercise reduces tension and anxiety. It also gives your body stamina and strength. You will want to find an exercise buddy to be with while you work toward better health.

FRIENDLY people don't like social scenes, especially when they are tired, but several options exist for you to get exercise without all the hoopla. In order to continue supporting, giving, and helping others, managing your stress is paramount. Your FIT program can be one excellent way of doing just that.

RELATING TO THE OTHER PERSONALITY STYLES

Your communication style is slow, methodical, warm, and friendly. You enjoy allowing others to talk more than you do. You are a great listener and encourager. But because you are so quiet, others don't always know what you think and how you feel. You may expect them to understand, but they can only know what you tell them.

You are reserved and on the conservative side—which means that faster, more energetic people may dominate the conversation if you don't jump in. Because you need a little extra time to formulate your thoughts, you don't always get to speak what is on your mind. You also don't want to offend anyone, so you are more cautious as to the words you choose. Although listening is a great strength, sometimes you must stand up for yourself. Speak up!

Relating to FAST people

When talking with FAST people, be direct and to the point. They will appreciate you getting right to the bottom line. No need to break the ice or socialize with FAST folks. Use words and phrases that are results oriented and that answer the question "What is in it for me?", which is foremost on their mind.

Most FAST people do not like being told what to do. They prefer options and deciding for themselves, so don't tell them what to do. Instead, offer suggestions that are results oriented and challenging. If you have details or stories to share, simply ask, "May I share this with you?" This way, you get their permission and their undivided attention. You both win.

These people are your complete opposites. Relating to them will require the most work from you. Yet you can have a great relationship with them. They like to lead, and you love to support. If you make an effort to wear thicker skin and understand that they aren't trying to do anything rude to you but are just doing what they know, you will be just fine.

Relating to FUN people

When interacting with FUN people, be more energetic. You are speaking with folks who love a good story, so don't be shy. Tell a story or funny joke. Laughing it up with this group is what it is all about. Details will not be the focal point, so if you do need to get an answer about something, gently guide them back on track.

You may find it difficult to get a word in edgewise because you are accustomed to being more polite and waiting your turn. You will need to jump in and express yourself. Don't worry; you won't hurt their feelings. They really do want to talk *with* you, not *at* you. They just need your help in doing so.

Other FRIENDLY people

When communicating with other FRIENDLY folks, just be yourself! Give them the time they need to formulate their thoughts, just as you would appreciate them doing for you. Your soft, friendly, affirming approach works the best. Since you understand that silence is not always a positive response, ask questions. Pull other FRIENDLY people into the conversation. Building trust and rapport will be important, but they will quickly discover that you are a loyal, dedicated person, so they'll open up to you.

Other FRIENDLY folks make great companions for you because you think alike. However, one of you may need to take charge, or you'll get stuck in "whatever you want is fine with me" quicksand.

Relating to FACTUAL people

When engaging with a FACTUAL individual, give 'em "just the facts, ma'am." Your naturally slow pace will allow them time to process, and they need that. In fact, you may need to give them additional time to think things over before they respond. Don't be disorganized or too personal. Try to present your idea systematically. They want you to stick to business and are more concerned with receiving correct data than getting to know you better. These folks are analytical and structured, so don't make a lot of sudden changes. Steady as she goes!

THE ULTIMATE WORKOUT PLAN FOR THE FRIENDLY PROFILE

Now that you have gained a basic understanding of yourself and how to interact with others, let's get down to the meat and potatoes of this book: working out with style—your style! We will take all this temperament information and relate it to how you will approach your cardio exercise, weight training, stretching, and even nutrition.

Remember, how you are wired *does* affect everything. Your FIT profile, as it relates to fitness, is what makes this book unique. You will now have the opportunity to customize a program—a lifestyle—based on who you are as an individual. No more one-size-fits-all approach, and no more failure. Success and good health are in your future. Ready to revolutionize your exercise?

How to raise your energy level

Most FRIENDLY profiles are quiet people living structured lives. You move slowly and don't always feel you have the energy to exercise. In order to establish a fitness program that will work for you and that you're energized about, you will want to include someone you care about. You will need to focus on helping that other person accomplish his or her goals. This way, you will help someone while you are helping yourself. Answering the question "Why do I need to do this?" will be important to you and will help you stay on track one day at a time. Do you want to:

- Play with your children without getting winded?
- See your children graduate from college and get married?
- Travel with your spouse?
- Continue in your profession into the golden years, contributing and helping others?

When it comes to staying with a fitness program, fellowship with a friend will be important for you. Don't set yourself up to fail by trying to exercise alone. Chances are you won't stick to it. You will find other things to do and other people to help out—and exercising will become the last item on your priority list. Try to use your exercise program as a way to spend quality time with a loved one or friend.

■

YOU WILL NEED TO FOCUS ON HELPING

ANOTHER PERSON REACH HIS OR HER GOALS.

■

Review chapter three and utilize the information for goal setting and achieving. What will you gain by being more healthy and fit? Who will you be able to help out more? How much more energy will you have to serve others? Those who care about you want you to be around a while, and living a healthy lifestyle is the only way to increase your longevity.

Let's pause for just a second and see what kind of shape you are presently in. Go ahead and take the following measurements:

Waist-to-hip ratio

Waist measurement = _____ (WM)

Hip measurement = _____ (HM)

WM _____ divided by HM _____ = _____Ratio

If you are a man and the ratio is greater than .95, you are in the high-fat category; you have greater risk for heart attack, and you need to lose weight. If you are a woman and the ratio is greater than .85, you are in the high-fat category; you have greater risk for heart attack, and you need to lose weight.

This is just a reference. Don't give up hope before you even start. Even if your measurements are acceptable (that is, your ratio is less than these numbers), you must continually include cardio exercise into your routine in order to prevent future health problems.

You don't want to end up like so many overweight people I see at the store who are completely out of breath and sweating because they got out of their car and walked in the store. They are walking time bombs.

Since you keep a fairly structured schedule, make it a point of including fitness into your life. Remember, when you include a friend or loved one in your workouts, you have the opportunity of helping that person out. I'm sure you want those special people to be around for a long while, too. When you focus on reaching out to someone else while exercising, you will ensure that you both win! Together you *can* do it.

THE PERFECT CARDIO PROGRAM FOR **FRIENDLY** PEOPLE

On the following pages there are potential healthy heart programs for your FIT profile. They are designed to set you up for success, not failure. They will involve other people and allow you to care for them as you take care of yourself. Try these workouts, and adapt them as you see fit. I understand that this is a lot to take in at once, but start somewhere—start today. I care about your health!

Chart 8.1 | FRIENDLY Cardio Programs

Exercise	Frequency	Intensity	Time	Tips for Your Style
Group aerobic classes: you can come with a friend, meet friends, or simply attend and leave.	3–5 times a week	Level 8–9½ (Most classes will work you at level 8 and visit the 9½. It's up to you, though, to ensure you get there.)	1 hour	Try to have a friend attend with you each time. Plan on driving together, working out together, and supporting one another during the workout.
Indoor cycling: a group environment, but you are independently working. No pressure to perform!	3 times a week	Level 8–9½ (You determine how hard you work. Watch your breathing, and visit those 9 and 9½ levels.)	1 hour	Again, the key here for you is to sign up with a buddy. As long as you have someone counting on you to be there for him or her, you will make it a priority.
Street cycling: an outdoor activity that is enjoyable and can involve your family.	1–3 times a week	Level 8–8½ (Challenge yourself with hills and speed to ensure you work at the 8 and 8½ levels.)	1 hour	Bike with a friend, and pick scenic routes that are enjoyable but challenging. Sign up for races together—not to compete, but to enjoy the journey together. This is a great activity for an entire family to enjoy together.
Sports activities: groups of friendly people.	1–3 times a week	Level 8 (Sports are more up and down. Try to get in some spurts of level 8.)	1 hour or more	Join a team with a friend, and commit to participate through the entire season. You will also meet more people on more manageable terms. Fitness class participants change out often, but teams are set for months at a time. You'll like the structure of team sports. These are also great for the entire family.

Exercise	Frequency	Intensity	Time	Tips for Your Style
Power walking: another way to get outside!	3–5 times a week	Level 8–9½ (Again, include hills to challenge yourself to the higher levels.)	At least 1 hour	Find your walking partner, and get outside for some fresh air and exercise. If your walking partner is a pet, make sure it can and will keep up. You will need to make sure you are working out hard enough. Check the Workout Intensity Chart on page 54.
Hiking club: club is a key word and provides the opportunity to make new friends.	1–3 times a week	Level 8 (Most hikes will offer great opportunities to challenge yourself in a fun way.)	1 hour or more	Again, another way to get outside with someone you care about. Research shows that hiking is one of the best activities for overall good health, strength, and endurance. You can pack a lunch and have a relaxing picnic in the great outdoors.
Swimming: a solo activity that anyone at any level can do.	3–5 times a week	Level 8 (Keep swimming, and you will reach this target range.)	30 minutes to 1 hour	Because you are patient and methodical, swimming probably appeals to you. It requires focus and the ability to stick with the same routine. Although it doesn't involve another person, it is a great option for you when you travel or don't have someone to join you.

Notes

- *Group aerobic classes* are the perfect way to work out and catch up with your friends. By meeting in advance and driving together, you ensure that you both get a workout and visit with one another. Some gyms have their group fitness classes as the "center of attention" at the facility. If this is the case, you may opt for a more exclusive club such as as one just for women. Smaller fitness studios usually don't put their class members on display. Find the right club for you, the one that offers you a comfortable environment.

- *Indoor cycling* is a phenomenal way to burn a lot of calories. A typical one-hour class can burn 600 to 900 calories. Most classes have formats that warm you up, work you hard, and cool you down at the end. This is a very individual workout, and you are not competing against anyone else. Everyone's fitness level and goals are different. You can go in with your friend, work out, and leave. Cycling classes are usually conducted in a private room with a closed door.

- *Street cycling* gets you out into nature and provides the opportunity to include your entire family if you want—even the dog! Cycling is one of those activities that people of different fitness levels can enjoy together. Select routes that are scenic but challenging. Bring a snack and plenty of water. Plan on taking a break midway to "smell the roses."

- *Sports activities* (basketball, volleyball, baseball, softball, tennis, and the like). Sports teams are a superb way of involving the entire family and many friends. Not all sports are created equal, though, so do not limit your entire cardio routine to just sports. Weave in some of the other suggestions as well. Organized teams are structured, exist for a finite amount of time, and are professionally run. You will like the predictability of the game schedule and the stability that comes from seeing the same people over the course of a couple of months.

- *Power walking* is still one of the best exercises out there. We were made to walk. Get a walking buddy, and hit the pavement with purpose. Walking during daylight hours is safer and more enjoyable. I know neighborhood groups that set a time each morning to meet at a certain corner, and whoever comes, walks. Start your own little walking group, and get to know your neighbors better.

- *Hiking club.* As with any other club, hiking clubs require that you commit in advance to participate. Join with a friend or loved one. You will receive details prior to the hike on what to bring and what to expect. Someone coordinates and plans the entire event, so you just have to show up! It's a phenomenal workout that offers gorgeous scenery and the opportunity to relate with others.

- *Swimming.* If you don't mind cold water and chlorine, swimming is an excellent cardio workout that utilizes your entire body without impact, which means it is easy on your joints. Many health clubs have lap pools. With swimming you can get a good workout in just thirty minutes.

Cardio success log

On page 176 is a success log to track your progress. I encourage you to use it—especially if you have trouble getting your cardio workout in each week. This will act as somewhat of an accountability partner or success record. Some people love cardio and get plenty of activity in each week. If, however, you struggle with cardio activities, log your attempts so that you start to plan with a friend or buddy in advance. Again, when someone is depending upon you, you will be more likely to show up.

On the log, "mode" refers to how you worked out. Examples are listed above. I recommend you make copies of this form and use it as needed. Others may prefer to log their cardio exercise on their wall calendar. Do what works for you. Just get that exercise in. We want you to be around for a long while! ☺

Chart 8.2 | **FRIENDLY Cardio Success Log**

DAY/DATE	CARDIO MODE	TIME	STRETCHES	NOTES
Monday				
Tuesday				
Wednesday				
Thursday				
Friday				
Saturday				
Sunday				
Monday				
Tuesday				
Wednesday				
Thursday				
Friday				
Saturday				
Sunday				
Monday				
Tuesday				
Wednesday				
Thursday				
Friday				
Saturday				
Sunday				
Monday				
Tuesday				
Wednesday				
Thursday				
Friday				
Saturday				
Sunday				

The Perfect Weight-Lifting Program for FRIENDLY People

If you are like most FRIENDLY folks, you probably don't like lifting weights at all. You don't like to sweat, and frankly, you don't really see the point of it. Remember my story in chapter four about the little tree that couldn't stand up to the strong wind? Your bones are like tree branches and trunks. If no resistance comes against them, they have no need to grow thick and dense. Like the wind against the young tree, weight lifting causes your bones to get thick and dense, thus becoming stronger and healthier.

It *is* important to have some weight-bearing exercise in your fitness program in order to live a healthy life. But you don't have to go to the weight room or join a class. You can work your muscles in the comfort of your own home with little expense. Remember the "swimming" routine I mentioned in chapter four? Look at that again, because in a short time and using only handheld weights you can work your entire upper body. If you add some leg exercises with resistance, you can complete your weight-training program in twenty to thirty minutes, tops.

If you can work out with a friend, you will enjoy the process more. If not, you can do your routine to music or in front of the television. In muscle resistance your goal isn't to get your heart rate to a certain place; rather, you are concentrating on muscle contractions. So you can multitask and take your mind off of your workout—as long as you're using correct form.

I recently spoke to a group of small business owners over their lunch hour. My topic was creating a healthier lifestyle. I urged the audience to take care of themselves for the sake of those they loved. A month later I spoke to this group again. One lady approached me with a sparkle in her eye. She was overweight but had just committed to working out and lifting weights—for her son's sake. She wanted to see him become a man. In her current health condition, she knew she wasn't loving him as she could. She needed to give him the gift of *her* good health. I was so proud of her. She had finally decided to make a change for the better and incorporate it into her life. She started with small steps—and you can, too!

A great leg routine for you to do with hand weights is the lunge. (See page 85 for further details.) You must watch the front knee and ensure that it doesn't move forward. Instead, push through your back knee toward the floor. Imagine a pole running through your head and spine and out your back knee. Each hand has a weight to add resistance. Lunge twenty times on one leg, and then switch. Feel the burn! You've just worked out your hamstrings, quads, and glutes.

If you have extra money, you may want to invest in a "total gym" machine that addresses all the basic muscles of the body in one piece of equipment. A well-known brand is the Smith machine, and you can usually find one on sale when the newer models come out. This will require more room, but you would also be able to involve more friends and/or family members.

If you want to know how to properly use the equipment you bought, then I suggest you hire a personal trainer to work with you. This way, you will know exactly how to perform each exercise and have a partner to encourage you with your goals. A personal trainer will outline your work-out each visit and explain why it is important to exercise properly. You will enjoy the process much more with someone than if you attempt to lift with machines on your own.

I would also recommend a circuit training class or program. These classes incorporate cardio fitness with resistance training and usually run one hour. You get everything done in one shot…BAM! The best-known program for women is *Curves*, but many health clubs have similar programs that are not gender specific. It's a good workout, and usually the groups aren't very large due to equipment restrictions. The circuit stations don't change too often, so you will become very familiar with what is expected for each class. You can count on working hard!

Weight-lifting victory log

On the following page is a weight-lifting victory log for you to record your progress in resistance training. I suggest you make ample copies of this and begin using it for whatever program you select. Log your seat settings and weight so that you can refer to it each time. Don't waste your time try-ing to figure out what you did previously. Record it, and build from there.

On this log, the "mode" refers to how you actually worked that muscle. For instance, "leg press" might be the mode for your quads and "15-pound barbells" could be your mode for biceps. Don't forget to change up the mode every now and then to challenge the muscle and prevent boredom.

Chart 8.3 | FRIENDLY Weight-Lifting Victory Log

Muscle	Mode	Seat/Settings	Weight/Reps #1	Weight/Reps #2	Weight/Reps #3	Notes
Quads						
Hamstrings						
Glutes						
Calves						
Inner thigh						
Outer thigh						
Biceps						
Triceps						
Shoulders						
Deltoids						
Pecs						
Lats/rhomboids						
Erector spinae						
Ab						
Obliques						
Stretch						

The Perfect Stretching Program for **FRIENDLY** People

Take a look at the stretches I outlined in chapter five. Stretching is great for your muscles, but it also soothes your soul. Use it as a way to bring balance and harmony to your life. Combine it with breathing techniques or meditation on Scripture if you like. Because of your slower pace, you will be drawn to stretching.

Be sure to do both your upper and lower body. Add in a "cat" stretch for your back, which means you are on all fours (elbows and knees). Push your spine up toward the ceiling, which creates an arched spine. Breathe in, and then lower your back until it forms a curve. Repeat this several times.

If you are actively involved in sports or outdoor recreation, I suggest you add a quad stretch (bring the heel of your foot up behind to your glute and push out through your knee) and a hamstring stretch (put one leg out in front of you with your heel on the floor and toe up; the other leg is bent at the knee, and you lean on your quad with your hand as you press your chest toward your quad). If you have trouble with your Achilles tendon, be sure to stretch your calves out (dorsiflexion, which is lifting your toes up, and plantarflexion, which points your toes downward).

You will love how stretching improves your overall health and performance. Stretching before and after exercise prevents injury by preparing muscles for work, warming them up and elongating muscles that have been worked or contracted. It also gets blood flowing back to the proper areas of the body, preventing the blood from pooling, which can cause clots. Stretching will help reduce stiffness and soreness from exercise, which can be a deterrent for you. Don't let it! Stretch it out.

PUTTING IT ALL TOGETHER:
YOUR ULTIMATE FRIENDLY WORKOUT PROGRAM

This is where the rubber meets the road. Now I would like you to actually spell out your weekly program. In this chapter I have provided an array of ideas and options for you to consider. Although I may understand your unique FIT profile, I still have not had the privilege of meeting you face-to-face. I do not know your personal schedule or the challenges you face. I am only the coach, guiding and directing you.

To help get you started, I've provided an example of one person's weekly schedule:

Chart 8.4 | FRIENDLY Weekly Workout Schedule (Susan)

Day	Activity	Location	Time	Notes
Monday	Group fitness class	Women's Fitness USA	1 hour	5:30 to 6:30 p.m./stretch
Tuesday	Weight Routine	At home with family	1 hour	5:30 to 6:30 p.m./stretch
Wednesday	Swimming	Women's Fitness USA	1 hour	11:00 to 12 noon/stretch
Thursday	Weight training	Personal trainer at home	1 hour	4:30 to 5:30 p.m./stretch
Friday	Street cycling	With family	1 hour	6:00 to 7:00 p.m./stretch
Saturday	Power walking	With family	1 hour	6:00 to 7:00 p.m./stretch
Sunday	Off	Or join sports team with family	1 hour or more	Play…what do you like to do?

Susan represents a sweet woman in her mid-forties with a goal to lose 30 pounds and strengthen her muscular system. She has no desire to be a swimsuit model for *Sports Illustrated*, but she does want to improve her overall health and conditioning so that she can continue to teach elementary school for years to come.

She doesn't like big, fancy gyms but prefers a fitness club just for women. There she has established close friendships and meets up with her exercise partner. She enjoys the one-on-one style rather than the huge, high-energy groups. Susan invested in a personal trainer one time a week to ensure she is weight training properly. She uses her own equipment. Her PT encourages her and keeps her on the right track.

She has found that swimming is a great way to work out during her lunch hour, which frees up that evening for her family. Other nights Susan includes her family with her exercise so they all can be together. She likes the fact that they are getting healthy together. By being an example to her family, she is helping them be fit.

You will notice that Susan has four days a week of cardio exercise, and she is strength training twice a week. With this schedule, Susan is on her way to slimming down without sacrificing what really matters to her.

How about you?

Here is a blank weekly schedule for you to fill in. Make copies of it, and start filling in the blanks with what you believe will work best for you. Set yourself up for success with programs that work for your FIT. Remember to stretch before and after exercise each time. Try to include at least three days of cardio exercise.

Chart 8.5 | **FRIENDLY Weekly Workout Schedule**

Day	Activity	Location	Time	Notes
Monday				
Tuesday				
Wednesday				
Thursday				
Friday				
Saturday				
Sunday				

KEYS TO YOUR SUCCESS

Below is a summary of things to do or not do in order to ensure that you are successful with your new FRIENDLY fitness program:

- Commit to someone you trust, and ask them to hold you accountable.

- Remember that your health is of the utmost importance.

- When possible, include those you love and care about in your fitness program.

- Set times in advance to meet with your buddy.

- Avoid power gyms and trendy sports clubs.

- If lifting at home, watch television or interact with family members while you work out.

- If working out with family, make sure to work hard enough.

- If you get off track, don't beat yourself up: start again.

- Reward yourself now and again for sticking with it.

- Remember that you are loved and needed. Take care of yourself.

Congratulations, you now have your own FRIENDLY fitness program, personalized to your temperament. I know you're eager to start working out with your buddy, but don't skip chapter ten, "Eat Right, Feel Right," especially if losing weight is one of your goals. Chapter eleven will challenge you to commit to be fit (success contract) and will help you start implementing your plan immediately. It also provides some stories from people just like you.

Don't delay. Your family and friends are counting on you!

	BY THE BOOK—
NINE	MAKING FITNESS **FACTUAL**

AS MANY AS 25,000 lives are lost annually due to a sedentary lifestyle.[1] Physical inactivity is quickly becoming the number one killer in America,[2] just behind heart disease, which itself is related to obesity and inactivity.

In this book you have learned basic principles about the different personality styles and how each of us is created uniquely. You also took the FIT (Fitness Individuality Traits) Assessment to determine your particular style. Building on that foundation, you will now learn how your specific personality style influences your fitness routine: what you do, how you do it, who you do it with, and how long you will do it. *This chapter is the key to making logical steps toward implementing a fitness program into your life* in order to prevent excessive fatigue, illness, and premature death.

The more you understand yourself, the better equipped you will be to determine what a healthy life looks like for you. The more information you have about health and fitness, the easier it will be to make the right decisions in regard to your fitness lifestyle. Adequate exercise and proper nutrition are the right path to take in order to achieve good health. And with good health comes improved quality of life, both professionally and personally.

WHY SHOULD YOU GET FIT?

If you relate most with the FACTUAL profile, you understand that living a healthy life is paramount—that without your health, you can't do anything else properly. You have read this book thus far and have most likely conducted your own research to determine that a fitness program of some sort must be woven into your schedule. Some of the benefits you may have determined are:

- More energy as a result of increased cardio capacity
- Increased mental focus due to proper nutrition
- Strength and endurance from muscle conditioning
- Improved productivity from better rest and sleep
- Reduced sickness and illness from a stronger immune system
- Less stress from physical activity and mental concentration required by exercise

You are the type of person who likes to analyze and process everything, so you have probably weighed your options and begun to formulate some plans for how you will execute your fitness program. This chapter provides you with more details that will enable you to live a healthy lifestyle. As a FACTUAL person, you will want to make sure you are exercising correctly.

It is important for you to have all the facts in order to create proper procedures for your life. A book you may find extremely helpful is *Fitness and Health* by Brian J. Sharkey, PhD. In that book Dr. Sharkey does an excellent job of educating his readers on health and wellness, and he includes plenty of statistics to back up his claims. But do not analyze fitness to the point of being paralyzed. For each of us the time comes when we must say, "This is enough information. Now I must decide and take action." Go ahead and gather plenty of data, but set a specific date when you will end your research and begin implementing. Before you know it, you will have *the* right format for your exercise program.

■

AS A *FACTUAL* PERSON, YOU WILL WANT TO MAKE SURE YOU ARE EXERCISING CORRECTLY.

■

You are an orderly and logical person. I suspect you have thoroughly read the pages leading up to your specific chapter, underlining your questions and highlighting points of interest. I hope it has given you enough information on the importance of striving for a healthier life. Since you typically seek great detail, you may spend additional time researching magazines, Web sites, and books on the subject of health and fitness. Some additional resources:

- WebMD.com
- *Shape* magazine
- *Health* magazine

I won't be offended by your "outside research." In fact, I encourage you to learn as much as you like. You can never spend too much time learning how to be healthier. However, I will caution you to not hold a negative attitude toward any material in this book that is new to you. Since you are the type that questions everything, you can sometimes view new information negatively. Here's a great strategy for keeping an open mind. Would you read the following and agree to try it?

- *Wear thicker skin.* Remember that you are reading this book to learn something new about health and fitness. Do not get caught up in how everything is presented as much as what you can gain from it. Every attempt has been made to write this book effectively for you. Please focus on what you can get from this book's message.

- *Be receptive.* Read these pages with an open mind, especially this chapter since it has been specifically designed for your FIT profile. Even the brightest, most educated individuals can learn something new. Even if you have read or heard some of the principles found in this book before, find a new way to apply them to your life today.

- *Delay judgment.* Finish the book, and give it time to sink in before you make a final decision on whether it will work for you or not. Go a step further, and try some of the recommendations before you say it is helpful or not. Many people, especially FACTUAL folks, need time to absorb new information and determine how to best incorporate it into their lives.

- *Adapt it.* Take what I have provided, and customize it to meet your specific needs. As I have said before, I have not had the privilege of meeting you face-to-face yet, so I cannot know everything about you. Make this work for you.

- *Desire to improve.* Obviously you are interested in improving your health. Otherwise you would not have purchased this book. The attitude you have when you read it, though, will ultimately determine what you get out of it. If you approach it with a negative attitude, you will not get anything positive from it. On the other hand, if you read it with the sincere hope of improving your health and making a difference in your life, you will get what you seek.

- *Make a commitment.* If after reading the above and giving it some consideration you are ready to make a commitment, do so!

Since you will probably have many more questions about your health, I think you will enjoy chapter ten, which addresses nutrition. I know you like to be thorough before jumping into anything, so this book should provide the perfect opportunity for you to start mapping out your path to good health. Some additional facts you might be interested in:

- Thirty percent of the aging process cannot be changed, but that leaves 70 percent in our hands.

- Upwards of 70 percent of cancer illnesses are believed to be diet related, meaning they could have been prevented with better nutrition.[3]

- Eighty percent of Americans suffer from back pain; strengthening your back through exercise will reduce your risk of injury.[4]

- Seventy-five to 95 percent of all doctor visits are stress related; working out can relieve tension and stress, thus diminishing your chances of sickness.[5]

You know how important your health is, and I have no doubt that you will make it a priority in your life. Because you are thorough, you will identify possible obstacles and strive to create the ideal schedule to set yourself up for success. One way to ensure success in fitness is to make sure you have a workout plan that helps you to be consistent.

Don't focus on how to accomplish exercise correctly to the extent that you lose sight of why you are exercising in the first place. I'm sure you made notes in chapter three regarding your personal reasons why you should exercise, but you may want to revisit them and cement *your* motivation. Whatever your goals in life, you will need good health to get you there efficiently and effectively.

THE **FACTUAL** PROFILE

Now, what does being FACTUAL really mean? It means you are a slower-paced individual who prefers working on tasks. Since you are more reserved and analytical, you enjoy cognitive activities. Your relationships are more private and one-on-one. You may not have a high volume of people you let in to get to know intimately, but those you do let in, you are very close to. When you speak, it is clear and concise. You aren't into rambling or talking nonsense. You like to stick to the business at hand.

You prefer an environment that is structured and organized. You don't like chaos, especially when it could have been prevented with a little planning. You can work alone or in groups, depending on the project. Those you work with, however, must have their ducks in a row. You have little patience for disarray and disorganization.

You can speak in front of groups when required as long as you have been given ample time to gather all your facts and prepare thoroughly. Your presentation style is systematic and step-by-step; you cover all angles. You aim for perfection in just about everything you do. Accuracy is a must for you. You will go the extra mile to ensure that things are correct. This is a gift you bring to any group, whether it is personal or professional. You are the person people look to in order to confirm accuracy and correctness.

You honor established rules, laws, and procedures because you know they provide structure and create a dependable environment. You believe in and support proven and traditional methods, especially when you have confirmed them with your own analysis. You probably resist change, especially change for change's sake.

You will usually be the one asking probing questions that can appear negative to others, but you are simply getting the facts in order to assess whether the suggested change is doable or not. Once you have received the data you require, you will still need some time to process it thoroughly before you come to your own conclusion. You do not accept statements to automatically be true; you will want to prove or disprove them on your own. Although you may take a little longer than others to warm up to a change, you will be 100 percent on board when you have determined that the change is a positive one.

You find comfort in facts and figures. You love calculating, measuring, and attempting to prove or disprove just about anything. You are analytical by nature. To some, however, you can come across as cold and heartless. On the contrary, you are a very caring individual. The more you value something or someone the more research you will conduct. You want things to be right. You don't mean to be uncooperative, but you tend to focus on a different plane than most.

Others can find it hard to get to know you because you don't let your feelings show. You are usually pretty "even" and are a straight shooter. You may be overly cautious and protective at first, but once you let someone in and begin to establish a one-on-one relationship, you will usually open right up. In the right circumstances and with the right people, you can be quite talkative! The key word for you is *right*. You like to behave and conduct yourself appropriately for the situation.

When you are stressed, you can actually become critical and cold. You don't like your information or facts being questioned, and this can also push you toward negativity. Your mottos are "Facts are facts" and "Never argue with the data." You'd much rather validate data than gossip at the water cooler. You appreciate projects that challenge your intellect and require deep investigation. You are a disciplined, loyal, hard-working individual.

Right now, your view of fitness is most likely one of the following:

- I have not found the right establishment or program for me.
- I am still gathering information on the pros and cons of exercise.
- I have not blocked out or planned time to exercise as of yet.

In any case, your slower pace and task-oriented attitude affects how you approach fitness. You desire a FACTUAL way of working out that allows you to correctly perform a program that is right for you. Structure, details, and a schedule will help you on your fitness journey. Chances are that in the past you haven't felt you had gathered enough information to find just the right fit for you. This book will help you succeed where you have failed in the past.

How to quickly identify someone with your style

You can spot another FACTUAL person usually by their contemplative look. FACTUAL people make good poker players because they can mask their true feelings. You won't hear them talking much, but you can believe they are thinking and processing. When they do speak, they have a point or key question that is right on the mark.

FACTUAL people are often quiet, but they will come forward when the situation warrants it. They prefer to work on projects and may go it alone or participate on a team, again depending upon what is appropriate for the situation. FACTUAL folks have difficulty listening to FAST people's grand visions or FUN people's wild stories. It isn't that they don't care, but they'd rather talk about concrete matters. Their focus is on tasks, projects, schedules, systems, and processes rather than on the people involved.

Normally, they will wear "classic" colors and outfits that never go out of style. They will select clothes that are proper for the situation, meaning that they will never be overdressed or underdressed for the occasion. They aren't interested in the latest fashion trend because it may not fit the circumstance. Most likely, they are wearing glasses, and the frame style will be practical. Since they spend so much time conducting extensive research, they use their eyes more than most. They will wear jewelry, but it will be minimal and appropriate for the event. They like the traditional, conservative look.

They prefer smaller, more intimate groups of people and may avoid large gatherings unless they know it is the right thing to do at the time. FACTUAL folks believe in consistency with their relationships. They are dependable.

As a FACTUAL person you probably drive a very practical car that meets your specific needs at this time. If you have children, for instance, then you are likely driving a minivan that will accommodate those needs. If you commute, you will have something smaller and more economical. Your vehicle will be a tried and true color—or whatever you could get on sale.

FACTUAL folks tend to be frugal and love a good negotiation process. They want the right price and will do all the research necessary to determine what that is. They won't pay more than a fair price for anything. They'd just as soon not have the item and wait for the right deal to come along than pay too much or be taken advantage of.

FACTUAL folks can be very patient people. I imagine you are the type of driver who abides by the speed limit and other highway laws—unless you feel the situation warrants otherwise. For example, if the flow of traffic is going ten miles per hour over the speed limit, and it is safe to do so, you will drive with the flow of traffic. Most of the time, however, you will honor all traffic regulations to the letter of the law, maintaining safety because that is the right thing to do.

Your office is probably organized and clean, everything in its place. You have logical filing systems and thoughtful placement for key equipment. If you have pictures from home, they are probably close to your chair. Anything out or on the walls is clean. Bookshelves are organized either alphabetically or by size to keep the shelf clutter free. FACTUAL people know where everything is at all times. You won't typically have many projects out at once...just the one you are concentrating on at the time.

When under stress, FACTUAL folks will begin to withdraw and spend more time alone. At these times, you will seek even more cognitive activities to help you relieve tension. Most people would find it stressful to work out a difficult problem, but not so for a FACTUAL person. You find comfort in looking for the right answer.

People with FACTUAL profiles are:

- Al Gore
- Stephen Covey
- Sgt. Joe Friday

Just because these folks are FACTUAL doesn't mean they can't be friendly and warm. Remember that we can temporarily adapt our personality styles to respond to the needs of the moment. FACTUAL people simply feel more comfortable doing things this way, but they do utilize the other areas to function.

■

JESUS BECAME EXACTLY WHAT
HE NEEDED, WHEN HE NEEDED IT.

■

Often when I am training people on the concepts of personality styles, somebody asks me what temperament Jesus was. The answer is easy: He was all four. Jesus became exactly what He needed, when He needed it. He is the perfect example of how every one of us should be striving to balance and blend with people. We each have our strengths, but we must be careful not to live just there. We must attempt to improve all areas of our complex being. The more balanced you are, the more correct you will be.

Your many strengths

As a FACTUAL person, you bring your analytical mind to any group. You are precise and accurate in all you do, personally and professionally. People may not always appreciate your in-depth look at things at first, but once they see how you can prevent obstacles by following your standards of operation, they will be grateful for your insight. You are able to provide great assurances to people with your thorough research and understanding of any topic you take on.

You give your best to any project you are assigned. You strive not only for excellence but also to exceed expectations. Because you care so much about details, you may take longer than others to complete the project in order to ensure it is correct. This is a positive trait that can backfire on you, especially when you are working under a deadline. Strive to balance correctness with timeliness.

You can work independently quite well, but you do like to know that you are part of a team with a strategic plan. You are most comfortable when you know what is expected of you and are given detailed specifics of the desired outcome. Many people admire your logical mind.

You aren't very talkative. You tend to hide your emotions unless you feel it is appropriate to share them. You listen intently and deliberately, looking for specific details and information to make your assessments and decisions. When you communicate, you are methodical and precise. You don't rush into anything and can almost be inflexible at times when changes are made quickly or without explanation.

Although FACTUAL people may hold a myriad of careers, they are a perfect fit for:

- Accounting
- Computer programming
- Scientific research
- Statistical data analysis
- Engineering

How to conquer challenges

FACTUAL folks are sensitive when it comes to details. If someone relates a story with incorrect information, FACTUAL people will have difficulty looking past it. They will probably correct the person, which can hurt your FUN person's feelings since he or she is more concerned with being animated than accurate. Try to focus on the person and not the data, which is a challenge for you.

FUN folks are your complete opposites and will require the most effort in your interactions. One way to improve relationships with them is to be more open and honest about your feelings. Switch from discussing *things* and begin sharing thoughts and feelings, and you will warm right up to your FUN and FRIENDLY folks.

You despise mistakes, mediocrity, sudden changes, clutter, and disorganization. If you find yourself dealing with this on a regular basis, you may become quite critical, negative, and unsociable. If you find yourself becoming more rigid and unaccommodating, take a step back. Reflect on what is causing this uneasiness, and attempt to refocus your energies on the things that *are* going right. Don't get so picky that you can't see the forest for the trees.

FACTUAL individuals can tend to impose their high standards on others. They can expect way too much of others who are not the same personality, a habit that causes strife and division. As much as I love my mother, when I was growing up she was very critical. I remember coming home with six As and one B on my report card one time, and she was very angry with the one B. Another time I cleaned the entire house from top to bottom for her as a surprise, but I forgot to dump the kitchen garbage. Without a word of appreciation, she criticized me for not dumping the trash. I was heartbroken.

Accepting what someone gives when it isn't how you would do it is tough, but if you want meaningful, long-lasting relationships, you must master this concept. You must learn to focus on the human element, not just the task element. Don't turn away a gift someone gives you because it doesn't measure up to your standards.

For a short time when I was younger I roomed with a FACTUAL gal. She ripped up the letters and cards she received from her boyfriend. Rather than relish the love he sent with his thoughtfulness, she got her red ink pen out and marked up his spelling mistakes. To make matters worse, she would show him. Some twenty years later, she is still single, unhappy, and miserably alone. Don't lose sight of what is important. Being right is not always the best path to choose.

When under stress, FACTUAL people can become vengeful. Pent-up feelings of dissatisfaction and disappointment in others become hostility. In order to prevent doing the wrong thing, you must take time to de-stress yourself. Time alone is important to you, but you must not sacrifice time with people. Although your way of showing that you care for someone is to do something for them, many people need to hear kind words, feel your touch, or share their hearts with you. The right thing to do is to show your affection the way the recipient would like you to. Take the time to find that out, and then take the necessary steps to do it right.

Because you are drawn to things more than people, you can use that as an escape. You may avoid conflict or relationships by working on projects. Although it feels good at the moment to stare at your computer for hours, you may be neglecting the very person who matters most to you. When you balance time alone with warm conversation with those you care about, everyone wins.

As long as you aren't stressed, you are very consistent. Your thorough approach gives others comfort and security. They know if you say, "This is a good product," that it is! They know you have done the research and would not make a mistake. They depend upon your accuracy with information. When something is in question, you are usually the one who is right.

A caution here is to not hang that over other people's heads, especially in a conflict. Nothing makes people angrier than a person who is right and knows it. Don't use your gift of gathering data as a tool to prove others wrong. Use it to help people make good decisions and stay on the right track.

When changes are made on you, you can often become inflexible and critical. You will find everything that can go wrong and then assume it *will* go wrong. Try asking questions first to get the specifics you need in order to understand the change before you dig your heels in. Remember that the team wins when everyone is on board and doing their job correctly.

Don't avoid changes or new projects just because you aren't familiar with them. This is called procrastination and can cause you intense pain, frustration, and disappointment. It can also prevent you from doing things right and on time. Instead, enjoy the journey of growing and learning something new. Knowing you, it won't take you long before you are a real pro at it.

If you find yourself constantly asking for more time or not finishing projects because you fear they aren't quite right yet, you are struggling with perfectionism. I'd like to share with you the difference between perfectionism and excellence. When people aim for perfection, they usually do so in order to say, "Hey, look at what I did. I did it! I am right." This mind-set is self-centered and self-destructive. When you can't achieve perfection, your self-worth is damaged. To you it means you are no good; you failed. And, since perfectionism is nearly impossible to obtain, you are in a vicious cycle.

Excellence, on the other hand, is doing your very best. It is accepting that this is good enough for this particular project at this particular time in these particular circumstances. When you strive for excellence, you are focusing on the end result rather than your self-esteem. Your value is separate from what you do. Just knowing that you did your best under the circumstances is good enough. It is the understanding that you never have all the time in the world and must act now. Everyone wins when you shoot for excellence.

Understanding the difference between perfectionism and excellence has changed my life, and I hope it will have a positive impact on yours.

In order to do this, you will need to temporarily visit your FUN or FRIENDLY side. This will enable you to focus more on the big picture rather than the intricate details. FACTUAL people can often forget to look up while they are in the trenches. This can cause them to get discouraged. Take a break to smell the roses once in a while to remain positive.

Because you like things done right, you can spend too much time on the *tasks* of life and not much time with people. Remember the biblical story about Martha and Mary? FRIENDLY folks relate with Mary: they enjoy the company of people rather than running around making things perfect. FACTUAL people, however, are running around like Martha, getting everything ready and just right. If you aren't careful, you can find yourself always getting everything right—only to find out you missed the most right thing of all.

If you aren't familiar with the story, look at Luke 10:38–42. Martha was a whirlwind of activity, preparing food for her special guests. She wanted everything to be perfect. Mary, on the other hand, decided to be with her guests. Martha was irritated with Mary and confronted Jesus, saying, "I've done all this work, and she is just sitting there at Your feet." Jesus replied, "She has chosen wisely." The moral of the story is that the dirty dishes would be there the next day. Jesus was only going to be there for the evening. Choose wisely, and you will have a lot less stress in your life.

How to beat stress

Stress is a part of life. To manage it, FACTUAL people need time for cognitive activity alone. They want to focus on something they can dissect, understand, process, and analyze. If they don't take this time, they can become moody, critical, and unsociable. Their tension can push them to the point of being mean and vengeful, saying heartless things that, while possibly true, are nonetheless hurtful.

Remember when I said that any strength pushed to an extreme is a weakness? Every temperament has a negative side, and it usually rears its ugly head when we are stressed. Since you are a FACTUAL person, watch for these warning signs:

- Are you getting more critical of others?
- Are you experiencing more fear than normal?
- Are you becoming more inflexible and rigid?
- Are you getting uptight over little details that really don't matter?
- Are you getting negative?
- Are you becoming completely unsociable?

When this happens, stop everything and do something for yourself. In my book *A Healthier, Happier You: 101 Steps for Lessening Stress*, I provide a wealth of ideas for reducing your stress quickly. I suggest you pick up a copy for more ways to recover from your stress.

One way to proactively manage your stress and also move toward better health is to exercise. Exercise is proven to reduce tension and anxiety. It also gives your body stamina and strength. You will want to find just the right program to implement, which is what we will be talking about in just a few pages.

FACTUAL people care about the health benefits they will receive from any exercise program and whether or not the program has been proven to work. As long as the evidence leads them to believe it is right for them, they will engage in it. The initial process of researching, investigating, and deciding will be the most difficult. Once the path is chosen, FACTUAL people will hold their course. In this chapter we'll design a FIT program that is just right for you!

RELATING TO THE OTHER PERSONALITY STYLES

Your communication style is slow, thoughtful, and precise. You spend time listening and processing what you hear before you speak. You probably believe in giving each person time to talk because you believe it is polite. You will ask logical questions to ensure you correctly understand what is being conveyed. You will gather details throughout the conversation but will probably not let the other person know how you feel. You enjoy holding your cards close to your vest and will require time to respond properly.

If expected to respond immediately, you may come across as cold and calculating. You are reserved and on the conservative side, which means that faster, more energetic people may try to rush you. Because you need extra time to formulate your thoughts and feelings, you will sharply retreat if pushed too hard. Although taking your time to thoroughly process something is one of your strengths, you must learn to respond in a timely manner. Waiting so long for the right information that it is too late to act makes it wrong, and nobody wins.

Relating to FAST people

When talking with FAST people, be direct and to the point. They will appreciate you getting right to the bottom line. They don't want you to break the ice or socialize with them, which is fine with you. They will want you to dive right into business. Use words and phrases that are results oriented and that answer the question "What is in it for me?", which is foremost on their mind.

Most FAST people do not like being told what to do. They prefer options and deciding for themselves, so don't tell them what to do. Instead, offer suggestions that are results oriented and challenging. You will have more details available than they are probably interested in, but simply ask them, "May I share this with you?" If they understand what is at stake and how these details can benefit them, you will have their undivided attention. If you wear thicker skin when around FAST people and prepare yourself for a faster pace, you will do just fine.

Relating to FUN people

When interacting with FUN people, be more energetic. You are speaking with folks who love a good story, so don't be too shy or quiet. Tell a great story or funny joke. Laughing it up with this group is what it is all about.

Details will not be the focal point, so if you need to get an answer, gently guide them back on track. You may get frustrated with all their "global" talk. You prefer talking about concrete matters. FUN folks are your direct opposites. You will need to be patient and not worry about details so much. Don't be too abrupt or cold, or you will hurt their feelings. They are just as people oriented as you are task oriented. Be kind.

Relating to FRIENDLY people

When communicating with FRIENDLY people, be warmer and more personable. Give them the time they need to formulate their thoughts just as you would appreciate them doing for you. They appreciate a friendly, soft approach that affirms them, so try to concentrate on the person first. Since you understand that silence is not always a positive response, ask questions. Pull FRIENDLY people into the conversation, and let them respond on their timetable.

Building trust and rapport will be important, but you are a credible person and will have no difficulty here. FRIENDLY people make great companions!

Other FACTUAL people

When engaging with other FACTUAL individuals, just be yourself! Focus on the facts. They will want time to process before they respond, but you will expect that since you are the same way. Being organized and systematically presenting your idea will work best. They want you to stick to business instead of being personable and are more concerned with receiving correct data than getting to know you better. These folks are analytical and structured just like you, so they don't like a lot of change. Steady as she goes!

THE ULTIMATE WORKOUT PLAN FOR THE FACTUAL PROFILE

Now that you have gained a basic understanding of yourself and how to interact with others, let's get down to the meat and potatoes of this book: working out with style—your style! We will take all this temperament information and relate it to how you will approach your cardio exercise, weight training, stretching, and even nutrition.

Remember, how you are wired *does* affect everything. Your FIT profile, as it relates to fitness, is what makes this book unique. You will now have the opportunity to customize a program—a lifestyle—based on who you are as an individual. No more one-size-fits-all approach, and no more failure. Success and good health are in your future. Ready to revolutionize your exercise?

How to raise your energy level

Most FACTUAL people are quiet, living organized, structured lives. You probably move slowly and may feel you haven't gathered enough information yet to make a decision regarding exercise. The fitness industry is constantly improving and changing, so you will have to apply your newfound motto, "This is enough data for now," and move on in order to establish a fitness program that will work for you. You can always revise it later.

You will want to select the right cardio exercise for your life and schedule. If you travel a lot, you will want something that can be done on the road. If you work evenings, you will want something that you can do during the day alone. This way, your program is appropriate for your life. Answering the question "How should I accomplish my fitness goals?" will be important to you and will help you stay on track one day at a time.

Putting your exercise on your calendar like any other appointment will help you incorporate it into your schedule. Don't set yourself up to fail by trying to exercise at times you know aren't convenient. If you do, chances are you won't stick to it. You will get frustrated and annoyed when you miss your scheduled time. Rather, place it on your calendar at a time you know you can honor.

■

SCHEDULE YOUR EXERCISE AT A CONVENIENT TIME ON YOUR CALENDAR.

■

Review chapter three, and utilize the information for goal setting and achieving. I'd also recommend that you skim through chapter four again for additional facts that might help you with your fitness decisions. Ask yourself, "What will I gain by being more healthy and fit?" and "What is the right exercise program for me?" I know your research has shown that working out is simply the right thing to do in order to be healthy—plain and simple.

This is a good time to pause for just a second and see what kind of shape you are presently in. Take the following body measurements:

Waist-to-hip ratio
Waist measurement = _____ (WM)
Hip measurement = _____ (HM)
WM _____ divided by HM _____ = _____Ratio

If you are a man and the ratio is greater than .95, you are in the high-fat category; you have greater risk for heart attack, and you need to lose weight. If you are a woman and the ratio is greater than .85, you are in the high-fat category; you have greater risk for heart attack, and you need to lose weight.

This is just a reference, a starting place. As you progress with your program, you can look back and tangibly see your improvement. Even if your measurements are acceptable (that is, your ratio is less than these numbers), you must continually include cardio exercise into your routine in order to prevent future health problems.

You don't want to end up like so many overweight people I see at the store who are completely out of breath and sweating because they got out of their car and walked in the store. They are walking time bombs. You want to be a living example of how we should all be: healthy and fit!

THE PERFECT CARDIO PROGRAM FOR FACTUAL PEOPLE

On the following pages are some energizing programs for your FIT profile. These programs will challenge your intellect as well as your physical stamina. They will provide you with structure so that you may monitor your progress and chart your course to success. The *Intensity* column refers back to the Workout Intensity Chart on page 54. Try these programs, and adapt them as you see fit.

I understand that this is a lot to take in at once, but start somewhere—start today. You know it is the right thing to do, and getting fit is an action that shows you care.

Chart 9.1 | FACTUAL Cardio Programs

Exercise	Frequency	Intensity	Time	Tips for Your Style
Step aerobics: very methodical	3 times a week	Level 8–9½ (Adding risers can intensify this workout to a 9½)	1 hour	By its nature, step aerobics require great concentration and thought. You will enjoy memorizing movements and getting the steps just right in order to maximize your workout.
Indoor cycling classes: structured	3 times a week	Level 8–9½ (Adding more gear or picking up your pace will increase your intensity)	1 hour	Cycling is a proven cardio workout that requires consistency. In order to see improvement, you must stick with it.
Stationary cycling: programs available to monitor your workout	3 times a week	Level 8–9½ (You determine on the front end what levels you want, and then the machine charts the course for you.)	30 minutes	All the exertion without the big class environment. You plot your own course and determine how you will ride. Again, this exercise has lots of things to keep track of and monitor throughout your workout. Just make sure you are working at the right intensity level. Check the Workout Intensity Chart on page 54.
Street cycling: outdoors and requires thought and planning	1–3 times a week	Level 8–8½ (Include hills and straight-aways for sprints to get your level up.)	1 hour	Outdoor cycling is a great sport. Plot out safe yet challenging routes. Keep track of your revolutions per minute (RPM) as well as your miles per hour (MPH), and watch your improvement.

Chart 9.1 | FACTUAL Cardio Programs (continued)

Exercise	Frequency	Intensity	Time	Tips for Your Style
Running: requires concentration and proper form	3 times a week	Level 8–9½ (Again, hills will change up your workout. Visit the 9½ with a sprint.)	30 minutes	Running requires discipline, determination, and focus. You can monitor your miles per hour (MPH) and see if you can shave off time, running farther each 30-minute block of time.
Sports activities: structured with rules and regulations	1–3 times a week	Level 8 (More interval training, but concentrate on getting a steady level.)	1 hour or more	Joining a team will provide a structured and scheduled workout for you. You may even volunteer to keep score or track statistics.
Power walking: set a goal, plan out your path, and enjoy.	3–5 times a week	Level 8–9½ (Use your arms to help keep your level up. Add hand weights, and it is even harder.)	At least 1 hour	Walking is still *the* best exercise. We were designed to walk. You will need to make sure you are working out hard enough. Check the Workout Intensity Chart on page 54.
Swimming: requires skill. Practice your form.	3–5 times a week	Level 8 (Keep swimming, and you will get into your zone.)	30 minutes to 1 hour	Because you are patient and methodical, swimming probably appeals to you. It requires focus and the ability to stick with the same routine. It is a great option for you when you travel.

Notes

- *Step aerobics* classes are challenging for the mind and the body. Complicated steps require concentration and thought. Once routines are mastered, the workout level continues to increase as you add more risers.

- *Indoor cycling* is a phenomenal way to burn a lot of calories. A typical one-hour class can burn 600 to 900 calories. Most classes have formats that warm you up, work you hard, and cool you down at the end. This is a very individual workout, and you can compete against yourself by monitoring your RPM and MPH. Cycling classes are usually conducted in a private room with a closed door.

- *Stationary cycling* is not for everyone. It challenges your ability to stay focused and work at a high enough level to get a health benefit. But it's filled with a bunch of statistical data, and it provides an excellent way to monitor cardio progress.

- *Street cycling* gets you outside into nature and provides the opportunity to plot out routes and set strategic goals. Select routes that are scenic but challenging. Bring plenty of water and a snack.

- *Running* is another independent exercise that allows you to compete with yourself through improved MPH. Work on distance or speed. Either way, you are getting a spectacular cardio workout. It also provides the perfect opportunity to focus on deep things.

- *Sports activities* (basketball, volleyball, baseball, softball, tennis, and the like). Sports teams are structured, organized, and scheduled. They allow you to plan appropriately, and you know what to expect each time. Your position on the team will be clearly defined. Not all sports are created equal, however, so do not limit your entire cardio routine to just sports. Weave in some of the other suggestions as well.

- *Power walking* is still one of the best exercises out there. Devise a walking route that includes some hills to push your heart rate up into the appropriate levels. Wear appropriate footwear, and you are on your way to good health!

- *Swimming.* If you don't mind cold water and chlorine, swimming is an excellent cardio work out that utilizes your entire body without impact, which means it is easy on your joints. Many health clubs have lap pools. With swimming you can get a good workout in just thirty minutes. This is a focused sport. You will enjoy learning how to improve your strokes and swim more smoothly and more consistently.

Cardio success log

On the following page is a cardio success log for you to use to track your cardio workouts. On the log, "mode" refers to how you worked out. Examples are listed above. I recommend you make enough copies of this form to cover at least a few months. Once you create a schedule and make these activities "habits," you can plug them into your calendar. Each time you work out you move a step closer to being healthy.

Chart 9.2 | **FACTUAL Cardio Success Log**

DAY/DATE	CARDIO MODE	TIME	STRETCHES	NOTES
Monday				
Tuesday				
Wednesday				
Thursday				
Friday				
Saturday				
Sunday				
Monday				
Tuesday				
Wednesday				
Thursday				
Friday				
Saturday				
Sunday				
Monday				
Tuesday				
Wednesday				
Thursday				
Friday				
Saturday				
Sunday				
Monday				
Tuesday				
Wednesday				
Thursday				
Friday				
Saturday				
Sunday				

The Perfect Weight-Lifting Program
for FACTUAL People

You may not have lifted weights before because you didn't really know how to do it properly. Now that you have read about proper technique, safety tips, and have pictures for reference, you should feel ready to jump in.

If you are still hesitant, reread chapters four and five. Better yet, conduct your own research on the Web or pick up a fitness magazine. Don't procrastinate on starting and blame it on a lack of information, though. You really should have enough data by now to at least start a basic program. In earlier chapters I've given you options for weight lifting, and I suggest you select one that fits your lifestyle.

If you have the time, lifting at a gym will give you the most choices of equipment. You will be able to focus on specific muscle groups by utilizing machines designed to do just that. These machines usually have pictures and instructions to help ensure proper technique.

If your schedule does not permit you to work out at a health club or you don't have one nearby, then you can install your own weight system at home. I know you are disciplined enough to stick to a workout program in a home gym, and they are certainly convenient. You won't have to wait in line or deal with large crowds of people. Do the homework, and make sure that the system you get is adequate for your needs today and your future requirements as you get stronger. I like the Smith system because it has safety spotting, which allows you to work out alone. I know you will get a good deal!

■

LIFTING AT A GYM WILL GIVE YOU THE MOST CHOICES OF
EQUIPMENT AND USUALLY HAS PICTURES AND INSTRUCTIONS
TO HELP ENSURE PROPER TECHNIQUE.

■

You can lift alone or with a partner. If you have aggressive goals that involve heavy free weights, you should have a partner to help with spotting. It's the safe thing to do. Because you will want to give the right amount of attention to each muscle, I suggest that you dedicate one day for your upper body and another day for your lower body. This will ensure that you work every muscle and do it correctly. You will also see incredible results by doing it this way.

Another option for you is to attend group weight-lifting classes such as Body Pump or REP Reebok. Just like a step aerobics class, these classes are structured and organized. Each movement is choreographed and timed perfectly to the music. By the end of one hour, you will have worked your entire body. Attending two of these a week will ensure a proper workout that is a very efficient use of your time. Routines are usually a month long, so you have plenty of time to become familiar with the program. They change monthly in order to provide a new challenge to your muscles.

I would also recommend that you set aside some money to hire a personal trainer to work with you. This way you will learn exactly how to perform each exercise. Whether you are working out at a health club or your own home gym, a personal trainer will outline your workout each visit and explain why it is important to exercise and how to execute it properly. A personal trainer will be happy to answer any of your questions and help you learn more about fitness.

Weight-lifting victory log

On the following page is a weight-lifting victory log for you to record your progress in resistance training. I suggest you make ample copies of this and begin using it for whatever program you select. Log your seat settings and weight so that you can refer to it each time. Don't waste your time trying to figure out what you did previously. Record it, and build from there.

On this log, the "mode" refers to how you actually worked that muscle. For instance, "leg press" might be the mode for your quads and "15-pound barbells" could be your mode for biceps. Don't forget to change up the mode every now and then to challenge the muscle.

Chart 9.3 | FACTUAL Weight-Lifting Victory Log

Muscle	Mode	Seat/Settings	Weight/Reps #1	Weight/Reps #2	Weight/Reps #3	Notes
Quads						
Hamstrings						
Glutes						
Calves						
Inner thigh						
Outer thigh						
Biceps						
Triceps						
Shoulders						
Deltoids						
Pecs						
Lats/rhomboids						
Erector spinae						
Ab						
Obliques						
Stretch						

The Perfect Stretching Program for FACTUAL People

Take a look at the stretches I have outlined in chapter five. Stretching is mandatory if you want to improve your performance and prevent injury. Make sure you schedule some stretching before and after your cardio exercise as well as before and after your muscle resistance work.

Aerobics and Fitness Association of America guidelines recommend three to five days of stretching a week.[6] Personally, I don't think we can get enough stretching. As a FACTUAL person, your slower pace will be drawn to stretching and the opportunity to contemplate while exercising.

Make sure to stretch both your upper and lower body. Add in a "cat" stretch for your back, which means you are on all fours (elbows and knees). Push your spine up toward the ceiling, which creates an arched spine. Breathe in, and then lower your back until it forms a curve. Repeat this several times.

If you are actively involved in sports or outdoor recreation, I suggest you add a quad stretch (bring the heel of your foot up behind your glute and push out through your knee) and a hamstring stretch (put one leg out in front of you with your heel on the floor and toe up; the other leg is bent at the knee, and you lean on your quad with your hand as you press your chest toward your quad). If you have trouble with your Achilles tendon, be sure to stretch your calves out (dorsiflexion, which is lifting your toes up, and plantarflexion, which points your toes downward).

Stretching improves your overall health and performance. Stretching before and after exercise prevents injury by preparing and warming up muscles as well as elongating muscles that have been worked or contracted. It also gets blood flowing back to the proper areas of the body, preventing the blood from pooling, which can cause clots. Stretching allows your body to perform at its best the next time you ask it to do so. It will help reduce stiffness and soreness from exercise by preventing lactic acid buildup. It's the right way to end any workout.

Putting It All Together: Your Ultimate FACTUAL Workout Program

This is where the rubber meets the road. Now I would like you to actually spell out your weekly program. In this chapter I have provided an array of ideas and options for you to consider. Although I may understand your unique FIT profile, I still have not had the privilege of meeting you face-to-face. I do not know your personal schedule or the challenges you face. I am only the coach, guiding and directing you.

To help get you started I've provided an example of one person's weekly schedule:

Chart 9.4 | FACTUAL Weekly Workout Schedule (Pete)

Day	Activity	Location	Time	Notes
Monday	Stationary bike and upper body lifting	Fitness Club USA	1 hour	5:30 to 6:30 p.m./stretch
Tuesday	Running	Outside	30 min.	7:00 to 7:30 a.m./stretch
Wednesday	Lower body lifting and swimming	Fitness Club USA	1 hour	12 noon to 1:00 p.m./stretch
Thursday	Indoor cycling	Fitness Club USA	1 hour	4:30 to 5:30 p.m./stretch
Friday	Weight lifting	Home gym w/PT	1 hour	4:00 to 5:00 p.m./stretch
Saturday	Step aerobics	Fitness Club USA	1 hour	8:00 to 9:00 a.m./stretch
Sunday	Off	Or join sports team	1 hour or more	Play…what do you like to do?

Pete represents a logical man in his mid-forties with a goal to lose 30 pounds and strengthen his muscular system. He has no desire to be a "he-man," but he does want to improve his overall health and conditioning. He doesn't necessarily care where he works out. He is more concerned with getting the right workout in and having a schedule he can count on. He likes to be consistent, so when he develops a schedule he sticks to it.

He invested in a home gym for convenience as well as a personal trainer one time a week to ensure he is weight training properly and effectively. His PT provides ways to correctly use his equipment and answers any questions he may have about living a healthy lifestyle.

He has found that combining some cardio with weights allows him to concentrate on his upper and lower body, giving them a thorough workout. He is primarily working out alone, but he does enjoy the step aerobics class. It is very organized and structured.

You will notice that Pete has five days a week of cardio exercise and is weight training three times a week. He'd rather maintain this schedule and do everything 100 percent than sacrifice quality. With this schedule, Pete is exercising properly and safely, and he is on his way to great health.

How are you doing?

Here's a blank weekly schedule for you to fill in. Make copies, and start filling in the blanks with what you believe will work best for you. Set yourself up for success with programs that work for your FIT. Remember to stretch before and after exercise each time. Try to include at least three days of cardio exercise.

Chart 9.5 | FACTUAL Weekly Workout Schedule

Day	Activity	Location	Time	Notes
Monday				
Tuesday				
Wednesday				
Thursday				
Friday				
Saturday				
Sunday				

Keys to Your Success

Below is a summary of things to do or not do in order to ensure your success with your new FACTUAL fitness program:

- Gather data on all the options and become familiar with the programs you like.

- Don't get stuck in the selecting process; commit to decide and take action.

- Set your routine, and schedule it.

- If lifting at home, make sure you have enough space.

- If you select a lifting partner, make sure he or she is reliable and dependable.

- Don't be afraid of trying new things; it is good to change it up now and then.

- Continually learn more about being healthy, and implement new information as appropriate.

- Remind yourself that exercise is required for quality and quantity of life.

Congratulations, you now have your own FACTUAL fitness program, personalized to your temperament. I know you're eager to get busy, but don't skip chapter ten, which addresses nutrition, especially if losing weight is one of your goals. Chapter eleven will challenge you to commit to be fit (success contract) and will help you start implementing your plan immediately.

Don't procrastinate any longer. The data show that the time is right for you to get fit.

FIT FOR LIFE

TEN | EAT RIGHT, FEEL RIGHT

BY NOW, YOU should have your personalized FIT workout program that incorporates cardio exercise, weight-resistance training, and stretching. Congratulations! You are halfway there.

"What!" you say. "Only halfway?" Sure. We can't expect to be healthy if all we do is *use* our bodies. Certainly exercise will make a huge improvement to your overall health, but you must also watch what you eat.

Many people hate the nutrition component of fitness because it is so much fun to eat! Many people want to believe that because they work out they can eat anything they want. Others don't eat much food at all, confusing *thin* with *healthy*. These are all false views of nutrition. You could be in serious trouble if you are adopting one of them.

Based upon your FIT, you will probably relate with one of these scenarios more than another. Here's some good news: just as we customized a workout routine based upon your FIT, here we will provide nutritional suggestions for your specific FIT. Read on.

Eating too much increases body fat. Being overweight is hard on the joints and organs because everything has to work twice as hard. That is why many overweight people have heart attacks. Their hearts, clogged and overworked, can no longer perform the extra work. Even those who exercise a lot are at risk if they don't also watch what they eat.

And if you think all thin people are healthy, you are mistaken. Those who eat very little to avoid exercise are putting their bodies at extreme risk. The body still needs nutrition, even if you aren't exerting yourself. These people are losing bone mass and may become so frail that their bones will snap in half like toothpicks. The best approach is to balance both exercise and nutrition. Let me explain why.

GARBAGE IN, GARBAGE OUT

Consider your automobile. You can wash it to be sure its outer appearance is sharp. You can put new tires on it. But if you haven't put the right stuff *in* it, such as oil and brake fluid, your car *will* break down.

We have a friend in Colorado who was so pleased to finally purchase a nice-looking Bronco. For years he'd had a beat-up car that looked like it would fall apart at any second. In his excitement and haste, however, he forgot to care for a small problem on the *inside* of the new vehicle. He failed to check the oil as he should have. On a long road trip, his engine burned up, and the car died. He saw warning signs like the oil light and diminishing power, but he ignored them even though he knew the vehicle had oil leak problems in the past. Although his car looked good on the outside, it was starving on the inside. It didn't have what it needed to run properly. Our bodies are the same way. We must be careful with what we put in.

Have you heard the saying, "Garbage in, garbage out"? Computer programmers often use this phrase, but it also helps us understand what happens with the foods we eat. If we supply our bodies with nutritional food, we will receive healthy benefits. But if we fill ourselves up with junk, we will feel poorly. It really is that simple.

So many of the ailments we face are our own doing. Research has shown that upwards of 70 percent of all cancers could be prevented by better nutrition.[1] In other words, if people ate better, their bodies would be healthier. If we give our bodies what they need, they are very capable of fighting off disease and illness. But when we deprive them of what they need, we are setting ourselves up for sickness.

I know you want better than this, and you definitely deserve to live a full and happy life. Proper nutrition must be an instrumental part of your new FIT program.

I'LL DRINK TO THAT!

Water is also vital to our overall health. No, a Diet Pepsi does not count! Most people do not drink enough water. Many times when you feel hungry, your body is actually telling you it is dehydrated. See, your body doesn't have a mechanism to signal dehydration, so it uses hunger pains to get your attention. Unfortunately, most of us eat food rather than drink water. The next time you are hungry midday, drink a glass of water first. You might find that it does the trick.

Ever get the "sleepies" late in the afternoon? Drink a glass of water. Water helps keep your brain—itself 80 percent water—functioning and will keep you focused. Our bodies need water for cell production, regulation of body temperature, and toxin excretion.[2]

How much water is enough? The Aerobics and Fitness Association of America suggests that for every 1,000 calories you consume, you should take in one quart (32 ounces) of fluid, primarily from water.[3] Since bottled water containers usually hold 8 ounces, you are looking at four bottles for every 1,000 calories you consume.

Your specific caloric need is based upon your gender, age, and activity level, but the American Dietetic Association recommends no fewer than 1,200 calories per day for women and no fewer than 1,400 calories per day for men.[4] Think of calories as fuel for your body. If you are exercising, you need to increase your caloric and water intake.

We should all start off the morning by drinking a glass of water. Our bodies have been dehydrated for six or more hours and a tall glass of H_2O is a great way to start off the day. I start drinking more water immediately after lunch in preparation for my exercise in the evening. I then drink a full 8 ounces during my exercise and another afterward. I always know when I am fully hydrated if I urinate before I leave the house, when I arrive at the gym, and immediately after my class! (I know, I know: too much information! ☺)

NUTRITION SNAPSHOT

Let's take a quick look at how you are doing right now with your nutrition and eating habits. Please fill out the profile below. Be honest! This is simply providing us with a starting point. No one has to see it but you. Remember, you are embarking on this journey for you. Basically, all we are doing is taking a snapshot of your eating habits *today*. After you have read this chapter, I know you will want to make adjustments to your diet.

NUTRITION AND WEIGHT PROFILE

Name: _____ Date: _____

What is your current weight? _____

What is your desired weight? _____

What is the *most* you have weighed as an adult? _____

What is the *least* you have weighed as an adult? _____

What is the lowest weight you have maintained for a year? _____

How many times have you lost and regained weight (10 pounds or more)? _____

What types of diets have you tried? _____

_____

If you have high blood pressure or high cholesterol, at what weight did these problems develop? _____

Is this a good time in your life to commit to a weight-loss program? _____

What obstacles are in the way of achieving your goal?

_____

_____

Which do you eat regularly (check all that apply)?

        Breakfast _____
        Midmorning snack _____
        Lunch _____
        Midafternoon snack _____
        Dinner _____
        After-dinner snack _____
        Late-night snack _____

How often do you eat out each week? _____

How many of these are fast food? _____

What size portions do you normally eat?

        Small _____

        Moderate _____

        Large _____

        Supersize _____

How often do you eat more than one serving?

        Always _____

        Usually _____

        Sometimes _____

        Never _____

How many minutes does it usually take you to eat a meal? _____

Do you eat while doing other activities (e.g. watching TV, reading, working)? Yes/No

How many times a week do you eat or drink the following?

    _____ cookies, cake, pie

    _____ candy

    _____ doughnuts

    _____ ice cream

    _____ muffins

    _____ regular soft drinks

    _____ potato chips, corn chips, etc.

    _____ fried foods

    _____ peanut butter, nuts, or seeds

    _____ crackers

    _____ fast food (McDonalds, Taco Bell, Arby's, etc.)

    _____ cheese

    _____ whole milk, cream, nondairy creamer

    _____ red meat (beef, pork, lamb)

    _____ butter, margarine, mayonnaise

    _____ breakfast meat or luncheon meat (bacon, sausage, hot dogs, etc.)

    _____ convenience items (frozen foods, instant potatoes, canned items)

    _____ refined grains (white rice, white breads)

    _____ more than one serving of alcohol per day (4 oz. wine or 12 oz. beer)

_____ more than two servings of a caffeine beverage in a day

How many servings of the following foods do you eat each day?

_____ fruit (fresh)

_____ vegetables (fresh)

_____ bread (wheat)

_____ cereal (whole grain)

_____ pasta, rice, other grains

_____ dairy products

_____ meat

_____ peas, tofu, dried beans, etc.

MAKING GOOD NUTRITION DECISIONS

I am sure just filling out this simple form has raised some red flags for you. It is very easy for us to sink into bad habits. We start off with a special treat once in a while, and before we know it, we have made it a regular menu item. Each of us should take inventory once in a while to see how we are doing.

It is hard for many, though, to even know if they are doing well or poorly. The word *diet* has been so misused that people don't understand the concept. Did you know that weight loss is a multi-billion-dollar-a-year industry? Do you know why they make so much money? Because we keep buying products in hopes of a miracle cure!

I'm going to say something that will sound heartless, but I'm actually being loving. I care for you enough to be honest. Here it is: *don't look for the quick fix.* Why? Because it doesn't exist. Unfortunately you will hear a completely different message just about everywhere you turn. Too many companies have too much money invested to let you know otherwise.

I do not know how it happened, but somehow our society has decided it is acceptable to not take responsibility for our own actions. If someone burns himself with hot coffee, he blames it on McDonald's. Coffee *is* hot, and it can burn you, especially if you are drinking and driving. Are we going to start suing our employers because we have to drive to work? It seems to be the same with those who are overweight. People are now blaming the fast-food industry for their obesity.

Whatever happened to just saying no? We must all take responsibility for our actions. Each one of us has the same opportunity to say yes or no to food. I'm not saying it is always easy, but *we* must make good decisions.

We are responsible for our own health. If we are in good health, then we can pat ourselves on the back. If we are in poor health, then we really don't have anyone to blame but ourselves.

Now, I do understand that some diseases attack without warning or cause. I'm not speaking of these types of illnesses but of those we *do* have control over. You would be surprised at how big that list is. We really can change our health by changing what we do.

Don't be misled into thinking that some pill, drink, powder, or bar will "fix" your problems. Often, *we* are the problem. Eating is just like any other addiction: we use it to ease the pain. Depending upon your profile and your background, you may find yourself relating with this.

Does food comfort you? Do you use it to enhance your moods? If you do, you are probably caught in a vicious cycle. The cycle begins with feeling down. Feeling down leads to eating. Eating helps you feel better, so you eat more. But after you have overeaten, you feel horrible about yourself. And what do you do when you feel down about things? You eat!

When the cycle gets completely out of hand you soon find you can't fit into your clothes anymore. That's when you may decide to buy a quick-fix solution. Depending upon what you buy, you might actually lose some weight. But the problem is that you don't keep it off, so you look for something else to try. And the weight-loss industry continues to get rich.

If their pills, powders, drinks, or whatever actually worked, you would only need to purchase it *once*. It would cure your weight problem once and for all. Unfortunately, this is not the case. Many people are led to believe that what they buy will actually work. They believe what they are told in advertisements.

My mother fell for this. When Healthy Choice first came out, they introduced their line of cookies, which were prominently labeled "fat free." My mother didn't even like cookies, but because they were supposed to be healthy she bought them. She began to eat lots of cookies—and she gained weight. Folks, *fat free is not calorie free.* In fact, many fat-free products add incredible amounts of sugar to compensate for the absence of fat. Often, you would be better off to stick with the regular version and just eat less.

That is the other temptation: "I can eat more of it because it is fat free." Please, if you get anything out of this nutritional section, understand that you cannot trust advertising claims. Advertisements are *selling* you something. These companies are in the business of making money, and it is at your and my expense unless we decide to take the one and only real way to health: proper nutrition and exercise.

220

Diets, whether new fad programs or systems that have been around for a while, simply don't work. By their very nature, diets require us to restrict or remove something. The moment you decide to deprive yourself of something, you can't help thinking about it. Don't believe me? Don't think about the color blue. Nothing blue. Don't picture a single thing blue. Don't let your eye stray to that blue thing on the table. OK, if you are like me, you immediately saw the sky or something blue. Our brains are strange that way. The more we tell ourselves not to do something, the more we fixate on it. Whatever your diet restricts, that is what you crave, and you will ultimately fail. Worse yet, you will feel discouraged and thus probably eat more.

A Balanced Diet

God didn't design us to be deprived, nor did He want us to participate in these vicious cycles. He has great plans for each of us. His desire for us is *balance*. Through the years we have forgotten the basics, but what we should be striving for is a well-balanced diet. The word *diet* should not refer to a program or plan you start and quit. Rather, your diet should simply mean what you eat. And what you eat should be well balanced. So before we go further, let me explain what a well-balanced diet actually looks like.

I am not a certified nutritionist. I have not dedicated my life to nutrition. But I have undergone extensive study through my personal trainer certifications as well as conducting my own research, not to mention that I try to live by what I teach. I used to starve myself when I was younger, for fear of gaining weight. I have seen the negative effects of poor nutrition firsthand. The good news is that whatever condition you are in today, you don't have to be in that same condition six months from now. Our bodies are amazing. They will respond if we do the right things.

What I am about to present is not new, trendy, or controversial. The Food and Drug Administration defined a well-balanced diet many, many years ago. You have seen the USDA food pyramid, right? We learned it in school. What the FDA has developed is a step above that includes more current research. With some minor updates and modifications, I believe it is still the best route to take. It doesn't require us to stop enjoying good food. It simply helps us fuel our bodies so that they run properly. And if our bodies are operating at their best, we can continue to enjoy life to the fullest.

Nutrition Guide

CARBOHYDRATES = 55–60 percent of diet
PROTEINS = 12–15 percent of diet
FAT = 25–30 percent of diet (no more than 10 percent saturated fat)[5]

Carbohydrates

The energy systems of your body—those processes that enable you to conduct your cardiovascular exercise—require carbohydrates. Carbohydrates are the body's main source of energy. They come in two forms: simple (sugars) or complex (vegetables, grains). They include both sugars and starches such as fruits, vegetables, potatoes, bread, cereal, pasta, rice, and beans.[6]

Diets that dramatically restrict your carb intake are dangerous. Your body *will* get what it needs, one way or the other. If you don't provide what it needs, it will take it from your organs, most likely your liver. Since the body will do what it needs to in order to operate, wouldn't you rather give it what it needs in the proper form and amount?

You should make carbs 55 to 60 percent of your diet. They can be simple or complex, which means they are either easier to digest or a little tougher, respectively. Examples of simple carbs:

- Sugars (natural and refined)
- Fruits
- Some vegetables (lettuce, tomatoes)

Examples of complex carbs:

- Potatoes
- Carrots
- Broccoli
- Corn
- Rice
- Beans
- Grains

Refined or processed sugars (found in most junk foods but also in boxed and frozen foods) should be limited to only 10 percent of your total carb intake.[7] Although they will help give you a quick boost of energy, they have no nutritional value. The body will still be craving the nutrition it needs, which is why you feel the need to eat more right away. Your hunger pangs never seem to be satisfied.

Ever hear the term "carb junkie?" Carbs are many people's favorite, and it is very easy to get addicted to them. The body learns that it doesn't have to burn your stored fat because it is getting plenty of carbs. This doesn't mean you won't gain weight. In fact, it means just the opposite. Your body isn't working efficiently. You will feel the need to eat more and more (usually a feeling of completely running out of gas) in order to sustain your energy systems. It will not use what it already has stored up. And all your excess carbs will be stored as fat. It is another vicious cycle.

The best way to approach carbs is to make sure you eat more complex or nutritionally packed carbs versus the empty ones in refined or processed sugars. And watch the add-ons that can accompany carbs, such as butter, sour cream, mayonnaise, toppings, salad dressings, and the like. These add additional fat calories and get you in trouble quickly.

Fat

Speaking of fat, that's something else that is important for your energy system. Fat is used for future work. Women need a higher percentage of body fat than men for their reproductive system. Fat also helps protect your body against cold temperatures. Insufficient body fat can lead to amenorrhea (lack of menstrual cycle), which can then lead to osteoporosis (bone loss).[8]

Too much fat, and you are at a greater risk for heart attack. Not enough fat, and you are damaging your muscular and skeletal structures. The key is to eat enough of the right kind of fat (unsaturated fat) and avoid the worst kind (saturated, which comes from animal fat). Twenty-five to 30 percent of your total diet should be fat, but no more than 10 percent of that should come from saturated fats.

The quickest way to reduce your saturated fat is to pledge to never eat fried food again. Fried foods have all the negatives and none of the positives (other than taste). I usually recommend that a person decide to give up just one type of fried food at a time. Taking on too much at once only sets you up for failure. For instance, eliminate french fries. Ouch! I know this is a tough one, but if you can conquer it, you will find it easier to kick other habits. Replace fries with a side salad or baked potato. Most fast-food restaurants are now offering these as alternatives at no additional charge.

Once you are over the cravings, once you don't need the fries and don't miss the fries, you are ready to tackle another item. This could take a couple of months, so don't get discouraged when you fall off the wagon. Each time you make a better choice, you are winning!

Consume the following high-fat foods sparingly:

- Fried foods
- Vegetable oils
- Butter/Margarine
- Sweets
- Cheese

Again, fat is necessary for your body to be healthy, but you want to guard yourself against saturated fats and triglycerides, which come from nonanimal fatty products (in other words, unnatural foods). The number one contributor to saturated fats in the typical diet of our nation is the good, old American hamburger.[9] Saturated fat raises cholesterol levels more than anything else in our diets.

Here are examples of fats that help reduce our LDL (known as bad cholesterol) and help raise our HDL (good cholesterol):

- Olive oil
- Canola oil
- Peanut oil
- Omega-3 fish oils (halibut, salmon, albacore tuna)
- Avocados
- Green olives

Protein

Our muscles need protein in order to grow and remain strong. How much protein you require will be determined upon how hard you work out, but roughly 12 to 15 percent of your diet should be protein. Most Americans eat way too much protein and don't even know it.

Your body does need some protein to fuel your exercise. Eat more or less of it based on how hard you're working out. If your workouts are registering low on the intensity scale (see page 54), then use the lower end of the protein range (12 percent). If you are exerting yourself, use the higher end (15 percent).

Many sources of protein also include fat, so be careful in selecting your proteins. Some diets are high in protein, which will ultimately cause hardening of the arteries due to the high percentage of fat. Other diets restrict protein. What you want to strive for is balance.

Here are some sources of protein:

- Beans
- Beef (watch fat content)
- Cheese (high in fat)
- Chicken
- Fish
- Milk (choose low-fat or rice/soy milk enriched with vitamins)

Now let's determine your exact percentages so you have something to shoot for on a daily basis. Take a moment to fill out the following calorie counter. If you are not trying to lose weight, simply put the same number for current weight (CW) and desired weight (DW).

CALORIE COUNTER

To lose weight at a safe rate and ensure the highest possible chance of keeping it off, women should expect to lose only one to two pounds per week, and men can expect to lose two to three pounds a week.[10] Be realistic, and manage your expectations.

Don't get too hung up on a certain weight. Rather, aim for a certain clothing size or know what you want to feel like in certain clothes. And remember, muscle weighs more than fat. I personally threw my scale away years ago. I strive for being toned, strong, and fit. I know what size I want to be and concentrate on that more than on my weight. Nonetheless, calories matter.

CURRENT WEIGHT (CW) _____ minus
DESIRED WEIGHT (DW) _____ (Difference or goal is _____ pounds)
GOAL _____ pounds divided by _____ pounds per week = _____ weeks to reach desired weight.

Now, let's determine how many calories you should be taking in (or consuming) each day. This formula is based upon your activity level, so choose the one that describes you (moderate lifestyle or active exercise):

DW _____ x 13 calories (moderate exercise) = _____ total calories (TC)
DW _____ x 18 calories (active exercise) = _____ total calories (TC)[11]

TC represents the required number of calories you will need to consume in order to *maintain* your weight—but you aren't there yet. Until you reach your desired weight, you will want to *reduce* your daily caloric intake.

For example, if you want maintain a weight of 120 pounds and you are exercising moderately, you need to consume in a single day the amount of food that will give you no more than 1,560 calories (120 x 13). If you're really working hard in your fitness program, you need more fuel. In that case, you'd need 2,160 calories (120 x 18) a day to maintain your weight.

To get to your desired weight, you will need to consume fewer calories per day than you are used to. The Aerobics Fitness Association of America suggests subtracting anywhere from 300 to 1,000 calories per day to achieve weight loss that will stay off. I have found that 400 calories per day is doable and basically requires giving up only one thing per day: a bagel, a Starbucks latte, or a burger.[12]

CCI _____ – 400 calories = _____ adjusted calories (AC)

In this formula, CCI is your current caloric intake. It's the number of calories you're currently consuming as you eat the foods and amounts you tend to eat every day. Use food labels and calorie counters to figure out your CCI. To get to your desired weight, we're going to drop that daily intake by 400 calories. If you're currently eating 3,000 calories a day, your AC will be 2,600. This is your target for total calories to eat per day. (Weight loss will be accelerated by exercise—because you're burning off additional calories—but for now we're just looking at calories from food.)

In order to help reach this target, you may find it easier to break your daily AC out into three meals:

AC _____ divided by 3 meals a day = _____ calories per meal (CPM)

If your AC is 2,600, your CPM is roughly 867. If your AC is 2,100, your CPM is 700. This gives you something to shoot for. You can think of these CPM totals as pools to draw from. If you don't use up all of your breakfast calories because you only had a fruit bowl, then you have extra calories to use for lunch or dinner. Just remember, the less calories you bring in, the less you will have to burn off. Trust me, it is easier to *not* take the calories in than to burn them.

Let's take your adjusted calories for the day (AC) and determine what kinds of food you should be eating. Remember, I do not support trends, fads, or quick weight-loss diets. I am a firm believer in a healthy, well-balanced diet as God intended it to be with proteins, carbs, and fat. What you want to do is make sure you are getting the right amount. Multiply your AC by the percentages to get your daily percentage of each category.

AC _____ x 55% or 60% = _____ carb intake
AC _____ x 12%, 13%, 14% or 15% = _____ protein intake
AC _____ x 25% or 30% = _____ fat intake

For example, if your AC (your target caloric intake for the day) is 2,000, and if 55 to 60 percent of those calories should come from carbohydrates, you should get between 1,100 and 1,200 calories from carbs. You should get 240 to 300 calories a day from proteins. And fats should comprise 500 to 600 calories of your daily diet. If you're coming from a high-fat diet, start at 30 percent and slowly ease back to having only 25 percent of your calories come from fats. We are blessed to live in a time and country in which we have this information on the labeling of our foods.

Note that no more than 10 percent of your *carbs* should come from processed foods. In the same way, regarding *fats*: no more than 10 percent of your daily fats should be from saturated fats ("bad fats"). As I mentioned before, your *protein* calorie intake should be adjusted based on the intensity level (and frequency) of your exercise program. The more exercise and weight lifting you're doing, the more protein you will want in your diet. And again, all protein isn't equal. Avoid high-fat protein options when possible.

I know numbers aren't always fun, but you have to do this only once. When you have your target (your daily AC), try to stay within those boundaries. I'm not suggesting you count every calorie, but do try to estimate what you are eating. Any steps you take will be better than taking no steps, eating at will without any regard to calories.

CALORIE CALENDAR

I like the caloric estimate from the Aerobics and Fitness Association of America because it takes into account your activity level. When you read food packaging that says, "Based upon a 2,000 calorie diet," it is not accounting for whether you are active or not. Start watching labels and begin keeping track of *your* calories. Be cautious of serving sizes on the labeling as well. Many times a package will have more than one serving inside, which means you have to multiply the calories by the number of servings to know how many calories are in the whole package.

To give you an idea of how quickly calories add up, here are some foods with their estimated total calories:

Chart 10.1 | Calorie Estimates for Sample Foods

Food	Total Calories
English muffin with jelly	155
Bran muffin	320
Hot cocoa	180
Apple juice	145
Turkey sub sandwich with no mayo	655
Dannon fruit yogurt	260
Plain baked potato	240
1 slice of bread	200
2 cups of spaghetti with sauce	520[13]

See how quickly calories can add up? That's 2,675 calories right there. The good news is that by giving up only one of these, you will be closer to your calorie total for the day. Watch what you put in your mouth one item at a time, and you will get smarter and be more aware of your nutrition. Baby step by baby step! Remember, you are eating to live, not living to eat.

The Calorie Calendar on the next page will help you keep track of your daily caloric intake. Put your CPM (your calories per meal, which is your AC divided by three) at the top of each meal's log. Use this as your guideline when shopping and eating:

Chart 10.2 | Calorie Calendar

BREAKFAST = _____ (CPM)

Food	Quantity	Calories	Time

LUNCH = _____ (CPM)

Food	Quantity	Calories	Time

DINNER = _____ (CPM)

Food	Quantity	Calories	Time

If this looks like too much work, try just journaling what you eat. Remember, if you burn more calories than you take in, you *will* lose weight.

NUTRITION JOURNAL

With these forms I am trying to help you understand the relationship between calories (what you put into your body) and what you burn (through exercise). When you take in more than you burn, you will gain weight. When you burn more than you take in (by watching what you eat and burning those calories with your workouts), you will lose weight. It is the only safe and effective way of reaching your weight goal.

Below is an example of a day's journal. Note that between-meal snacks are OK so long as you don't go over your daily allowance. Note also that this person, though allocated 800 calories a meal (based on 2,400 calories daily), didn't eat those amounts every meal—but the daily bottom line was still within the limits of the AC intake.

Chart 10.3 | Nutrition Journal (Debbie)

Name: <u>Debbie</u>
Monday, 5/1/06
Breakfast: 800 calories

Portion	Description	Calories	Time
1 small bowl	Mixed fresh fruit	200	9:00 a.m.
1 8-oz. cup	Diet Rite w/1 slice lemon	10	9:30 a.m.
1	Multivitamin	5	10:00 a.m.

Midmorning

Portion	Description	Calories	Time
1 8-oz. cup	Water w/1 slice lemon	10	10:30 a.m.

Lunch: 800 calories

Portion	Description	Calories	Time
1 small bowl	Fresh green salad w/fake crab	450	12:00 p.m.
1 tbsp.	Vinegar dressing	50	12:00 p.m.
3 each	Calcium/Mag/Zinc	5	1:00 p.m.

Afternoon

Portion	Description	Calories	Time
1 8-oz. cup	Water w/lemon	10	2:00 p.m.
1 handful	Unsalted nuts	200	3:00 p.m.

Dinner: 800 calories

Portion	Description	Calories	Time
1 small bowl	Fresh green salad w/ 1 tbsp. vinegar dressing	250	7:00 p.m.
1 small piece	Meatloaf (made with soy meat) w/1 tbsp. ketchup	350	7:00 p.m.
1 medium helping	Fresh green beans w/1 tbsp. butter	150	7:00 p.m.
1 8-oz. cup	Club soda w/1 slice lemon	10	7:30 p.m.

Evening

Portion	Description	Calories	Time
1 8-oz. cup	Decaf iced tea w/1 slice lemon	50	9:00 p.m.
3 pieces	Small chocolate pieces	300	9:00 p.m.

In this example, Debbie has a 2,400 daily caloric intake because of her desired weight and activity level. Divided by three, this means she can consume 800 calories per meal. How did she do? By my calculations, she ate 2,050 calories worth of food, which is 350 less than her requirement. This is good if she's trying to lose weight. If she's trying to maintain or if she's going to exercise strenuously, it might actually be too few calories to keep her motor running.

Notice the small amount of condiments. Condiments add more than flavor to your food: they also add a ton of calories. Many fast-food places have great salad options now. But if you add the full packet of ranch dressing on the salad, you have just consumed as many calories as one of their big burgers. Be smart, and you can make an immediate impact on your diet.

In this example, if she also exercises, she will have had a great day of moving toward good health! Journaling is a great way to track your eating habits.

A note of caution to those who are superactive: make sure you get enough of the right calories to sustain your activity level. Don't fuel up on junk and sugar just because you will be exercising. "Garbage in, garbage out" still applies to you.

On the next page is a blank nutrition journal form for you. Copy it as necessary. Highlight or circle those things you know you can reduce or eliminate right away, like heavy dressings. Replace them with light Italian or plain vinegar. Personally, I'd rather have as little calories in my salad as possible so I can enjoy something else later. It is all about choices—one by one.

Chart 10.4 | **Nutrition Journal**

Name: _____

Date: _____

Breakfast _____ (CPM)

Portion	Description	Calories	Time

Midmorning

Portion	Description	Calories	Time

Lunch _____ (CPM)

Portion	Description	Calories	Time

Afternoon

Portion	Description	Calories	Time

Chart 10.4 | Nutrition Journal (continued)

Dinner _____ (CPM)

Portion	Description	Calories	Time

Evening

Portion	Description	Calories	Time

I have said several times now that you need to burn more calories than you take in, so I thought it would be helpful to give you an idea of how you burn calories during various forms of exercise.

Chart 10.5 | Estimated Calories Burned During Daily Workouts

Activity	Estimated Calories Burned
Indoor cycling—1 hour at level 8½	600–900
Running on treadmill—30 minutes at 6 mph	330
Hiking with a backpack—2 hours at level 8	1,300
Elliptical—30 minutes at level 8	300

Remember that the exact number of calories burned will be determined by the time you put in and the intensity level at which you are working.

THE FOOD BANK

Taking all this information a little further now, let me show you how you can get the right amount of nutrition per week. I like to train people to think of their calories just like a bank. You start off each day with a full account by food category, which has been assigned points. (Points don't replace counting your calories; they are simply a way to monitor the right foods.)

Remember when you calculated your carbs, proteins, and fats? This idea breaks it down into smaller groups to help you achieve proper nutrition.

As you eat, you deduct points out of your food bank—just as you deduct funds from your bank account when you use your checkbook. When you run out of funds in your checkbook, you are broke, right? The logical thing to do is to stop spending money. Apply this same principle to your eating habits. When you are out of food bank points, stop eating! For example, if I were to eat ⅓ cup of nuts every day of the week, I have fulfilled my beans, nuts, and seeds category. That means no sunflowers on the salad, too. That would be overdrawing the account.

Most diets work in just the opposite way. With those you are adding your way up to your total calories allowed for that day. I believe the checkbook model will work better for you.

Here is a food bank with descriptions to give you an idea of how you can spend your food bank points:

Chart 10.6 | **Food Bank Standard Servings**

Category	Servings	Description
Sweets	5 per week	1 cup low-fat yogurt, ½ cup frozen yogurt, 1 tbsp. sugar, syrup, or jam
Beans, nuts, seeds	7 per week	½ cup beans, ⅓ cup nuts, 2 tbsp. sunflower seeds
Oils/dressing/mayo	14 per week	1 tbsp. oil, 1 tsp. mayo or 2 tbsp. low-fat mayo, 1 tbsp. salad dressing, or 2 tbsp. light salad dressing
Low-fat dairy	14 per week	1 cup low-fat milk or yogurt, 1½ oz. cheese
Seafood/poultry/meat	14 per week	3 oz. broiled or roasted seafood, skinless poultry, or lean meat
Whole grains	56 per week	1 slice bread, ½ cup dry cereal, ½ cup cooked rice, pasta, or cereal
Veggies and fruits	70 per week	1 cup lettuce or ½ cup other veggies, 1 medium fresh fruit or ½ cup frozen or canned fruit, ¾ cup fruit juice[14]

It is amazing how quickly some categories add up without much effort. You really don't have to worry about restricting your fruits and veggies. Eat to your heart's content! But monitor your sweets very closely, as well as your dairy and meats.

Below is a blank form you can use to keep track of your own food bank. One of my clients put this on her Palm Pilot and keeps track as she goes, meal by meal. With a few clicks, she knows exactly how many more points or servings she has left. If she splurges on one meal, she knows she will need to reduce her points or servings at the next one. Her goal is to end up just right by the end of the day and week.

Weight Watchers is very similar. You are given a total for your day, and you keep track of your points. If you are considering Weight Watchers, I encourage you to join. They are supportive and encouraging, and they apply most of the same basic principles I have discussed here. FRIENDLY folks will appreciate the group mentality—all for one and one for all. You will not be alone on your journey. If you're another temperament, you might want to track each meal precisely. Decide what works for you. Just so long as you're watching what you eat!

Chart 10.7 | **Food Bank Serving Record**

Category	Servings	Mon	Tues	Wed	Thur	Fri	Sat	Sun	Total
Sweets	5								
Beans, nuts, seeds	7								
Oils, dressing, mayo	14								
Low-fat dairy	14								
Seafood/poultry/meat	14								
Whole grains	56								
Veggie and fruits	70								
TOTAL	180								

TIPS FOR EATING OUT

One of our problems in our culture is that we eat *supersized* portions. (I was very pleased to see McDonalds' decision to phase out their supersize options.) A serving portion the size of your fist is just fine. If you have made more than that or are given a larger portion than that, save it for another meal. Don't feel as if you have to eat everything in front of you. I know many people were raised to believe that it was impolite not to clean their plate, but do you want to be polite or healthy?

One of my dear friends says that I amaze him. He noticed that with every meal I eat, I leave food on my plate. One day he asked me why, and I simply said, "I stop when I am full." Even if I take too large a portion to begin with, I quit when I have had plenty. It drives my husband nuts sometimes. I will literally leave just one more bite on my plate. Maybe you're thinking that one more bite wouldn't do any harm. Well, a lot of "one more bites" will! Watch your portions, and stop when you are full.

Here are some tips that might help your eating habits when you're eating out:

- Drink a glass of water before you eat.
- Ask for a small, lunch, or half-size portion. (Some restaurants have smaller "senior" portions they'll let anyone order.)
- Eat your salad first (but go easy on the dressing).
- Eat your veggies first.
- Put your fork down after each bite.
- Chew slowly.
- Cut up only one piece of meat at a time.
- Don't eat bread.
- Drink a glass of water midway through your meal.
- Ask for a "to go" box before you are finished; this puts pressure on you to actually have leftovers for the box.
- Skip dessert by asking for the check before they show you the dessert tray!

FIT-FRIENDLY FOODS

I believe in eating a diet that is not only well balanced, but also realistic. Most of the people I work with have a full schedule and want to live a normal life. They work, have families, and have many commitments and things they want to do. They don't want their nutritional program to be so rigid that it takes them hours of planning and work, nor do they want to sacrifice all fun foods.

The concept of moderation works if you have the discipline. I call it the 80/20 rule. Eat right 80 percent of the time and fudge 20 percent of the time. If you eat three meals a day seven days a week, that leaves you roughly four meals a week to "let go." I caution you, though, not to lump together all four of those meals over the weekend. I have a client who would lose weight during the week and regain it on the weekend by fudging on four meals in a row. You will never get ahead this way.

I created what I call FIT-Friendly Foods to help balance what you eat. The table on the next page includes suggestions for you to try. For each meal I've given you some ideas to help you go from what you may be eating, the *Avoid* column, to just one step healthier, the *Good* column. When you've moved to the *Good* column, you might then be ready to try a few things from the *Better* column. And so forth.

The idea is to make one good choice after another. Each *no* you say to the *Avoid* column—and each *yes* you say to items in the *Good*, *Better*, or *Best* columns—is a step closer to better health. And with each step you will gain strength and confidence. Before you know it, you will be eating right and living well all the time!

Chart 10.8 | FIT-Friendly Foods

Breakfast

Avoid	Good	Better	Best
Processed sugars (i.e. cereal bars, cinnamon rolls, Pop Tarts, waffles, pancakes)	1 bowl canned fruit or a handful of dried fruit	1 bowl frozen fruit	1 bowl fresh fruit
High-fat milk products (such as regular yogurt, real milk)	1 Slim Fast breakfast drink	1 Jamba Juice smoothie	Fresh fruit blended with ice and water
Egg yolks, which have twice the cholesterol as meat	Fried eggs or omelets	Scrambled eggs	Egg Beaters
Processed sugar (like most boxed cereals) or high-fat milk	1 English muffin w/ light jam or 1 bagel w/light butter	1 bowl low-sugar, whole-grain cereal	1 bowl hot oatmeal with minimal butter and rice milk
High-sodium and high-sugar drinks (any juice that isn't 100 percent…even then, watch calories)	1 glass fruit juice	V8 low-sodium vegetable drink	1 glass freshly squeezed fruit juice or vegetable juice
Energy bars (I've noticed that most of these are really high in saturated fat)	1 Nutri-grain breakfast bar	1 bran muffin	1 banana and 1 small low-fat yogurt

Chart 10.8 | FIT-Friendly Foods (**continued**)

Notes

You can have black coffee or hot or iced tea with breakfast basically calorie free. You should also have one glass of water first thing in the morning to hydrate.

Midmorning (a.k.a. "I'm still waking up!")

Avoid	Good	Better	Best
Sweets (avoid store-bought muffins, doughnuts, cinnamon rolls, or any desserts brought in to the office)	1 Nutri-grain breakfast bar	Handful of carrots or celery sticks	1 apple, banana, orange, tangerine, plum, etc.
Yolks and high-sugar drinks (regular pop)	1 glass fruit juice	Protein drink	Hardboiled eggs (whites only)

Notes

If you had protein for breakfast, you probably won't need it midmorning. Remember, we often take in too much protein, so watch yourself carefully here. But if you had only fruit and grains for breakfast, you might consider a protein option.

Have some water.

Chart 10.8 | FIT-Friendly Foods (continued)
Lunch

Avoid	Good	Better	Best
Fried chicken, heavy/creamy dressings; biscuits, bread, or crackers	Oriental Chicken Salad at Jack in the Box or other fast-food restaurant	Grocery store packaged salad mix	Freshly made green salad with crab, or fresh salad bar
Wheat bread or low-fat white alternative (check labels); potato chips and other fried chips	Egg salad sandwich with light mayo; veggies or pretzels	Tuna sandwich with light mayo; veggies or pretzels	Turkey sandwich with no mayo; veggies or pretzels
Crackers and bread full of sodium	Teriyaki chicken bowl or other rice bowl from Jack in the Box	Bowl of canned, low-sodium vegetable, turkey, or bean soup	Homemade bowl of vegetable, turkey, or bean soup
Heavy sauces, any fried sides, and too much bread	Ham and cheese sandwich; fruit or veggies on the side	Grilled chicken breast sandwich (hold the mayo); fruit or veggies on the side	Veggie burger; fruit or veggies on the side
Supreme burrito with large amounts of sour cream and cheese	2 tacos	Baked potato with light butter and fresh mushrooms only	Fresh veggie wrap

Notes

Go light on the bread at lunch if you had bread in the morning. If you didn't have any grains in the morning, bread is fine. Remember, bread is considered a processed sugar unless it consists mostly of grains.

Chart 10.8 | **FIT-Friendly Foods (continued)**

Beware: not all wheat breads are created equal. Some of them are higher in sugar than white bread. Watch the labels.

Whenever possible, replace fried or questionable sides with fruit or vegetables.

Have some more water.

If you travel a lot, you now have much healthier options while on the road. Don't use traveling as an excuse to eat poorly. It may take a little extra effort, but you can still eat healthy while away from home.

Afternoon (a.k.a. "I'm ready for a nap!")

Avoid	Good	Better	Best
Sweets and salty snacks	Carrots or celery sticks	1 apple, banana, orange, tangerine, plum, etc.	Bottle of water
Sweets and salty snacks	1 handful of pretzels	Lightly salted or unsalted nuts: almonds, walnuts, or pecans	Bottle of water
Sweets and salty snacks	3 pieces of candy or chocolate	Handful of trail mix or dried fruit	Sugar-free gum

Notes

If you had sugar in your breakfast or lunch (juice included), go easy on the sugar now. Natural sugars like fruit can usually satisfy the craving.

Drink more water.

Chart 10.8 | FIT-Friendly Foods (continued)

Dinner

Avoid	Good	Better	Best
Fried fish and heavy sauces; lots of condiments	Boxed/frozen fish (not fried); add brown rice, veggies, or baked potato	Frozen fish packages in seafood section; add brown rice, veggies, or baked potato	Fresh fish; add brown rice, veggies, or baked potato
Chicken with the skin on	1 chicken fajita; add steamed vegetables for side	1 soy burger with wheat bun; add steamed vegetables for side	1 broiled skinless, boneless chicken breast; add steamed vegetables for side
Fatty cuts of meat	Grilled pork chop; add mashed potatoes, turnips, or cooked yams	1 broiled turkey leg; add mashed potatoes, turnips, or cooked yams	1 piece soy meatloaf; add mashed potatoes, turnips, or cooked yams
Bread; lots of condiments	1 small bowl spaghetti or other pasta in light sauce	1 piece lean steak	Baked potato with grilled chicken slices

Notes

I didn't list it because it is a big jump for most, but steamed squash (acorn, butter, or spaghetti squash) makes very nutritious meals when combined with a nice salad.

Have a small dinner salad and light dressing with any option.

Again, if you have already had bread today, try to avoid it now.

Chart 10.8 | FIT-Friendly Foods (continued)

Evening (a.k.a. "I'm bored!")

Avoid	Good	Better	Best
Sweets/desserts (like regular ice cream, chocolate cake, éclairs, etc.)	1 frozen fruit bar	Soy ice cream	Fresh fruit
Anything with too much salt	1 handful of pretzels or microwavable popcorn	1 handful of trail mix or dried fruit	1 handful of nuts: almonds, walnuts, pecans, or air-popped popcorn without butter or salt
Big portions of any snack	3 pieces of candy or chocolate	Popcorn with light butter and light or no salt	Bottle of water
Sweets and salty items	1 glass fruit or vegetable juice	Carrots or celery sticks	1 apple, banana, orange, tangerine, plum, etc.

Notes

It is OK to be "bad" for up to four meals a week if you use the 80/20 rule, but try to be good the other days.

If you cannot be trusted with sweets around the house, don't buy them!

MAKING BETTER NUTRITION CHOICES TODAY

The rule of thumb on *when* to eat carbs is prior to exercise, like the night before. Then after exertion, when your muscles need to recuperate, eat protein. Most schools of thought suggest tapering your carbs as the day goes:

limit your carbs in the evening and get your protein in. Muscles repair while we sleep, so protein helps the process. Our muscles are 80 percent water and 20 percent protein,[15] so it is important to get both in, especially when you are active.

And just to be clear, you shouldn't be eating everything I suggested at one sitting. These are menu items to select from at each meal. I'm trying to help you realize that you don't have to give up living and enjoying food altogether. You simply need to make smart choices.

Here are some quick ways to make better choices *today*:

- Opt for healthy side dishes instead of fried ones.
- Choose fresh over frozen and frozen over canned or boxed.
- Pick bright, rich-colored vegetables, and don't overcook them. (The more color the vegetable has, the more nutrients it has.)
- Select lean cuts of meat.
- Reduce portion sizes.
- Limit bread, and select whole grains over white or traditional wheat.
- Make homemade meals when possible.
- Read labels carefully.

I have provided a ton of information on nutrition, yet I have really only scratched the surface. I hope you realize that an entire book could be dedicated (and many have been) to just this subject alone. I am trying to give you an overall picture by sticking primarily to the basics. I believe in the basics. They work!

As I write this book, Christmas is just around the corner. 'Tis the season to overeat! I used to avoid participating in holiday festivities for fear of gaining weight, but I now partake and enjoy myself. I'm in better shape and the same weight. I simply make sure that I—you guessed it—burn more calories than I take in. When we are busy or stressed, one of the first things to go is our exercise. Don't sacrifice the one thing that will ensure everything else is at its best. You will enjoy life much more if you are burning your stress and maintaining a healthy weight.

NUTRITION AND THE TEMPERAMENTS

This book is not only about fitness and nutrition. It also acknowledges the role of personality type in staying healthy. With that in mind, here are some FIT-specific tips that will help you eat right to live.

Nutrition for FAST people

- Drink plenty of water. You have the tendency to not stop long enough to even drink water.

- Eat your fruits and veggies. These are the original fast food. They are quick, easy, and healthy!

- Take the time to eat! You most likely see eating as an inconvenience. Make it easy on yourself, and bring along healthy foods. You can eat while you work, but do eat!

- Remember that your body needs fuel in order to function properly. If it isn't getting what it needs, you won't be 100 percent.

- Multitask. Schedule business meetings or times with friends around a meal to ensure you will have the time to eat.

- Watch your intake of salt, fat, and sugar. If you are eating on the run, you might be more likely to reach for frozen, boxed, or fast food, but these are high in salt, fat, and sugar.

- Go easy on heavy dressings and condiments.

- Eat your greens first. If you run out of time, at least you filled up on the good stuff.

- You have to burn 3,500 calories to work off one pound of fat, so choose your food fats wisely.[16]

- Avoid anything fried.

- Burn more calories than you take in!

Nutrition for FUN people

- Drink plenty of water.

- Roughly estimate what you eat. Use the nutrition journal, not the calorie counter.

- Be good six days a week, then give yourself one day off. On that day, don't worry about tracking food. Eat, and be merry.

- Eat your fruits and veggies. These are the original fast foods. They are quick, easy, and healthy.

- Start with the food you like best, and then move on to the rest of the meal. If you are full, you are more likely to stop eating. If you save your favorite for last, you will stuff yourself.

- Stop when you are full! This way you can talk more.

- Keep your portions small. Dish out the right portion, and immediately store the remaining food in the refrigerator so you won't be tempted for seconds (or thirds).

- Slow down. The faster you eat, the longer it will take your "gauge" to determine that you are full. Give your body a chance to decide if it has had enough. Slow down, and enjoy the company.

- Go easy on heavy dressings and condiments.

- You have to burn 3,500 calories to work off one pound of fat, so choose your food fats wisely.

- Garbage in, garbage out.

- Avoid anything fried!

- Burn more calories than you take in!

Nutrition for FRIENDLY people

- Drink plenty of water, especially before a meal.

- Eat your salad first—with light dressing, of course.

- Start with the food you like best, and then move on to the rest of the meal. If you are full, you are more likely to stop eating. If you save your favorite for last, you will stuff yourself.

- Be good six days a week, then give yourself one day off. On that day, don't worry about tracking food. Eat, and enjoy the company.

- Stop when you are full.

- Keep your portions small. Dish out the right portion, and immediately store the remaining food in the refrigerator so you won't be tempted for seconds (or thirds).

- When you are hungry, ask yourself, "Am I really hungry, or am I bored, tired, anxious, nervous, or upset?" Drink water to curb the craving.

- Write down what you find yourself eating when you are blue or sad. Use this as a guideline to help you eliminate certain foods from your diet.

- You like to eat with friends, but you've got to watch how many times you eat out each week. It is much harder to eat healthy when you're eating out. Dine in!

- Go easy on heavy dressings and condiments.

- You have to burn 3,500 calories to work off one pound of fat, so choose your food fats wisely.

- Garbage in, garbage out.

- Avoid anything fried.

- Burn more calories than you take in!

Nutrition for FACTUAL people

- Drink lots of water, especially before you eat, to hydrate and fill up.

- Keep your meal portions small.

- Track your calories using the calorie counter and calendar.

- Journal your eating habits to determine where you can make the most improvement.

- Read labels, and watch nutritional value.

- Eat just one helping!

- Eat until you are full, not until your portion is gone.

- Eat three meals a day or seven small ones (keeps metabolism high).

- You have to burn 3,500 calories to work off one pound of fat, so choose your food fats wisely.

- Garbage in, garbage out.

- Go easy on heavy dressings and condiments.

- Avoid anything fried.

- Burn more calories than you take in!

EAT TO LIVE

I hope you have found this nutrition information helpful. It will take some adjustments and some time, but I know you can do it. Start off with the *Good* options, and experience success there before you move over to the *Better* ones. You may find yourself mixing up some of all three in your diet. Each *Best* decision you make is one step closer to your goal.

If you can recruit your entire family and you all begin to follow these basic principles, you will have greater chances of success. Any time you embark on new eating habits but still try to cook for or surround yourself with those with bad habits, you will find yourself slipping. I knew a very obese man who decided once and for all that he was going to lose weight. He joined Weight Watchers and began to see progress immediately. His wife and children, however, did not want to participate. They continued to eat cake, ice cream, and pies after very large meals. They were actually quite negative about his change because he wasn't joining them. Instead of receiving support, he got ridiculed. Within six months, he gave up and went back to his old eating habits. If he is still alive, he is probably obese and unhappy.

I would like to tell you that everyone will support your decision for good health, but I can't promise that. Unfortunately, any time we change a pattern, we create waves. Some people will decide that the new pattern is good and will accept it. Some may even cheer you on or join you. But others will not like the change. They will resist it, even if it doesn't affect them. If you haven't read it yet, pick up a copy of *The Dream Giver* by Bruce Wilkinson. It's an awesome book that will encourage you to stay on course, no matter what comes your way.

We are strange creatures in that we like things to remain the same. I have learned that when we make personal improvements, others are forced to look in the mirror. If they don't like what they see, they get angry with us for forcing them to look. "If you hadn't embarked on your new journey," they say, "everyone would have just stayed in the same place. Things would have been just fine." Well, you know better. You know where poor eating habits and a lack of exercise will lead you.

You now have knowledge and a customized plan of attack. You have the ability, motivation, and willpower to succeed! It's your choice to make: eat to live, or live to eat.

I'm with you on the journey. I am cheering you on. The next chapter will help you with the choices you must make. God be with you.

Eleven

CHOOSE WISELY

THROUGHOUT THIS BOOK I have shared with you many reasons to exercise, ways to exercise, and even suggestions on how to improve your diet. We have discussed what motivates you and why you might want to change your current lifestyle to a healthier one. As your personal trainer, I have tried my best to give you enough information to make wise choices—yet not overwhelm you with facts or jargon.

But this is as far as I can take you. The rest is up to you. It is now up to you to take this wealth of information and apply it to your life. The choice is yours. You can decide to discard it and shrug it off as nonsense, or you can take what you have learned and make it work for your particular situation. I hope and pray you choose the latter. I am concerned for our nation's health, and that includes your health.

■

MAN DOES NOT SIMPLY EXIST, BUT ALWAYS DECIDES
WHAT HIS EXISTENCE WILL BE, WHAT HE WILL
BECOME IN THE NEXT MOMENT.

—VIKTOR FRANKEL

■

OPPORTUNITY COST

We make choices every day. At this moment, you are reading this book. That was a choice. What did you have to give up in order to take the time to sit down and read this for a while? I'm guessing a lot of things. In fact, you gave up *everything* else in order to spend time with me in this book. I appreciate it! That is what is called "opportunity cost." Choosing to do one thing means choosing not to do everything else.

Life is full of options for us. We are constantly looking at a menu of possibilities:

- Where will I eat lunch and with whom? Can I even afford to stop and eat?
- Do I have time to pick up the dry cleaning before the kids' soccer game?
- Should I stop by and see my folks or get home and put the dishes away?
- I need to write my sister, but the clothes need folding…
- I should call my friend, but the kids have homework…
- I really want to exercise, *but*…

Like a scale, we are weighing out every option and then determining what we want to do or should do. Everything has a different value, so you might actually be willing to pay the cost of procrastinating organizing your closet if you can live with the disarray.

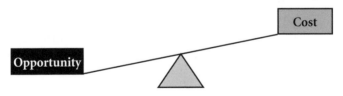

Each opportunity has a price to it. If you do opt to visit your folks, the dishes might sit another day. If you do pick up your dry cleaning, you may miss the kids' soccer game. Opportunity costs. Only you can determine if the cost associated with the decision for your particular circumstance is worth it.

The question I have for you is this: how much is your health worth? Is it worth giving up a show on television? Is it worth giving up french fries? The flip side of this is another question: what can poor health cost you? Answer: *everything*. Without your health you won't be able to do the other things you want or need to do. Your health supports your lifestyle. What kind of lifestyle you have will be up to you.

Decisions aren't always easy, especially today. We are busier than we have ever been. We have more options, more choices, more distractions. But you must prioritize. You must decide what matters most and choose wisely.

■

IN FORTY HOURS, I SHALL BE IN BATTLE, WITH LITTLE INFORMATION, AND ON THE SPUR OF THE MOMENT WILL HAVE TO MAKE THE MOST MOMENTOUS DECISIONS. BUT, I BELIEVE THAT ONE'S SPIRIT ENLARGES WITH RESPONSIBILITY AND THAT, WITH GOD'S HELP, I SHALL MAKE THEM, AND MAKE THEM RIGHT.

—*GENERAL GEORGE S. PATTON*

■

When I'm teaching my cycling classes and we are about to embark on a serious climb up a steep hill, I challenge my students to decide right here and now that they will make it. I encourage them to decide that they will do whatever it takes to make it. While you are *on* the hill is the wrong time to think about how important climbing it is to you. The obstacles might be too great and the grade too steep. But if before you ever ascend the hill you decide you *will* make it, you have already succeeded. You must see yourself at the top of the hill.

Visualize yourself healthy. See yourself already doing the things it takes to improve the quality of your life. Decide here and now that you will live a better life. Create those habits now.

THE POWER OF HABIT

FRIEND OR FOE?

I can be your friend and companion
Or immediately turn into your enemy if me you abandon.
I can push you onward and help you set sail
Or I can hold you back only to fail.
Friend or foe—only you know.

If you turn things over to me,
I'll get them done quickly, you'll see.

I'm easy to manage, but you'll need to be firm.
Just show me precisely what you want, and I will learn.

I have run with giants—each and every one.
But huge failures, I have also done.
I can make you great,
But know what is at stake.
I can be your foe or your friend.
You ultimately decide in the end.

Use me for whatever you want, I care not.
Just remember whom I am—forget not!
I am a habit, bringing the world to your feet,
Or unraveling everything into massive defeat.

Treat me wisely and with great care.
Ignore me only if you dare.

—Lorraine Bossé-Smith

Your Success Contract

One way to ensure that you make your new FIT exercise program a real habit is to commit to it in writing. If you are serious about becoming healthier, I encourage you to fill out the following form, sign it, and have someone you trust witness your signature. Choose someone who cares enough to check on you and hold you accountable if you begin to slip.

A personal trainer can be that person for you, if you are willing and able to make the financial commitment. Chances are I don't live near you, but perhaps you are close to a gym or private studio. At least get some information on personal training. It might be just the ticket to helping you on your journey to good health.

Chart 11.1 | Success Contract

SUCCESS CONTRACT

AS YOUR PERSONAL trainer and coach, I can do only so much. The responsibility lies with *you* to actually make the necessary behavior modifications to your lifestyle to obtain the results you seek.

I, _____, hereby make a commitment to myself and to _____ to change my behavior and make the necessary modifications to my lifestyle as suggested and outlined in *Finally FIT!* to reach my SMART goals.

I agree to stick to an exercise program for at least _____ weeks.

I commit to doing cardio exercise _____ times a week for at least _____ minutes at _____ intensity in order to improve my overall level of physical activity. I will also include _____ days of resistance training, along with _____ days of stretching.

Ways I will honor this agreement: _____
_____
_____
_____

Potential obstacles I see that will try to prevent me from reaching my goal:
_____
_____
_____
_____

Ways I will combat these obstacles and overcome the challenges:
_____
_____
_____
_____

When I have kept this agreement, I give myself permission to celebrate! I will reward myself by _____.

Signature _____ Date _____

Witness _____ Date _____

SUCCESS STORIES

The clients I work with have made the decision to work with a personal trainer. Although they represent different personality styles, they all saw the value of working with someone who cared about their health enough to encourage and challenge them. Here are some of their stories.

Harvey

Harvey is a FAST profile. When he came to me, he had just started exercising aggressively again. He is very goal oriented, and his purpose for exercising is to be in shape for rock climbing. He loves the challenge and adventure of pushing the envelope with climbing. Exercise is a *means* to an end for him. He wants to lose a little weight and strengthen his body in order to improve his climbing technique.

We weight train hard together once a week, and he lifts on his own for one or two other days a week, depending upon his schedule. He attends my Monday night cycle class at the gym and either runs or cycles three other times a week. He doesn't really like running, but it has proven to be a fast, down and dirty workout for him. He can run inside or outside, and he gets it done in a relatively short amount of time.

Once Harvey decided he wanted to work out, he has stuck to it. He keeps his motivation on the forefront of his mind. Everything he does or doesn't do is to help his climbing.

Harvey struggles with nutrition, though. He is having difficulty with balancing this part of the equation. Because he is always on the go, he rarely eats breakfast. This affects his metabolism for the day. If he eats lunch, it is late in the day. By then, he is starved and tends to select something heavy rather than a light meal. He doesn't like fruits and vegetables, and he eats a late dinner. Afterwards, he may snack or eat dessert.

If you are a FAST person, you may relate. As I tell Harvey, you need to eat *something* for breakfast. Boil up a dozen eggs and eat two hardboiled eggs (without the yolk) on your way out the door. This will give your body some pure protein and energy to make it to lunch. You won't be as starved at lunchtime and may be able to choose a better option. Try chicken salads, shrimp salads, crab salads, or tuna salads. These have more substance to them. With these you will get your needed greens and have something that will stick to your ribs. If you work out hard like Harvey, you'll need that protein. And don't forget your carbs.

In three months, Harvey has lost half an inch off his waist and increased his muscle mass in his arms and legs. He's on his way to climbing to the top!

Karis

Karis is a FUN personality. She is very sociable and has a lot of friends that keep her schedule full. Karis came to me wanting to lose a little weight and tone up. She had been very active in soccer until a knee injury prevented her from playing. Without this team sport, she found herself in a fitness slump.

Karis likes to exercise with a friend or a group because it is more fun that way. We started her in my Wednesday cycle class, and she had a friend meet her there. Afterwards, they would have dinner together. Karis enjoys kickboxing classes at the gym, as well. We train hard together one time a week, working on toning and trimming. We have a good time talking and sharing over the course of the hour. Karis tries to get her second weight-training day in but struggles when she doesn't have someone to meet with.

If you are a FUN person, you can probably relate to this scenario. You might want to invest in a second session with your personal trainer or make sure you have a lifting partner.

Karis has seen results. She is getting her cardio exercise in and eating right. By making wiser choices with her meals and giving up a few fatty foods, she has lost inches in her hips, glutes, and thighs. Her upper body is slimming down, too.

Her motivation to stick with it right now is her upcoming wedding. As long as we continue to make it fun, Karis will walk down the aisle in the size wedding dress she wanted. It will be a dream come true!

Cathy

Cathy is a FRIENDLY person. She has always enjoyed playing sports with friends, but she struggled with working out at a gym. She doesn't like the mob mentality, especially when lifting weights. If you have a FRIENDLY temperament, you can probably relate to her. She came to me knowing she needed to lose weight and strengthen up as she was having knee problems. The doctor had advised her to lose some weight. Her motivation was to get healthy and be able to enjoy her sports.

Because of Cathy's knee problems, she is limited to what she can and cannot do. She also has horrible allergies, which prevent her from exercising outside. Stationary cycling was just the ticket for her. She started cycling with me three days a week. At first, it was tough for her to finish a class, but once she stuck with it, she found the workout to be challenging and beneficial. She also got to meet some people in class. Cycle classes aren't huge and out of control. They are limited to the number of bikes, and we have twenty-five.

I then set Cathy up for a resistance-training program she can do at home with handheld weights. Cathy can watch television, listen to music, or even talk with family while she is working out. Her objective is to strengthen. With new softball teams forming, she is motivated to be in shape. Cathy lost weight immediately, although she has more to go. Additional knee surgery slowed her down a bit, but with choosing better meal options, Cathy will stay on track, and so can you!

Rayce

Rayce is the FACTUAL type. He came to me with his own resistance program already outlined. He had three different programs that worked different muscles each time. He had outlined his estimated amounts of weights to be used and spelled out his goals for improvement. We began training together to ensure he was lifting properly.

Rayce wanted to lose a little weight, especially around the middle. He enjoys lifting weights but doesn't like many forms of cardio exercise. I showed Rayce how to jump rope, which is an efficient way to burn calories in a short amount of time. He loved to cycle, so I gave him guidelines for his heart rate to ensure he was working hard enough. Rayce makes excellent choices when it comes to nutrition. He knows what his body needs, and he provides it. You might relate with him.

The key for Rayce is to continue to schedule time for his cardio. He must keep it on his calendar and protect it. If he does, he will be right on track for good, overall health.

Lorraine

I thought you might want to hear a bit about how I made my way to good health. I have always been an active individual. I loved anything outdoors: hiking, biking, tennis, softball, volleyball, and so on. I had the cardio portion of the equation down, attending the gym faithfully.

However, I wasn't eating right, nor was I weight training. I didn't provide my body with enough fuel to sustain my level of fitness. In 1997 my life's stress-ometer was off the chart. I dropped down to 97 pounds at 5 feet 10 inches. I looked like a cancer patient! (See my Web site, www .thetotalyou.biz, for pictures.) I had pencil arms and 6 percent body fat, which is dangerously low for a woman.

Being thin. Oh, what a problem to have, right? But let me tell you something: being underweight is just as serious as being overweight. My heart could have given out at any moment just like someone who is obese.

It sustained huge amounts of stress. Just like someone who is overweight, I had to choose a different route. I needed to take action if I was going to be healthy.

My body was barely able to function—and one day, it almost didn't. I was lying in bed and literally did not have the physical strength to get up. I prayed to God to give me the strength because I had none of my own left. My body was empty. On that day, I realized I had to make some drastic changes. I knew I had to first of all manage my stress better (read my first book, *A Healthier, Happier You: 101 Steps for Lessening Stress* from Barbour Publishing, to see a few things I learned), and I committed to eating right and weight training. I didn't want to be frail and weak, so I embarked on my journey to good health.

I began to eat breakfast every day, which I had not done in the past. I loved to eat salads, but now I added protein to them and ensured I was getting enough nutrients through healthy foods. I gave up boxed foods, frozen foods, and most canned items (other than soup). It took me well over a year to gain my weight back properly and build up my muscles, but baby step by baby step I did it.

Today the only fried food I eat is french fries once in a blue moon. My typical week is five days of cardio exercise, and I actually teach four classes at the health club. That started because I would get extremely frustrated with the signup process and waiting lists for classes. I decided to teach classes so I would always have a spot! Besides, I like being the one "in charge." And I get to listen to the music *I* enjoy. Gee, what profile am I?

In addition to my cardio workouts, I lift weights twice a week. I do my entire body each day in order to keep it fast. On Fridays, I do a lot of floor exercises, core muscle work, and toning exercises to complement my other weight days. I cycle, run, hike, bike, play tennis, rock climb, scuba dive, and snow ski to have fun on top of that! Oh yes, and I stretch as often as I can.

Today I am stronger than I have ever been. Since 1997, I have gained 35 pounds of solid mass. I am also pleased to say that I don't get sick very often. Best of all, I still fit in a small size, even though I have more toned muscles. I know women who worry about becoming "huge" if they lift weights. But my testimony is that resistance training rids your body of the layer of fat that lies over your muscles. When you thin that layer out, you actually lose inches, even though you are building stronger muscles.

As I worked on improving myself, I got inspired to help others. Here I am today writing a book so that you too may experience good health.

You Can Do It

I hope one of these stories helps you to know that you can do it. With some dedication, hard work, and time, you can reach your health and fitness goals. No matter your motivation and purpose, you can achieve success if you decide to and make wise choices that support it.

My conclusion is short, but it does wish you great health and success toward your goals.

You are on your way, and I am proud of you!

CONCLUSION | IMPROVE THE QUALITY OF YOUR LIFE

A MAN WAS walking to work one morning via his usual route when he suddenly fell into a pothole the size of a small car. "Where did this come from?" he exclaimed. "I have found myself in a pothole. How ever shall I get out?" He managed to scratch and claw his way up to the top, but he was a mess. He proceeded on to work.

The next morning, he took the same route to work. As he turned the corner, he fell into the same pothole. "No way!" the man yelled. "I can't believe this. I've fallen in the same big hole." He was eventually able to crawl out, but he had to exert a lot of effort, and he had to go to work again all dirty and grimy.

The next morning, the man thought to himself, *Ha, I won't fall for that same trick today. I will make sure I walk to the side of that stupid pothole.* So, walking down the same path, he moved over to the edge of the pothole. Little did he know, though, that the edge was wet and slick. He lost his balance and began to slide—right into the pothole once again. Frustrated and muddy, he got himself out of the hole and headed to work.

The man's wife, hearing the tale every night of his horrible crashes into the dark, messy hole, made a suggestion the next day: "Sweetheart," she said, "you have fallen into a large pothole on the same path to work for several days now. There appears to be no way around it."

Her husband nodded.

"Well," she said, "wouldn't it be better to take a different route to work?"

GO A DIFFERENT WAY

So often we get frustrated and even downright upset over things that seem to always happen to us. Unfortunately, complaining about them won't change them. Only action will. Why *try* to avoid a pothole in your life when you can be certain to avoid it altogether? By doing things the same way you have always done them, you will get the same results. It's a fact. If you are tired of falling into that deep, dark pothole, you have to take another route. Give the concepts in this book a try.

I do hope you have enjoyed our time together as much as I have. I am blessed with the ability to do many different things, but the one thread that weaves them all together is my passion and purpose to improve the quality of people's lives. My hope and prayer with this book is that you have been touched, inspired, and motivated and will take the necessary steps toward better health.

We are given only a short amount of time on this earth, and I believe we should make the most of it. Our bodies are gifts from God, and I believe we should take very good care of them. We've spent a lot of time talking about how you can do that, but please don't forget your spiritual condition. Without God's light in our lives and His promises of hope, our physical health pales in comparison.

I know we often feel like our physical bodies are a curse more than a blessing, but how could we function without them? Imperfections and all, your body allows you to live.

Some years ago, God gave me this advice, and the older I get the more I appreciate its wisdom: "Be thankful for every body part, and be grateful for its purpose." Hardly a night goes by that I don't thank God for my strong legs. They may not be as thin as a sixteen-year-old girl's, but they enable me to climb mountains. I thank God for my eyes, their color, and their ability to see all that He has created, even though they are getting older and wearing out. I go through a list of body parts and what they do, which creates awareness and a heart full of gratitude. Have you thanked God for your body lately?

Don't focus on what your body *doesn't* do, but rather be thankful for what it *does*. Yes, we need to care for it and perhaps redefine it, but we can always appreciate what it does for us. As you take better care of your body, you will appreciate the ability to perform at higher levels with less sickness and illness. The healthier you are, the better you will feel.

Remember, it is all about balance: exercise and a healthy diet. Track your progress using the FIT Journal page I have included at the end of this conclusion. Make as many copies as you need. This journal will remind you of your *why*. It will allow you to look back and see how far you've come.

If you keep your eyes looking ahead toward your goals and your motivation in your heart at all times, you will be well on your way to a brighter tomorrow.

I pray this book will be an instrument that helps you become *Finally FIT!*

FIT Journal

Name:

Date:

_____

_____

_____

_____

_____

_____

_____

_____

_____

_____

_____

_____

_____

_____

_____

_____

Briefly describe your desired feedback.

Did I get my cardio exercise done today?
    ☐ Yes
    ☐ No

Did I get my stretching in today?
    ☐ Yes
    ☐ No

Have I gotten proper nutrition today?
    ☐ Yes
    ☐ No

Did I get my resistance training in this morning?
    ☐ Yes
    ☐ No

Comments:

"SUCCESS IS OBTAINED ONE DAY AT A TIME."

—LORRAINE BOSSÉ-SMITH

NOTES

Introduction

1. JoAnn E. Manson, MD, DrPH, et al., "The Escalating Pandemics of Obesity and Sedentary Lifestyle: A Call to Action for Clinicians," *Archives of Internal Medicine* 164, no. 3 (February 9, 2004): 249–258.

2. Julie van Roden, *A Guide to Personal Fitness Training* (Sherman Oaks, CA: Aerobics and Fitness Association of America, 2001), 6.

3. David Schwartz, *Speaker's Sourcebook II* (Englewood Cliffs, NJ: Prentice Hall, 1994), 345.

4. Advanced Personal Training Conference, San Diego, CA, Aerobics Fitness Association of America, 2002.

5. van Roden, *A Guide to Personal Fitness Training*, 1–6.

Chapter 1: Discover Your FIT!

1. Robert Rohm, *Positive Personality Profiles* (Atlanta, GA: Personality Insights, 2003).

2. Marita Littauer, *You've Got What It Takes* (Minneapolis, MN: Bethany House Publishers, 2000).

Chapter 3: Understanding Why You Do What You Do

1. Hyrum W. Smith, *The 10 Natural Laws of Successful Time and Life Management* (New York, NY: Warner Books, 1994), 30.

2. Karla Worley, *Growing Weary Doing Good?* (Birmingham, AL: New Hope Publishers, 2001), vii–viii.

3. Lorraine Bossé-Smith, *A Healthier, Happier You: 101 Steps for Lessening Stress* (Urichsville, OH: Barbour Publishing, 2004).

Chapter 4: Fitness Facts

1. Brian J. Sharkey, PhD, *Fitness and Health* (Champaign, IL: Human Kinetics, 1997).

2. For an array of articles on this subject, do a search on "cardio capacity" and "blood pressure" on http://pubs.ama-assn.org.

3. van Roden, *A Guide to Personal Fitness Training*, 6.

4. Paul T. Williams, "Relationships of Heart Disease Risk Factors to Exercise Quantity and Intensity," *Archives of Internal Medicine* 158 (February 1998): 237–245.

5. Peg Jordan, RN, *Fitness: Theory & Practice* (Sherman Oaks, CA: Aerobics and Fitness Association of America, 1997), 60.

6. Advanced Personal Trainer Certification, San Diego, CA, Aerobics and Fitness Association of America, 2003.

7. Ibid.

8. Jordan, *Fitness: Theory & Practice*, 174.

9. Ibid., 176.

10. Advanced Personal Trainer Certification.

11. Ibid.

12. Jordan, *Fitness: Theory & Practice*, 110.

13. Personal Trainer Certification, San Diego, CA, Aerobics and Fitness Association of America, 2002.

14. Jordan, *Fitness: Theory & Practice*, 126–127.

15. Aerobics Instruction Primary Certification, Camarillo, CA, Aerobics and Fitness Association of America, 2001.

16. Jordan, *Fitness: Theory & Practice*, 56.

Chapter 5: Seeing Is Believing

1. Personal Trainer Certification.

2. van Roden, *A Guide to Personal Fitness Training*, 5.

3. Jordan, *Fitness Practice & Theory*, 103.

4. Personal Training Certification.

5. van Roden, *A Guide to Personal Fitness Training*, 5.

Chapter 8: Together We Can Do It—Making Fitness FRIENDLY

1. Henry Cloud and John Townsend, *Boundaries* (Grand Rapids, MI: Zondervan, 1996).

Chapter 9: By the Book—Making Fitness FACTUAL

1. Sharkey, *Fitness and Health*, 3.
2. Personal Training Certification.
3. Ibid.
4. van Roden, *A Guide to Personal Fitness Training*, 5.
5. Schwartz, *Speaker's Sourcebook II*, 346.
6. van Roden, *A Guide to Personal Fitness Training*, 87.

Chapter 10: Eat Right, Feel Right

1. Personal Training Certification, 2002.
2. Jordan, *Fitness: Theory & Practice*, 225.
3. Ibid., 226.
4. van Roden, *A Guide to Personal Fitness Training*, 105.
5. Jordan, *Fitness: Theory & Practice*, 225–228.
6. van Roden, *A Guide to Personal Fitness Training*, 93.
7. Jordan, *Fitness: Theory & Practice*, 228.
8. Ibid.
9. van Roden, *A Guide to Personal Fitness Training*, 95.
10. Jordan, *Fitness: Theory & Practice*, 244.
11. Ibid.
12. Ibid.
13. Ibid., 235–236.
14. Ibid., 230–231.
15. Advanced Personal Training Certification.
16. Personal Fitness Training Certification.

BIBLIOGRAPHY

Buzzell, Dr. Sid, ed. *The Leadership Bible* (New International Translation). Grand Rapids, MI: Zondervan Corporation, 1998.

Cook, John. *The Book of Positive Quotations.* Minneapolis, MN: Rubicon Press, Inc., 1993.

Jordan, Peg, RN. *Fitness Theory & Practice.* Sherman Oaks, CA and Stoughton, MA: Aerobics Fitness Association of America and Reebox University Press, 1993, 1995, 1997.

Littauer, Marita. *You've Got What It Takes.* Minneapolis, MN: Bethany House Publishers, 2000.

Rohm, Robert, PhD. *Positive Personality Profiles.* Atlanta, GA: Personality Insights, 2003.

Sharkey, Brian J., PhD. *Fitness and Health.* Champaign, IL: Human Kenetic, 1997.

van Ekern, Glenn. *Speaker's Sourcebook II.* Englewood Cliffs, NJ: Prentice Hall, Inc., 1994.

van Roden, Julie. *A Guide to Personal Fitness Training.* Sherman Oaks, CA: Aerobics Fitness Association of America, 1997, 2001.

A HEALTHIER, HAPPIER YOU

You can't read the newspaper or watch the news without seeing something about stress. Americans work an exhausting 1,815 hours per year compared to 1,459 in France or 1,707 in Great Britain. Because of stress, people are overeating, drinking excessive alcohol, and turning to drugs for relief. This unhealthy approach cannot continue. We must learn to manage our stress!

In her book *A Healthier, Happier You!*, Lorraine Bossé-Smith, has provided 101 steps for lessening stress in four areas: our mind, our emotions, our physical bodies, and our spirituality. In order to live a healthier, more balanced life, Bossé-Smith encourages readers to take care of their "total being."

If you don't do something with your stress, it will do something to you. Cancel chaos TODAY and replace it with balanced living! *A Healthier, Happier You!* is available at a bookstore near you. Or you can order it from my Web Site: www.thetotalyou.biz.

Strang Communications, the publisher of both Charisma House and *Charisma* magazine, wants to give you a FREE SUBSCRIPTION to our award-winning magazine.

Since its inception in 1975, *Charisma* magazine has helped thousands of Christians stay connected with what God is doing worldwide.

Within its pages you will discover in-depth reports and the latest news from a Christian perspective, biblical health tips, global events in the body of Christ, personality profiles, and so much more. Join the family of *Charisma* readers who enjoy feeding their spirit each month with miracle-filled testimonies and inspiring articles that bring clarity, provoke prayer, and demand answers.

To claim your **3 free issues** of *Charisma,* send your name and address to: Charisma 3 Free Issue Offer, 600 Rinehart Road, Lake Mary, FL 32746. Or you may call 1-800-829-3346 and ask for Offer # 93FREE. This offer is only valid in the USA.

---

www.charismamag.com